T0301502

Organizing Hope

Organizing Hope

Narratives for a Better Future

Edited by

Daniel Ericsson

Associate Professor in the School of Business and Economics, Linnaeus University, Sweden

Monika Kostera

Professor and Chair in Management at Jagiellonian University in Kraków, Poland and Professor in Management and Organization at Södertörn University, Sweden

Edward Elgar
PUBLISHING

Cheltenham, UK • Northampton, MA, USA

Published by
Edward Elgar Publishing Limited
The Lypiatts
15 Lansdown Road
Cheltenham
Glos GL50 2JA
UK

Edward Elgar Publishing, Inc.
William Pratt House
9 Dewey Court
Northampton
Massachusetts 01060
USA

A catalogue record for this book
is available from the British Library

Library of Congress Control Number: 2019951585

This book is available electronically in the **Elgar**online
Business subject collection
DOI 10.4337/9781788979443

ISBN 978 1 78897 943 6 (cased)
ISBN 978 1 78897 944 3 (eBook)

Typeset by Servis Filmsetting Ltd, Stockport, Cheshire
Printed and bound by CPI Group (UK) Ltd, Croydon CR0 4YY

Contents

PART TWO   EMPIRICAL AND IMAGINATIVE INSPIRATIONS

Contributors

George Cairns is Adjunct Professor at QUT Business School, Brisbane, Australia. He qualified and worked as an architect in the UK. He was previously Professor of Management and Head of the School of Management at Essex University, UK and RMIT University, Australia. He shares critical concerns with colleagues about the nature of business education but sees these as being set within a broad context of human existence (and concern) – culture, society, education and acculturation.

Christina Ciupke is a performer and choreographer based in Berlin, Germany. She develops projects and specific situations in collaboration with artists from dance and other fields of art. Tanzfabrik Berlin has been her partner in Berlin. In 2016 she joined the European apap – advancing performing arts project network. She has collaborated with Anke Strauß since 2015 on the Working Utopias project.

Stewart Clegg is Distinguished Professor of Management and Organization Studies at the University of Technology Sydney, Australia. He has published widely in the management, organizations and politics literatures in many of the leading journals. Widely acknowledged as one of the most significant contemporary theorists of power relations, he is also one of the most influential contributors to organization studies, recognized by his being chosen as an EGOS Honorary Member, a Distinguished Fellow of EURAM and a Fellow of the Academy of Management.

Miguel Pina e Cunha is the Fundação Amélia de Mello Professor of Leadership at Nova School of Business and Economics, Universidade Nova de Lisboa, Portugal. His research deals mostly with the surprising (paradox, improvisation, serendipity, zemblanity, vicious circles) and the extreme (positive organizing, genocide). He has published more than 150 papers on these and related topics. He recently co-authored *Elgar Introduction to Theories of Organizational Resilience* (Edward Elgar Publishing, 2018), co-edited *Management, Organizations and Contemporary Social Theory* (Routledge, 2019), and received the 2015 best paper award from the *European Management Review*.

Małgorzata Ćwikła is an Assistant Professor at the Faculty of Management and Social Communication, Jagiellonian University in Kraków, Poland. Her current research interests are focused on the future of work and the connection between socio-technological development and management practice, particularly in the field of culture and the arts.

Daniel Ericsson received his PhD from the Stockholm School of Economics and is currently Associate Professor at Linnaeus University, Sweden. He is particularly interested in understanding how entrepreneurship is constructed and organized in society, as well as the unforeseen consequences of entrepreneurship. In his latest project he studies how entrepreneurship is enacted in the cultural sector.

Anna Góral, PhD, is an organizational and management researcher, and Assistant Professor at the Institute of Culture, Jagiellonian University in Kraków, Poland. Her professional interests are heritage management, community building and governance, communities' self-organization and networking.

Michał Izak, PhD, is a Reader in Management and Business at the University of Roehampton, UK. His research interests include critical management studies, fiction as a reflection of organizational dynamics, and organizational storytelling. Most recently he has been researching neoliberal organizational flexibility discourses. He publishes regularly in peer reviewed journals and is a member of editorial boards as well as co-organizer of international conferences.

Markus Kallifatides is Matts Carlgren Associate Professor of Management at the Stockholm School of Economics, Sweden. He has recently contributed to *Environment and Planning A*, *Cambridge Journal of Economics*, *Scandinavian Journal of Management* and *Corporate Governance* and participated in multiple interventions in Swedish public debate organized by the union think-tank Katalys.

Monika Kostera is Professor Ordinaria and Chair in Management at the Jagiellonian University in Kraków, Poland and Professor in Management and Organization at Södertörn University, Sweden. She has also been Professor and Chair at Durham University, UK. She is the author, co-author and editor of over 40 books in Polish and English, and of numerous scientific articles. Her current research interests include organizational imagination, disalienated work and organizational ethnography. She is a member of Erbacce Poets' Cooperative.

Wendelin Küpers is Professor of Leadership and Organization Studies at Karlshochschule International University in Karlsruhe, Germany and

Associate Professor at ICN ARTEM, France. Previously, he taught at and pursued research with various universities in Europe, India and New Zealand. Combining a phenomenological and cross-disciplinary orientation, his research focuses on embodied, emotional and creative transformational dimensions in relation to more responsible and wise forms of organizing and managing. Furthermore, his research focuses on integrating artful and aesthetic dimensions of practical wisdom into organization and leadership.

Richard Longman is Lecturer in Organization Studies at Bristol Business School (University of the West of England). His research focuses on alternative organizing and his theorising (which is driven by social theory) is motivated by a desire to understand individual experiences of alternative organizational discourses and practices.

Karolina Matyjaszkowicz is a Polish visual artist interested in folk motifs and archetypes. She graduated from the Academy of Fine Arts in Lodz, Poland in 2008. She has been awarded several distinctions, including the award of Marshal of the Lodzkie Voivodship and the Wieslaw Nowicki prize for creative and social contributions to regional culture. She has taken part in a large number of exhibitions, and her artwork is part of the permanent exposition of the Museum of Lowicz, the Central Museum of Textiles in Lodz, the National Museum in Gdansk, and the Regional Museum in Brzeziny.

John G. McClellan, PhD is Associate Professor of Communication at Boise State University, USA. His research attends to organizing discourses that enable (and constrain) qualities of organizational life, with an interest in dialogic communication that can engender mutually beneficial organizational change. His work appears in *The Oxford Handbook of Critical Management Studies*, *The Handbook of Business Discourse*, and *Discourse Perspectives on Organizational Communication* as well as the journals *Organization*, *Management Communication Quarterly*, and *Journal of Change Management*.

Aneta Milczarczyk holds a PhD in entrepreneurship. Her research and professional interests focus on social entrepreneurship, corporate social responsibility, and humanistic management. Currently, she is conducting research in Poczta Polska S.A. related to the organization and operation of the company.

Agata Morgan holds an MA in political studies from Warsaw University and a PhD in humanistic management from the Jagiellonian University in Kraków, Poland. She is interested in management of public space, its symbols and suppressed meanings, and women's studies, as well as in interpretative and artistic representation of qualitative research.

Tali Padan founded the NGO Mellem Education in 2012 and has since been providing training in conflict, democracy and self-reflection, using experiential learning methodologies. She found there was a need for this work not just in the NGO world but also in management education, where students learn about social responsibility. The question, however, is how responsibility is 'learned.' From her experience giving workshops, it is not effective if learned as a theory or a concept but needs to be a process of questioning and reflecting, especially on areas where borders are drawn and 'the other' is created. These borders must be, in a sense, 'unlearned.' The often uncomfortable process of getting to this unlearning, and how to support this process in order to encourage a greater sense of responsibility among business students, is the focus of her current PhD research.

Martin Parker is Professor of Organization Studies in the Department of Management, Bristol University, UK. He writes about alternative organizations, politics and ethics, and culture and organizing.

Roland Paulsen is Associate Professor in Sociology at Lund University, Sweden. His first book, *Arbetssamhället* (Gleerups, 2010), is a meta-empirical study of how the meanings of work have varied historically. His second book, *Empty Labor* (Cambridge University Press, 2014), is an interview study that he carried out for his doctoral dissertation of employees who spend a large proportion of their working days on private activities. His third book, *Vi bara lyder* (Atlas, 2015), analyzes how employees obey rules of which they intellectually disapprove. He is also the co-author of *Return to Meaning* (Oxford University Press, 2017), which discusses the changing meaning of social science under the paradigm of 'publish or perish.'

Marta Połeć is a PhD candidate in humanistic management, Faculty of Management and Social Communication, Jagiellonian University in Kraków, Poland. She holds an MA in culture and media management from the Jagiellonian University, and a BA in both management and ethnology from the University of Warsaw. She is Project Manager for the Ethnography of Informal Organization of Street Artists in Poland (Polish Ministry of Science and Higher Education) Diamond Grant research project. Her research interests are focused on theory of organization, street performances, the urban sphere and ethnography.

Arménio Rego is Professor at Católica Porto Business School, Portugal. His work has been published in journals such as *Applied Psychology: An International Review*, *Human Relations*, *Journal of Business Ethics*, *Journal of Business Research*, *Journal of Management* and *Leadership Quarterly*, among others. His research examines positive organizational behavior. He is the lead author of *The Virtues of Leadership: Contemporary Challenges for Global Managers* (with Cunha and Clegg, Oxford University Press, 2012).

Ace Volkmann Simpson is Senior Lecturer in Organizational Behavior in the UTS Business School, University of Technology Sydney, Australia and a member of the Center for Business and Social Innovation, a leading research center. He has a strong interest in human well-being, flourishing and social justice, and his research brings a critical-social perspective to positive organizational practices such as humility, psychological safety, paradox and love. His main research focus is on the cultivation of organizational compassion, which he is currently studying as a critical missing factor in most programs aiming to address the persistent problem of workplace bullying. His research has been published in journals such as *Journal of Management*, *Journal of Business Ethics* and *Journal of Management Inquiry*.

Anke Strauß is a critical management and organization researcher based in Berlin, Germany. Her research interests are the situation between art and (business) organizations, including the mutual influence of art and business, interdisciplinary forms of collaboration, alternative ways of organizing and the role of affect and aesthetics for organizing (work)lives. Since 2015, together with Christina Ciupke, she has developed collaborative ways of researching, creating and presenting knowledge.

John Vaughan studied undergraduate sociology and economics at the University of Leeds, UK, under Professor Zygmunt Bauman among others, after which he became a computer programmer at a car factory. He later went into the teaching of English as a foreign language and worked in Japan, the Middle East and many European countries. After an MBA, he continued working in business schools in the UK and Asia, focusing on organizational behavior and international human resource management. During this period he developed the multi-cultural group learning model. His fourth career involves writing and helping individuals focus on their direction and values.

Karl E. Weick is Emeritus Professor and the Rensis Likert Distinguished University Professor at the Ross School of Business at the University of Michigan, USA. He has introduced the concepts of loose coupling, mindfulness and sensemaking and developed several ideas of organizational imagination used in many theoretical as well as practical contexts. He is the author of many fundamental books on organizing and organizations, including the classic *The Social Psychology of Organizing*.

Prologue

Anke Strauß and Christina Ciupke

Hope is a paradoxical place. It is where we store what we long for and what we are fearful of at the same time. It is where we acknowledge the fragility of our lives. Hope lies in uncertainty.

Writing poems can be a poetic expression of hope, but desire is a matter of the body. And so it needs to be read out loud so that hope can become an embodied expression that works as an integral part of our bodily sensorium. Hearing ourselves saying out loud "I hope" frames everything that follows it. How many facets of hope exist? It is our voices that tell us about it, that resonate with and interconnect various bodies. It can be firm and strong like the trunk of a tree or fragile and nearly non-existent like a breeze whispering in the foliage. But, even when it is nearly not there, this nearly is enough for hope to persist in the most hostile situations. Thus hope is the ultimate expression of life – and yet it has to be practised. Reading the following poem out loud as a practice of hope is directed towards what matters to people when thinking about their work lives.

Yet "I hope" can also be used as an incantation that evokes any other landscape of what really matters and concurrently what is really at stake in our lives. Becoming aware of this landscape might allow us to navigate through the dust that the collapse of our current (Western) worlds entails and reinvent how to live on our damaged planet.

Working Utopias[1]
I hope work as a relation is friendship.
I hope work as a relation becomes less dominated by fear.
I hope work as a relation is trying again.
I worry that work relations become increasingly strategic.
I worry work relations are undermined by competition.
I hope that work relations can be structured differently than merely through market logic.
I hope work as a relation is collective daydreaming.

I worry about the strategic cruelty of professionals.
I wonder what parasites do to work relations.
I worry that work as a relation is defined by efficiency.

I hope work as a relation can transgress networking logics.
I hope we start building packs.
I hope work as a relation is based on trust.
I worry that work as a relation is dominated by opportunism.

I hope that work as a relation is making space for togetherness.
I hope work as a relation has more time to unfold.
I hope that work as a relation can balance fears.
I worry about how much is excluded in current work relations.
I hope that decision-making is shared in work relations.
I worry about abusive work relations.
I wonder what complicity does to work relations.

I worry that work as a relation is affected by opportunistic strategies.
I worry that work as a relation is affected by an increasingly unequal
distribution of resources.
I hope that work as a relation embraces the unpredictable.
I hope that work as a relation gives shelter for the not yet fully grown, not fully
developed ideas, desires, plans and people.

I hope that work as a relation can also handle deals.
I hope that work as a relation can recuperate patience again.
I worry that work as a relation is overpowered by expectations.
I worry that work as a relation has been replaced by functions and positions.
I hope we can work side by side.
I hope that work as a relation gives more space to everyone.
I worry that intimacy can be abused in work relations.

I hope that we do not lose respect for the other.
I hope work as a relation nurtures solidarity.
I hope that work as a relation is growing.
I wonder how to think about the future of work relations.
I hope that work as a relation gives enough time for listening.
I hope that work as a relation leads to joint forces.
I hope work as a relation invites [ex]change.
I hope work as a relation becomes more caring.
I hope we can also let go of work relations.

I hope.

Hope as being committed to a proposal as a practice of respect.
Hope as listening.
Hope as witchcraft that names and invites those who are missing.
Hope as a sensing and working with different energy levels.
Hope as a practice to unfold something powerful.

Hope as picking up and joining ideas of different people as a practice of
mutual engagement.
Hope as sharing worries, dreams and personal longings as a practice of trust.
Hope as awareness of the importance of protecting, nourishing and letting the
inside grow to open up to the outside.
Hope as a being open and curious towards others as a practice of being
non-judgmental.

Hope as acknowledging the fragility of embryonic encounters as a practice of protecting.

Hope as making space despite fear.
Hope as a practice of spacing.

Hope as a practice of bricolage.
Hope as exploring the threshold that in- and excludes instead of reproducing it.
Hope as rejecting the power of the factual.
Hope as dancing as a practice of togetherness, that does not need words.
Hope as focusing on interest and fascination instead of achievement and expertise.
Hope as a practice of rendering the unknown as a lateral presence that does not give answers but determines action.

Hope as experimenting with transgressing one's own boundaries as a practice of taking risks.
Hope as being prepared to be disappointed.
Hope as remaining prepared to be affected and to affect.

NOTE

1. Working Utopias is a research collaboration between an organization studies scholar and a choreographer. It researches various artist-run organizations to explore the role of utopian imaginaries for organizing work lives based on solidarity despite conditions of individualization. This text has many roots, two of which are the writings of Ernst Bloch and our experiences with the process of the Artist Summit at Dance Platform 2018 in Germany. We would like to thank all participants and particularly the HOOD artist collective for their generous invitation for co-creating hope.

Introduction: Organizing hope: Narratives for a better future

Daniel Ericsson and Monika Kostera

According to thinkers such as Zygmunt Bauman (2017a) and Wolfgang Streeck (2016), the current social world is ruled by a crumbling, morbid system. Old social institutions are failing and no new ones have yet emerged. This state in between ruling institutions has been labeled *the interregnum* by Bauman (2012), using Antonio Gramsci's metaphor. "The crisis consists precisely in the fact that the old is dying and the new cannot be born; in this interregnum a great variety of morbid symptoms appear" (Gramsci, 1971, p. 276), Gramsci foretold. Rather than literally denoting an era after the death of one sovereign yet before the enthronement of a new monarch, in today's late global capitalism an interregnum denotes "times of uncertainty, and while [it is] raising many questions, three of them seem particularly pertinent to address at a time when rulers no longer can rule and the ruled no longer wish to be ruled: institutional disparity, the future of migrants and the endurability of the planet" (Bauman, 2012, p. 51).

The structures that once supported collective social action (Bauman, 2012) and which enabled more or less smooth self-regulation of economic mechanisms (Streeck, 2016) have lost their taken-for-granted character and often reveal their powerlessness to solve any of the mounting problems that face humanity and the planet. The usual resourcefulness and responsibility that seemed to be found at the bottom of modernity are giving way to direct violence and what looks like a relentless raid on the common good, blatant malice, greed, mounting fear, uncertainty and a sense of powerlessness. Humanity seems to have betrayed its values or, with the rapid dismantling and discarding of the institutions that once held memory and social identity, such as academia and eldership, it may even look as if it never really had them, as if it all were a dream or a lie.

Humans however depend on making sense of the world and life, perhaps as much as on nourishing their bodies for survival and so on. In times of rabid meaninglessness, we fill the unbearable void with whatever we are able to find, such as simplified and idolized images of "what it used to be like," a phantasmatic past that has never been. Modern countries, organizations and ideologies in this sense seem to go backward in time, engaging in a nostalgic yet politically consequential quest for a "retrotopia," in Zygmunt Bauman's word (2017a).

Without any structures linking us to utopias located in the future, humanity thus seems to have run out of faith. Instead, we have made a full U-turn and pursue pasts that would redeem us from the present and all the problems it presents. But it is not possible to turn back the clock and, even less, recreate a past that has never been. In the words of Zygmunt Bauman:

> There are no shortcuts leading to a quick, adroit and effortless damming of the "back to" currents – whether to Hobbes, to tribes, to inequality or to the womb. . . . We need to brace ourselves for a long period marked by more questions than answers and more problems than solutions, as well as for acting in the shadow of finely balanced chances of success and defeat. But in this one case – in opposition to the cases to which Margaret Thatcher used to impute it – the verdict "there is no alternative" will hold fast, with no likelihood of appeal. More than at any other time, we – human inhabitants of the Earth – are in the either/or situation: we face joining either hands, or common graves. (Bauman, 2017a, pp. 166–167)

In this book, we have gathered a collection of chapters that provide different answers to Bauman's call, considering what can be done to alter the direction of the dead course on which humanity seems to be set. The authors we invited to partake in our endeavor were encouraged to come up with ideas that would make it worthwhile for humanity to take itself through the abyss to the other side of the interregnum and dare to try to build a new system, hopefully better and more just for everyone and kinder to the planet we share, because, like Bauman, we believe that much now depends on our ability and courage to collectively rethink the state of the world and find hope – a gift and an ability that has nothing to do with optimism but much with the power of social imagination (Bauman, 2016).

In our call for contributions, we stressed the importance of *organizing* hope, partly because we consider the joining of hands in order to move beyond the interregnum to be essentially a matter of coordinating people, resources, energies, inspirations and aspirations, and partly because we believe that the social imagination of hope is especially crucial on the organizational level. Coupled with critical awareness and an active use of courageous thinking, it is in our organizations that new ideas will be formed (or old ones re-formed) to cope with our present-day dilemmas and problems. This is an activity at the heart of what organization theorist Heather Höpfl (2013) used to regard as the necessary, redeeming resistance against a morbid system, and for a desired future after the current system is abolished. As such, it brings hope in a situation defined by its hopelessness.

Our project unfolds in relation to a large and growing number of publications depicting the bleak state of the world and trying to draw attention to the shocking seriousness of our current situation. Concerned voices are raised from different perspectives and places in the political spectrum, from socialist sociologist Zygmunt Bauman (2017a), to environmental activist Naomi Klein (2014), to deep ecology author Clive Ponting (2007), to conservative philosopher Rafał Matyja (2018). Organization and management theory has its own abundant literature of this kind, including in recent years: Cederström and Fleming (2012), Alvesson (2014), Skoglund (2015) and Fleming (2017). These are very important and much needed, as is the growing interest in alternative organizations (for example Parker et al., 2007; Parker, 2011; Kostera, 2014; Reedy et al., 2016).

Few engaged social scientists and readers of social science need convincing that things are not as good as they were promising to be for many just a few decades ago, as David Graeber (2015) compellingly demonstrates. We do not think it is good or promising. Instead, we very much agree with Peter Fleming's (2019) diagnosis: the worst is yet to come. Overpowered by suicidal work ethics, planetary destruction, financial crashes and treacherous and completely irresponsible politicians we are, in fact, all together in the sinking ship of capitalism. A few billionaires are getting more outrageously rich every day, at the expense of all the rest of us. But there is much more to come, and there are no reasons to be cheerful. There are specters haunting the sociosphere: of all the good futures that never happened, the dreams we had, but also of the grisly future that has not yet materialized.

To face all this, we need a special mindset Fleming (2019) proposes, and he lists four possible responses. The first is *optimism*, and it suggests that things are improving – in fact, are quite good already – and makes use of different measures, mostly statistical, to make buoyant points. It may result in colorful and funny moving graphs, but the audience is increasingly hard to convince. The second is *nihilism*, which recommends embracing the destruction and bleakness to make a buck on it, or two. Misery can be profitable for those who know how to profit from it. Apart from being sadistic at best and psychopathic at worst, it is also extremely stupid. Not even the most expensive hideaway on New Zealand will save the rich from planetary destruction when the day comes.

The third response is *radical positivity*, preached by some energetic activists from the left. In the face of disaster, we should do whatever is within our power to resist it and save ourselves and the planet from the wreckage. As true as this message is, it is also, unfortunately, not encouraging: not much is within our power. The fourth and last proposition is Fleming's own, which he calls *revolutionary pessimism*. It is a response which "does [not] succumb to resignation, even in the face of insurmountable odds," but "anticipates the nastiest surprises that a derailed civilization has to offer, yet refuses the cult of futility" (2019, p. 39).

Revolutionary pessimism however is quite an Anglo-Saxon response. Being Swedish and Polish, we do not completely resonate with this mindset, even though we recognize both its beauty and its use. Instead, we propose a fifth response with Slavic-Scandi undertones: *radical mourning together with persistent hope*. Historically Slavs have not been the happiest of people, most of them (except Russians) constantly being attacked and occupied by not too friendly invaders from all sides. They have therefore developed a great talent for mourning and obstinacy, which is equaled by the Scandinavian stubbornness in the face of unforgiving natural conditions, poverty and darkness. Swedes know that the past is not going to come back, and, even if it did, this is no reason to celebrate. Poles (and Czechs) know that hope is nothing like fluffy optimism but can take the inelegant form of pigheaded refusal to accept that the dominant order is obvious or normal or, indeed, one with legitimacy to define the future. Vaclav Havel, who knew rather well what he was speaking of, said the following in *Disturbing the Peace*:

> Hope, in this deep and powerful sense, is not the same as joy that things are going well, or willingness to invest in enterprises that are obviously headed for early success, but rather an ability to work for something because it is good, not just because it stands a chance to succeed. The more unpromising the situation in which we demonstrate hope, the deeper that hope is. Hope is not the same thing as optimism. It is not the conviction that something will turn out well, but the certainty that something makes sense, regardless of how it turns out. In short, I think that the deepest and most important form of hope, the only one that can keep us above water and urge us to good works, and the only true source of the breathtaking dimension of the human spirit and its efforts, is something we get, as it were, from "elsewhere." It is also this hope, above all, that gives us the strength to live and continually to try new things, even in conditions that seem as hopeless as ours do, here and now. (Havel, 1990, p. 182)

Zygmunt Bauman (2017b), the Polish sociologist, held a similar view on the matter, explaining that, for a social scientist, hope is the desire and also the impulse to make our planet a more hospitable place to live. It is a radical act, because it is immortal, has its roots in the future, and needs no proof rooted in the past. It makes life worth living. Such hope needs no justification, no motivation and no cheerful state of mind – it is the desire to live, the lust of life even under the most dispiriting circumstances. In short, it is a refusal to make things easy for *them*, whoever they are, and give up and die.

Poles and Swedes in this vein simply don't give up, and this is not because they constantly feel like dancing. The Polish peasant Ślimak, for example, protagonist of the novel *The Outpost* by Bolesław Prus (1953), knows very well that the occupying Prussian empire is overpowering and that nobody will come to save him and his family. He is called Ślimak, the Snail, not because he is "stupid," but because he is slow to change his mind and sympathies. Ślimak thus refuses to sell his farm to German settlers, even though that would have profited him, because he does not want to change his identity and become a laborer. The farm stands out as an impossible outpost of Polishness and autonomy but is in the end saved by Ślimak with help from his poor Jewish friend Jojne.

Equally persistent are Swedish farmers Karl Oskar Nilsson and his wife Kristina, protagonists of the novel *The Emigrants* by Vilhelm Moberg (2013). Karl Oskar and Kristina are struggling to keep their farm in an almost barren land and unforgiving climate. Their hard work, loyalty and dedication, however, do not bring them a happy ending. When their son dies, they decide to emigrate to the USA, escaping poverty but never giving up on who they are and what they care about.

Radical mourning together with persistent hope is thus the overarching narrative we – Daniel and Monika – live by. Others narrate hope differently. Plato made Socrates speak of hope as of something that a person has little or no power over, something like fate (Plato's *Protagoras*). Aesop depicted hope as the swallow in his fables, the bird bringing spring but also, possibly, dying in the process, especially if it comes too early. But it speaks the truth, that spring is about to come, even if "one swallow does not make a summer" indeed. And then there is, of course, Pandora. The first woman received a jar which she was told not to open. Of course, she opened it, and out came all the miseries of the world. She tried to shut the jar but it was too late. The only thing left in it was – Hope. Blessing – or misfortune? There is no easy answer to this question. We suggest that it is, indeed, both, at the same time. At least that is what "our" hope – mourning and obstinacy – looks like. But it is also beautiful, because it is, at the very bottom, about devotion to something that matters, to life itself.

The narratives told by the contributors to this volume come in many shapes and colors. They are grounded in the contributors' different empirical and theoretical experiences, and guided by different philosophical, political, scientific and aesthetical underpinnings. As a consequence, many different notions of hope come to life in the following pages, as well as many different approaches to coping with the interregnum. This in turn is a reflection of our open call for contributions, in which we welcomed narrative explorations into the future on themes such as "alternative organizations for social inclusion and ecological blossoming," "compassion and organizing with the other," "meaningful work and workplaces" and "activists, social entrepreneurs and idealists."

The answer to our call was overwhelming, and – after having conducted a double blind review process[1] – we are proud to present 18 chapters that in different ways explore hope. The chapters have been arranged in two thematic sections based on our observation that the different chapters in varying degrees are exploring utopian hope in terms of "why," "what," "where" and "how." One group of authors follow philosophical and theoretical paths addressing "why" and "what" in order to rethink hope and outline an alternative future, whereas another group of authors seek empirical and/or imaginative inspiration in order to chisel a way (or a method) out of the interregnum, stressing "where" to look for guidance and "how" to go into the future.

The distinction between these two groups is of course not strict or mutually exclusive. Both within and between these two broadly defined groups there are overlaps, nuances and contradictions that speak against our thematic structure. We do however hope that the imposed structure could serve as a meaningful road map for all those interested in continuing the conversation initiated by thinkers such as Bauman (2017a) and Streeck (2016). There might be no grand narrative on organizing hope, yet the chapters in this book, taken together, send a strong message: Organizing hope to overcome the interregnum is a complex assemblage of emic and etic inspirations fueled by inter alia new empirical vistas, metaphorical thinking, social imagination and anarchistic approaches.

The prologue preceding this introduction is a poem by Christina Ciupke and Anke Strauss invoking such metaphorical thinking and directing attention towards the different notions and streams that come after.

First out in Part One is a short reflection by Karl E. Weick (Chapter 1, "Hopeful organizing in the crucible of the interregnum"), pondering the possible workings of hope in a macro interregnum and its implications for organizing, as something unfolding.

Then, in Chapter 2, "Alternative futures: 'Hope is a thing with feathers,'" providing philosophical and theoretical inspirations for the future, Martin Parker seeks to rewrite critical theory and critical management studies by endowing "critical" with less cynical connotations in relation to hope. Critical diagnosis and accounts of organizations and management are not enough, Parker argues; they are only the first step in a dialectic towards the envisioning of a better future to come. Without such envisioning, critical theorizing is not only without any (real) consequences but also intrinsically "boring" – in the sense of conservatively reproducing more of the same, i.e. exactly those things in life that deserve to be criticized. "We should be suspicious of utopia, but enthusiastic utopians," Parker concludes.

In Chapter 3, "The utopian quest for an alternative," Roland Paulsen picks up Parker's dialectical thread of thought and wonders if it is really possible to come up with an empirically grounded (and workable) alternative to the dominant modes of production and consumption. An array of different alternatives could indeed be envisioned, from Ruth Levitas via Fredric Jameson to Erik Olin Wright, but they all reveal a troublesome paradox: The more the alternatives are turned into realpolitik, the more they are inverted under the influence of bleak *There is no alternative!* rhetoric – and/or by their unintended consequences. The utopian endeavor, argues Paulsen, is therefore something other than a project of (merely) opposition: "It is a challenging quest, an appeal to hope, weighted by an impossible burden of proof."

In contrast to Paulsen's conceptualization of utopia as a never-ending quest for something that might never come into existence, John Vaughan seems to have found what he has been searching for: an intellectual (dis)-position that might enable business school teachers and researchers to regain control over their thinking and actions. In Chapter 4, "Epimethean hope or Promethean expectation? The role of organisational behaviour," Vaughan chisels out this (dis)position in terms of five interrelated themes or elements: a Baumanesque critique of neoliberalism, critical thinking according to John Dewey, ideographic methodology, a progressive understanding of organizational behavior, and multi-cultural group learning. Taken together, these elements represent "a celebration of diversity and humanness," and provide fertile soil for democratic "gardening" projects, according to Vaughan.

John G. McClellan is also into democratic "gardening," although of a slightly different kind. In Chapter 5, "Transforming work into 'play': Genuine conversations as hope for meaningful organizational change," he invites the reader to partake in transforming contemporary work life, from discursive practices of self-subordination and self-alienation to self-awareness and engagement. The inspiration for such an emancipatory and hopeful transformation comes from Hans-Georg Gadamer and his notion of genuine conversation in which the "otherness of the other" is embraced in a playful manner. By opening up conversations on "subject matters" such as work-related problems, fears, feelings of emptiness, and anxieties, not only does a hopeful horizon of otherwise hidden alternatives come into existence, argues McClellan, but also mutual appreciation and meaningful collaborations.

The democratic aspects of contemporary work and business life are also the center of attention in Chapter 6, "Hope in business organizing for societal progress: Three narratives." Here Stewart Clegg, Ace Volkmann Simpson, Miguel Pina e Cunha and Arménio Rego explore capitalist organizations and their role of providing betterment for society (or not). Their discussion is organized in terms of three narratives. The ethical narrative addresses the philosophical question of value, "What ought to be?"; the empirical narrative puts scientific focus upon the question of "What is?"; whereas the prudential narrative evolves around the political issue of "What can be?" The authors show how these three narratives have developed through history, and how they have ended up in providing contradictory answers to the posed questions. Despite the different descriptions of – and prescriptions for – corporate capitalism, the authors see hope in a nuanced and non-authoritarian understanding of business activities; and they see hope in societal and organizational democracy. Capitalist organizations may act well or badly depending on the strategic choices that they have made, but it is the responsibility of democratic governments to safeguard the public and the public good, the argument runs.

Issues of democracy and responsibility are also at stake in Wendelin Küpers's "Post-Pandoran hope for moving wisely beyond the neo-Promethean Anthropocene" (Chapter 7), which closes Part One, "Philosophical and theoretical inspirations." One could, however, argue that these issues are given even greater importance, as Küpers addresses the Anthropocene and its devastating consequences on our geo-bio-social becomings. Beyond the dystopic narratives of the Anthropocene, however, there is hope, Küpers argues, but it requires a turn to practical wisdom, "a form of enacted moral excellence to create flourishing and happiness." To inculcate this turn, Küpers interprets the Anthropocene in relation to the mythical stories of Prometheus and Pandora's box, and ends up envisioning a post-anthropocentric age, devoid of Promethean hubris and fueled by the release of Pandoran hope. Küpers calls this age the "eco- or *zoë*-cene," the era of "meanings of life in an ecological sense."

In Part Two, "Empirical and imaginative inspirations," Richard Longman follows suit with a study on alternative organizing, "'Hope-full purpose': Time, oblivion, and the strange attractors of Pandora's box" (Chapter 8). The explicit objective, for Longman, is to unite Pandoran hope with purpose because, as he argues, "retrieving the hope that is lodged at the bottom of Pandora's box must be a purposeful act." If so, then it "requires us to become agents of change, living out relationships and practices that remedy our present shortcomings and characterize a better future," as Longman puts it. The empirical location of investigation is *Medium*, an online site of social journalism, and, based on his readings of the case, Longman presents a "portmanteau construction" in terms of "hope-full purpose" – a construction that he hopes offers an organizational alternative to "short-term gain and individual egoism."

Similarly to Longman, George Cairns writes against the prevalent self-interest and discriminatory powers of contemporary forms of organization, looking for self-organizing communities working for the common good. His remedy to the situation in Chapter 9, "Against organization – farewell to hope?," is however different. The betterment of society, he argues, requires the de(con)struction of "hope" and "organization" as we currently know the two concepts, and the simultaneous rejection of how they currently are being used and appropriated by elite actors. Cairns sees potential in both Feyerabend's intellectual approach and Guillet de Monthoux's ideas on anarchism, but he is also empirically inspired by three very different community initiatives: a housing co-op, community facility services, and a parallel currency. "The key aim," Cairns concludes, "must be to find a minimum common ground within different world-views that will provide hope for a better shared future while enabling true diversity and individuality at the local level."

Also for Anna Góral, the local community is put in focus, as it is believed to form the basis for alternative organizations striving for resilience, sustainability and social inclusion. In Chapter 10, "Idealists and dreamers: Struggling for more resilient communities via alternative organisations," Góral tries to find out what makes people tick in such organizations, despite the many hardships they often encounter. She finds an answer to her query by studying three different empirical cases (a community center, a support agency for rural development, and an interest organization for disabled people), and she arrives at the conclusion that resilience goes hand in hand with people who firmly believe that their visions and engagement will have real social impact. They are idealists and dreamers, activists and altruists – and, as such, they function as the "axis mundi" of their local communities.

In Chapter 11, "Cadriste (R)Evolution," Markus Kallifatides shifts focus from local communities producing social good to nation-state democracies grappling with social injustices and environmental destruction. For these democracies to be successful, the capitalistic formula of "money, commodity, more money" must, according to Kallifatides, be replaced by an alternative formula in which "money must be invested in something other than commodities, and the 'return on investment' must be something other than more money." Kallifatides calls thus for a (r)evolution, and the inspiration for this he finds in the institutional particularities of Sweden and the so-called "Swedish model." Daydreaming away, Kallifatides conjures up a provisional utopia of institutional investments, and a class alliance of the urban middle classes and wage laborers. This cadre becomes a reformist avant-garde that enables a shift in the power balance from capital to labor – "and from those now alive to those not yet born."

Tali Padan is also occupied by the necessity of change in order to counteract the devastating consequences of crumbling institutions. Her focus however is on democratic citizenship education, i.e. the development of political, social and moral literacy, and she queries the type of learning processes that could make young people develop such skills, as well as prepare them to bridge the tensions between on the one hand the individual and the collective, and diversity and unity on the other. In Chapter 12, "The hope of discomfort: Using democratic citizenship education for transformative learning," Padan turns to Mezirow's concept of "transformative learning" for inspiration, and she reports from her own experiences in working with the Betzavta method. Centered around a "discomforting dilemma," this method encourages the participants not only to reflect upon their selves and their experiences but also to confront the very assumptions they make about the world and others – even if it hurts – because it is in the experienced discomfort, Padan argues, that hope resides; it makes the participants more open and emotionally able to change.

A different pathway to emancipation that might make it possible to move beyond the present-day interregnum is offered by Daniel Ericsson in Chapter 13, "Technologies of the commune: A bridge over troubled water?" Ericsson's point of departure is what Foucault called "technologies of the self," epistemological truth games that individuals use on themselves to attain a desired state of being, such as the sacrificing of oneself by subordination. From the perspective of capitalism's technologies of the self, Ericsson advocates an alternative epistemology that is "neither self-centred nor directed towards self-discipline," and sets out to narrate this in terms of "technology of the commune." The protagonist of his narrative is Toffler's utopian "prosumer," and the plot twists into the music industry and the phenomenon of "house concerts." Listening to the experiences of "prosumers" enacting such "house concerts," Ericsson chisels out the sense moral: the music industry is reconfiguring into a collective knowledge-making project that seems to free the actors from "(at least some of) the yokes of capitalism."

The field of culture is also the empirical vista for Agata Morgan. In Chapter 14, "'Dad, Do Not Cry': Imagination and creativity on their own terms in inclusive cities and communities," she challenges the concept of creativity, especially as it has been used by Richard Florida in his works on the "creative class," and argues for a more inclusive conceptualization of creativity. For inspiration on how to create a new narrative on creativity, in which creativity is enacted for a greater good rather than only serving a chosen elite, Morgan turns to visual artist Łukasz Surowiec and his mural paintings. In Surowiec's artwork Morgan finds a powerful story of social change that "restores our hope in better, more inclusive cities and communities," and through which otherwise silenced voices are being heard.

Marta Połeć also turns to the field of culture as she focuses upon a somewhat marginalized urban phenomenon: street performances. In Chapter 15, "Street performances in hope for the future of the urban sphere: Human interaction, self-realization and emotive enactment," she reports on an ethnographic study carried out in several Polish cities where she has followed tens of performers closely and attentively. She argues that street performances can be seen as inspiring and hopeful in many ways. Firstly, street performances inform us about what it means to be human, carrying values such as trust, cooperation and kindness, thus contributing to a humanistic atmosphere of public domains. Secondly, street performances express the right to live one's life regardless of any social and normative expectations. And, thirdly, street performances represent emotional enactment. If we could live as we learn at the street shows, Połeć concludes, our lives would definitely be "more friendly, interactive, mindful and trustful."

If street performances embrace the richness of life, then linearity kills it. Linearity is a "morbid activity," write Michał Izak and Monika Kostera in Chapter 16, "There is hope in organizing: Dialogic imagination against linearity," because it aspires "to cleanse the world of all ambivalence ... everything that is poetic and baroque." Izak and Kostera therefore set out to replace linearity and linear thinking with metaphorical thinking and dialogic imagination as an inspiration for alternative organizing into the future. Backed by extensive ethnographic field work carried out in a variety of organizations, their arguments unfold in the form of a compelling tale: where room is made for imagination, not only new organizational understandings and directions emerge but also meaningful interactions. Imagination releases and encompasses organizational dynamics otherwise suppressed, and allows otherwise unseen and silent actors to partake in organizational sensemaking. "And therein lies our hope," Izak and Kostera conclude, "as a desire motivated by the forlorn state of much of the organizational world as it is."

In Chapter 17, "Good labour: Affirmative work awareness and hope," Małgorzata Ćwikła brings "work" back into the discussion about the meaning and richness of life. Work, as it has been predominantly problematized within contemporary research, is most often associated with things like exploitation, inequalities, blurred boundaries and so on, but Ćwikła is eager to change this. By approaching work with an affirmative attitude, she therefore turns the research agenda upside down through simply asking people to describe what they find good about their jobs.

Her study reveals that the answers to this question could be categorized into elements in organizations such as "interpersonal relations," "range of duties" and "personal attitude." For Ćwikła, these elements indicate what might be missing in contemporary work life, and probably should form the basis for organizational projections into the future.

Aneta Milczarczyk also has an interest in the good aspects of life, but her interest is directed towards people who want to make the world a better place to live in for others – and who actually take actions to make their dreams and visions come true. In Chapter 18, "Actors of goodness and hope in action," Milczarczyk presents a case study of such people working at the Southend Credit Union, an initiative taken to tackle an experienced injustice in the local community, and geared at helping marginalized people to straighten out their lives by straightening out their finances. What comes out of Milczarczyk's interpretation is a kind of self-fulfilling prophecy of hope: The actors at Southend Credit Union are led by their hope of making things better, and their actions bring hope into the local community – which in turn fosters the notion of collective hope. All in all, argues Milczarczyk, hope is a stimulus for social change.

Pondering the mystery of writing, rock musician and poet Patti Smith (2017) asks herself why she is doing it. Her answer to the question is revealed in the book's title, *Devotion*. It is neither an optimistic mindset nor determination that defines it, but something quite different. In the author's own words:

> Things are slow moving. There is a pencil stub in my pocket.
> What is the task? To compose a work that communicates on several levels, as in a parable, devoid of the stain of cleverness.
> What is the dream? To write something fine, that would be better than I am, and that would justify my trials and indiscretions. To offer proof, through a scramble of words, that God exists.
> Why do I write? My finger, as a stylus, traces the question in the blank air. A familiar riddle posed since youth, withdrawing from play, comrades and the valley of love, girded with words, a beat outside.
> Why do we write? A chorus erupts.
> Because we cannot simply live. (Smith, 2017, p. 93)

What is writing for our contributors in this volume? It is now for you to find out.

NOTE

1. The editors would like to express the deepest gratitude to all of our colleagues who took their time to review one or several chapters: Sylwia Ciuk, Stewart Clegg, Mathilda Dahl, Krzystof Durczak, Daniel Ericsson, Malin Gawell, Anna Góral, Jenny Helin, Michal Izak, Tommy Jensen, Kenneth Mølbjerg Jørgensen, Markus Kallifatides, Monika Kostera, Wendelin Küpers, Richard Longman, Tomasz Ludwicki, Henrietta Nilsson, Daniel Nyberg, Tomasz Ochinowski, Tali Padan, Alexia Panayiotou, Roland Paulsen, Marta Połeć, Anette Risberg, Joanna Srednicka, Anke Strauß and Marta Szeluga-Romanska. Without your effort, the book would simply not have come into existence.

PART ONE

Philosophical and theoretical inspirations

1. Hopeful organizing in the crucible of the interregnum

Karl E. Weick

The unsettling gap known as an "interregnum" seems formidable, which may make it hard to see that it can be scaled down as well as up. The combination of an old dying order, intermediate flux filled with despair and possibilities, and an ineffable new order suggests that the gap between the old and the new is an interwoven mixture of hope, fear, and imagination. Equivalent structures are visible at more micro levels such as those associated with organizing in extreme contexts (Hällgren et al., 2018). It is the extremity of these latter contexts, as well as the progression of decline, confusion, and redoing, that makes it possible to use the micro example of organizing for high reliability (e.g. Ramanujam and Roberts, 2018) to see into the workings of hope in a macro interregnum.

Our working definition of hope is Rorty's modest description of hope as "imagined conjectures addressing specific purposes" (quoted in Carlsen et al., 2012, p. 294). The following discussion is grounded in losses of the old order in events such as the collapse of the roof over the B&O Railroad Museum and the destruction of several irreplaceable artifacts (Christianson et al., 2009), air traffic control thwarted by non-standard communication (Weick, 1990), and flawed pediatric heart surgery fostered by hubris and a slow learning curve (Weick and Sutcliffe, 2003). These examples focus on decline and a resulting gap of variable duration, but they are less clear about a new order. That lack of clarity is not unique to micro losses since it is also found in a macro interregnum.

The interregnums (plural) experienced in these more localized extreme settings are episodic, bounded, and transient, yet they retain the basics of a pause between regimes. They retain the fact of uncertainty, the felt intensity of important moment(s), the tenuous balancing of fear and hope, and the necessity to reconstitute an evolving present. Both organizing itself and foresight into a provisional order are reconstituted. The organizing takes the form of "reconstituting," and the "evolving present" is the provisional order. An evolving present can range from a heightened resolve to articulate and move toward utopias to a similar resolve to move toward more modest improvements.

Here is a sample of what we can learn about organizing in the interregnum when we watch people engage in reliability seeking.

First, when people engage with extreme contexts, their organizing is more like a stance than a place (organization). The stance is a disposition of activity guided by a grammar of rules and conventions that establish coordinated common ground (Weick, 1979, p. 3). In other words, the stance embodies shared recipes for action and interpretation. This means that hoping tends to be woven into the common ground of the conventions and the recipes. For example, a stance for managing in the face of threatening disruptions has been conceptualized as mindful organizing. This form of organizing is composed of a preoccupation with failure, a reluctance to simplify, a sensitivity to operations, a commitment to resilience, and a deference to expertise (Weick et al., 1999; Weick and Sutcliffe, 2015; Sutcliffe, 2018). Hope is embedded in this mindful stance in the form of *resilience* to keep going. Hope is embedded in a serious effort to capture detail rather than to *simplify*, a capture that opens possibilities and provides resources for imagination. Attention to *failures* likewise suggests openings, as does deference to *expertise*. Experts often spot options and possibilities that have been missed or normalized into invisibility. Finally, the stance is anchored by *current operations* in the present (Busby, 2006).

Second, activity in the gap between the declining old and the ineffable new is made more, not less, complicated by any successful achievement. John Dewey articulated a plausible mechanism. Every accomplishment

> effects a new distribution of energies which have henceforth to be employed in ways for which past experience gives no exact instruction. . . . From the side of what has gone before achievement settles something. From the side of what comes after, it complicates, introducing new problems and unsettling factors. There is something pitifully juvenile in the idea that "evolution," progress, means a definite amount of accomplishment which will forever stay done, and which by an exact amount lessens the amount still to be done, disposing once and for all of just so many perplexities. (Dewey, [1922] 2008, p. 197)

If this compounding of complications is the case, then hoping is part of a *sensitivity to current operations* and to the present in general. "[I]nstruction in what to do next can never come from an infinite goal, which for us is bound to be empty. It can be derived only from study of the deficiencies, irregularities and possibilities of the actual situation" (Dewey, [1922] 2008, p. 199). This is why, in extreme contexts, one often hears responders say "I've never seen this before, but I know what to do." Hope animates that sentence. In a macro interregnum, "knowing what to do" can feel like a much bigger problem. But it still lurks in the *deficiencies, irregularities and possibilities of the actual situation*.

Readers may object to Dewey's dismissal of an "empty infinite goal," arguing that ways out of the interregnum are neither infinite nor empty. That may be the case. But it is also the case that those exceptions are formulated and reformulated in an overdetermined present that is also changing.

Third, and again from John Dewey, we see that hopeful organizing is writ small and frequent, but with the capability to foster continued hoping.

> In every waking moment, the complete balance of the organism and its environment is constantly interfered with and as constantly restored. . . . Life is interruptions and recoveries. . . . [A]t these moments of a shifting of activity conscious feeling and thought arise and are accentuated. The disturbed adjustment of organism and environment is reflected in a temporary strife. (Dewey, [1922] 2008, p. 125)

In extreme contexts, whether created by uncontrolled wildland fire or by uncontrolled societal shortcomings, interruptions are abundant. What makes the interregnum a site for hoping is the conscious "accentuation of feeling and thought" produced by interruptions. In extreme contexts, this accentuation uncovers localized fears and options. And, if the organizing is sufficiently mindful, imaginative combinations of what is uncovered can be assembled. If we scale up this assembling to the level of Bauman's interregnum, interferences and accentuations continue to affect whether imagination can render the ineffable less so.

Fourth, G.L.S. Shackle's lovely phrase "haunted equilibrium" (1974, p. 77) captures the active quality of both a micro and a macro interregnum. Even though that interregnum is a gap, it is also an unsteady balancing of despair and hope. What is "haunted" about that equilibrium is that it can lose this balance without warning. Shackle puts it this way: Our adjustments

> are to the last degree fragile and unstable, because their basis is inevitably at all times partly figment. . . . [This state of affairs is "haunted" because] disillusion can call everything in question. What follows such a collapse must defy analysis, since reason for the time being recognizes its own defeat. . . . [This leads] to a new groping for adjustment and eventually to a new equilibrium of this peculiar kind. (1974, p. 77)

And, fifth, the recurring idea of possibilities enacted out of that which is troubling suggests that alertness and attention make a difference in the equilibria of an interregnum. Attention can be partitioned into at least three components. Attention is composed partly of its objects, which answer to the question: *To what* are they attending? Attention is also composed of resources, which answer to the question: *With what* are they attending? And attention is composed partly of goals, which answer to the question: *For what* are they attending? (Adapted from Dewey, 1989, pp. 333–340.) While the content of the answers to these questions provides insight into what is occurring in an interregnum, it may be even more crucial to assess the relative development and activation of all three. The interregnum may be a haunted equilibrium, but part of the "disillusion" that Shackle (1974) points to may be traced to a singular preoccupation with to, for, or with what. Pathways out of an interregnum should differ dramatically depending on the preferred component of attending.

To conclude, in the preceding discussion hope has been treated as a verb not a noun, and as a process not a state. The verb and the process can be generalized across levels of analysis and can connect macro and micro, at least in theory. Disruptions in an old order accentuate flux, thought, and feeling, which can be interwoven with hoping, thereby altering an evolving present. The very fact of interweaving makes it tough (and artificial) to pull apart an interregnum and focus on hope alone. It could be argued that the very inseparability of hoping is the feedstock of longing.

While the future is something of a mystery, what is less of a mystery is that it will be perceived from a stance in the present. That present stance matters a great deal. It can enrich an interregnum, a possibility that is evident in John Dewey's categorical imperative: "So act as to increase the meaning of present experience. . . . [S]tudy the needs and alternative possibilities lying within a unique and localized situation. . . . Till men give up the search for a general formula of progress they will not know where to look to find it" (Dewey, [1922] 2008, p. 196).

2. Alternative futures: 'Hope is a thing with feathers'

Martin Parker

HOPING: AGAINST HOPE

Hope isn't a very fashionable attitude right now.[1] When confronted with what already seems like irrevocable climate change, nativist politics, staggering global inequality and increasing corporate domination, only the stupid or naïve would invest heavily in the future. In any case, hope sounds cheesy and uncool. Hope is for the advertisers of mobile phones, or bright-eyed evangelicals waiting for the afterlife with a smile on their faces while the flames nibble at their toes. Hope is for children waiting for Santa. Realism and cynicism sound like much more adult attitudes to the present. In the *Divine Comedy*, Dante places the expression 'Abandon hope all ye who enter here' on the entrance to hell. I'm not sure why, because the best way to torture the damned would be to leave them with hope, not to let them know that there is no way out. What's the point of hope when the future is so clearly bleak?

However, one rather uncool genre of serious writing that is heavily invested in hope is futurological speculation concerning what our societies and economies might look like. This is a timid form of writing when compared to science fiction and fantasy, a sort of realism projected into the future but without any fractures or contradictions. When considering the shape of things to come, many writers have imagined the future as a totality, as a state of affairs that could be described with reference to some sort of unifying principle, whether ethical, economic or technological. Libraries of books have been written about post-industrialism, the digital economy, the service society, the sharing economy, post-capitalism, post-bureaucracy, the platform economy and many other neologisms. Serious futurology has been – since at least Bell, Drucker and Toffler – a big industry, and it sells lots of copies. This does suggest that people are interested in the future – after all they will be living there for the rest of their lives – but what is less often remarked is that these powerful stories are each based on the intensification of one particular dimension of the present age, and they usually (perhaps for rhetorical effect) do not describe future worlds that are multiple or variable, or that are based on a series of competing principles. To admit of such variety would surely damage the neat narrative that takes us from here to there, the configuration of the future unfolding with a grinding inevitability from the machineries of the present.

This lack of nuance within each futurology is echoed in the way that critics refer to current problems. There are a series of big words which are often enough used to point fingers at the present and they are totalizing but multiple, words that sweep matters together in order to point to the things that 'we' don't like. 'Hegemony', 'capitalism', 'industrialism', 'patriarchy', 'racism', 'colonialism', 'imperialism', 'bureaucracy', 'hetero-normativity' and (of course) 'neo-liberalism' are all terms which are a common part of critical and academic language and all involve the labelling of something to be opposed to.[2] In any particular argument or assertion, one or more of these words then becomes a shorthand for certain causes and consequences, establishing the terrain on which diagnoses and accusations can be deployed. This sort of utterance often establishes something about the authors too, about their positioning within particular academic or political communities. As with a swimmer pushing hard against the side of the pool, the solidity of the sins of the present allows for a powerful kicking away to somewhere else. It's a satisfying feeling, surging away from things 'we' don't like, but where do 'we' want to go?

My community, for the last quarter of a century, has been critical management studies (CMS), a heterodox movement within the globalizing business school, and it is (of course) against all of those bad things, but is also rather cynical about hope. It lacks the faith of the serious futurologists, or the creativity of writers of science fiction such as Ursula Le Guin, Kim Stanley Robinson or China Miéville. As a result it is unclear as to what CMS might be 'for', a fact which has resulted in much soul searching and many highly ranked publications. This short chapter is an attempt to think about hope in the context of critical accounts of organization and organizing, because any version of the future is also a description of social and economic arrangements. Ideas about ownership and control, about hierarchy and decision making, about markets and bureaucracies, about scale and responsibility, social and material technologies and so on, are all elements in a description of future worlds. These are also the core concepts of any organization theory. It seems to me that the proper task of a critical theory of organizations and management is to aim this theory at the future, in the hope of shaping things to come. In that sense, this chapter encourages less cynicism about hope in order to produce a radical futurology. To make the argument, I will meander through postmodernism, 'post-hope' and Ernst Bloch, before ending by claiming that hope is immanent within critique, but needs to become explicit in discussions about alternative forms of organization.

BACK TO THE POSTMODERN

If pushing against the present is the beginning of a trajectory, the problem is where to head, which island to swim to. The stories of the futurologists are usually far too neat, too predictable, and rarely tell us what we need to do to overcome inequalities of class, ethnicity, gender and so on. In any case, since postmodernism (at least), critical intellectuals have been wary of pinning their colours to any particular mast. It is much easier to complain about the multiple injustices of now than to argue for visions of a world that we might want to live in. Of course, this defensiveness about being definitive is understandable, because the dangers of blueprint utopianism have been extensively documented over the last century (Bauman, 1989; Scott, 1998; Parker, 2002a). Like the line drawings of modernist housing or shopping centres, which looked so good on paper, the reality is often less inviting, and the forms of authority required to produce the described future are usually totalitarian. The future looks better from a distance, a vague fantasy of something other which leaves the dull matter of colouring in the details and working out the problems for another day. There is a long tradition of radicals refusing such specifications on the grounds that they foreclose the possibilities of the future. Marx and Engels were notoriously reluctant to describe (even in something called a 'Manifesto') in anything other than rhetorical terms how a communist society might be organized, preferring instead to describe the programme needed to abolish capitalism (Ollman, 2005). Emma Goldman, anarchist and feminist, similarly refused to endorse 'an iron-clad programme or method on the future. . . . Anarchism, as I understand it, leaves posterity free to develop its own particular systems, in harmony with its needs' (in Marshall, 1993, p. 404).

We might see this as a generous and principled refusal to tell others what to do, but it could just as easily be understood as an infuriating refusal to be specific. From the Frankfurt School onwards, critical theorists have been much better at diagnosis than proposal, often preferring Adorno's 'negative dialectic' to being captured by saying something definitive or signing up to a vulgar manifesto. Yet it seems to me that shouty condemnations of the way that things are – such as those engaged in nowadays by the critical management inheritors to the critical theorists in the business school – logically suggest that something ought to be done. They imply (to put it weakly) that an alternative arrangement is possible. Otherwise we might as well dismiss the noise as mere wind, just bellowing at the storm and tides because it makes us feel better. Yet this is what many academics and critical thinkers do when they echo an academic style of condemnation without proposal, of principled outrage combined with equally principled insistence on saying nothing much about their desired shape of things to come. This takes us back to postmodernism, and a certain attitude towards ideas about social progress.

The idea that modernism – a faith in big theories and world-changing schemes – has led to various horrors and stupidities is not particularly controversial. But 40 years ago, when Lyotard (and then many others) questioned the *grands récits* which they claimed dominated our thinking, I don't think that they were intending to suggest that we should give up hope in the future. The suspicion of metanarratives was just that, a questioning of the idea that there is *one* story, a single understanding of the world that will save us. Reading this as a disavowal of progress *tout court* seems to be throwing the entire family out with the bathwater. Lyotard's famous *Report on Knowledge* ([1979] 1986) is shot through with gestures aiming at avoiding the twin problems of the terror of totalitarianism and the mercantilization of knowledge, both tendencies which express a dangerous clarity about 'what is to be done' (Lenin, [1902] 1975). Indeed, the closing sentence of Lyotard's book has a tone which is very like that of one of the manifestos written by Filippo Marinetti, the founder of the futurist movement:

> Under the general demand for slackening and for appeasement, we can hear the mutterings of the desire for a return of terror, for the realization of the fantasy to seize reality. The answer is: Let us wage a war on totality; let us be witnesses to the unpresentable; let us activate the differences and save the honor of the name. (Lyotard, [1979] 1986, p. 82)

Whatever this means (because it is not at all clear) it is not a demand that tomorrow be cancelled because it is too dangerous. This declamation is demanding a future – 'a politics that would respect both the desire for justice and the desire for the unknown' (Lyotard, [1979] 1986, p. 67).

Unsurprisingly though, and just like so many radicals of the page, Lyotard tells us little about what his future might look like. There is one mention in the book of the imaginative and inventive possibilities of the *petit récit*, and some comments on 'postmodern knowledge' (which 'refines our sensitivity to differences and reinforces our ability to tolerate the incommensurable') but no more detail than that (Lyotard, [1979] 1986, pp. 60, xxv). We are left with the idea that this is a modest, multiple and creative way of thinking, which all sound like positive features of thought, but not much else. The intellectual style which Lyotard practises can be recognized in many other thinkers too. Vattimo and Rovatti's 'weak thought'

([1983] 2012), Adorno's 'negative dialectics', Deleuze and Guattari's pref-
erence for rhizomatic over arboreal knowledge, Derrida's soliciting of the
counter-meanings in texts, and Foucault's insistence that everything is
dangerous are all impressive demonstrations of what thought can do to
explode the certainties of the present. These are anti-institutional thinkers,
writers of fluid and sparkling ideas who encourage restless questioning
and who express suspicions of any and all established arrangements and
authorities.

These forms of thought emerge in the shadow of the counter-culture of
the 1960s, and specifically of the events of France 1968. It was common
enough in this literature for some version of desire and freedom to be
counterposed to the baton- and syringe-wielding coercions of bureaucracy, police and state, and hence for 'organization', 'management' and
'business' to be words which provoked suspicion. Think about the forms
of organization that made the twentieth century: in the political machines
of Lenin and Hitler, both of whom use the word 'organization' continually
in their writings; in the death camp, Manhattan Project and supermarket;
or in the cultural criticisms of the obedience of 'organization man' (Whyte,
1961) or 'one-dimensional man' (Marcuse, 1964). A first reading of Michel
Foucault's histories, for example, might be understood to be saying that
'the great confinement' that produced prisons, hospitals, schools and so
on was a baleful social arrangement which classifies, stratifies, subjectifies
and so on. We see similar moves in Paul Feyerabend's account of scientific
institutions as structures which prevent innovation and free thought, Ivan
Illich's sustained arguments concerning the failures of the state and its
apparatus, and the growing influence of the work of critical theorists,
whether from Frankfurt or elsewhere. All, it seemed, had organizations in
their sights, and so perhaps it was not surprising that 'post-structuralists'
or 'post-Marxists' such as Baudrillard, Derrida, Badiou, Rancière and
others were often also understood in similar ways, as prophets of a libera-
tion which could be gained through reflexivity about the way that language
and power chained thought, but who rarely suggested how the world might
be better organized.

Of course, this is to homogenize with a very big intellectual blender,
and often to foreground the reception of a theorist over a detailed reading
of their work, but it seems fair to say that from the 1970s onwards many
critical thinkers were rhetorically opposing themselves to various senses of
organization, management and bureaucracy, usually in the name of some
sort of emancipation. Within organization studies, Burrell and Morgan
classified some of these as radical humanist 'anti-organization' theorists
(1979, p. 310), a current of anti-authoritarian scepticism that appeared
to occupy the moral high ground, insisting on an attitude of permanent

suspicion about the operations of power. 'Organization', it seemed, implied dominance, fixity, the ossification of thought. It was aligned with patriarchal and heterosexist forms of knowing, imperial political economies and a form of neo-liberalism that sought to financialize all our futures. There was nothing productive about it, just a jackboot stamping on a human face, forever.

This widespread caution against programmatic certainty has shaped critical work on management too, since it swims in the same intellectual currents as most of the human sciences. Whether the targets are right or left totalitarianism, or the market utopias of neo-liberals, if anyone starts shouting that they know what is best for us all, we should kick away their soapbox, deconstruct their language and check their privilege. I think that this is in many ways an admirable attitude to claim of authority, but there is a problem if it then leads to a refusal to engage in any serious talk about what the future should look like, to think about what sort of institutions might be needed in order to produce forms of life that could be seen to be desirable. The recent debates about 'performativity', or even 'critical performativity', within CMS are emblematic in this regard. The accusation is that critical management academics do not want to be useful and spend too much time developing oppositional theory (Spicer et al., 2009). However, instead of developing a concern for what better work, better organizations or a better economy might look like, academics engaged in this 'debate' have largely continued to argue about which theory is more radical, or which theorist deserves condemnation or celebration (Spicer et al., 2016; Parker and Parker, 2017).[3] However we might characterize it, and I do feel words like 'postmodern' are far too glib in this regard, this is writing and thinking without consequences. It is post-structural in the sense that it articulates a theory of language, meaning and history that assumes no underlying model or trajectory will be adequate. I happen to find these ideas very helpful for stimulating thought, but they often end up being post-structural in the sense that they hesitate to identify structure or structuring as the solution to any problem. That is to say, social, legal, economic, organizational practices tend to be treated as phenomena that always need to be overcome, repetitions that require disentangling to find the hidden oppressions at their heart.

It would be easy to be misunderstood here. I am not suggesting any sort of wholesale rejection of critical thought. That would be a profoundly conservative position, reactionary in the definitional sense. However, in the context of an understanding of the concept and practice of organizing, I think critique can only ever be treated as one moment in a dialectic. This means that the sort of doubt about the present that encourages a suspicion of common sense, of the taken-for-granted, is precisely what produces the

possibility of something else emerging. Soliciting the cracks in our now
by pointing to the inequalities and injustices of the contemporary world
encourages a rethinking of the categories that produce that thought, but
that does not mean, should not mean, that thought's work is then done.
Just as dystopias are warnings against utopias that have gone wrong, so is
critical thinking shot through with an often unacknowledged motive, that
the state of affairs which propelled it will no longer be the case (Benhabib,
1986). Otherwise, why bother?[4]

HOPE

So what does 'hope' have to do with all this? If we set aside the terrors of
starvation, persecution, forced migration and violence which beset large
numbers of the people on the planet and provide their own reasons for
hope and despair,[5] then I think a minimal version of hope probably begins
with a consciousness of boredom, of dull inevitability stretching into the
future. Contentment would not produce hope. At work, or even in leisure,
the repetitions of the present in the global north are often so deadening or
cruel in their rhythm and tone that it is easy enough to drift into daydreams
in which something else might happen: castles in the air built as defences
against the mundane. Fantasy, romance and glamour are ways of escape
from this boredom (Cohen and Taylor, [1976] 1992), and so are science
fiction, utopianism and forms of radical politics that imagine a different
future. These are methods of thinking and doing within which strangeness
might erupt and lives lived inattentively become present to hand and
urgent.

My complaint about what might be called 'post-hope', either in cynical
realism or in attitudes of permanent suspicion, is that it simply doesn't
take the future seriously enough. Ernst Bloch, a peripheral figure in the
Frankfurt School, seems to capture this nicely in his insistence on thinking
the 'not-yet', an 'anticipatory consciousness' which he claims is manifested
in many different forms. His huge, rambling and largely incomprehensible
three-volume *Principle of Hope* is an examination of human being (note
the verb) as an unfinished project aiming at a Hegelian resolution. The
book, originally to be called 'Dreams of a Better Life', provides a full and
varied documentation of daydreams and utopias, from foreign lands to
glossy magazines, and from sexual desire to films and theatre.

> How richly people have always dreamed of this, dreamed of the better life that
> might be possible. Everybody's life is pervaded by daydreams: one part of this
> is just stale, even enervating escapism, even booty for swindlers, but another
> part is provocative, is not content just to accept the bad which exists, does not

accept renunciation. This other part has hoping at its core, and is teachable. It can be extricated from the unregulated daydream and from its sly misuse, can be activated undimmed. Nobody has ever lived without daydreams, but it is a question of knowing them deeper and deeper and in this way keeping them trained unerringly, usefully, on what is right. (Bloch, [1959] 1986, p. 3)

Bloch doesn't tell us anything much about what the future will look like either, despite Marxism being his most developed form of 'not-yet', but he is determined that the future matters.

Why does this matter to those interested in organizing? Precisely because descriptions of the future are themselves descriptions of forms of organization, more or less stable social arrangements, which bring people and things together in particular constellations. Contemporary truths about organizing, told and sold by business schools, futurologists and politicians the world over, are largely intensifications of the same (Parker, 2018). The dominant forms in the global north (which can be summarized as 'market managerial') seek to produce a future in which the value produced by all production, consumption and exchange is captured by increasingly gigantic hierarchical structures. The language of 'care', 'passion', 'choice' and so on, routinely expressed by those who do the marketing and public relations for large organizations, is no more than an invitation to this capture. This, it seems to me, is boring in the sense that it produces a future of more of the same, just as so many serious futurologists do in their books. More inequality; more advertising; more carbon emissions; more hierarchy; more consumption; more waste; more dull jobs; more claims to be responsible, to care, to be passionate about choice. This is an organizational monoculture, a predictable landscape in which a fundamental repetition is camouflaged by bright colours, smiling faces and a soundtrack of jangling guitars. This is the future sold by Bloch's swindlers, a form of escapism which is basically a strengthening of the inexorable logic of the present.

The character Mark Renton in the original *Trainspotting* film (Boyle, 1996) parodies this as well as anyone:

> Choose life. Choose a job. Choose a career. Choose a family. Choose a fucking big television. Choose washing machines, cars, compact disc players, and electrical tin openers. Choose good health, low cholesterol and dental insurance. Choose fixed-interest mortgage repayments. Choose a starter home. Choose your friends. Choose leisure wear and matching luggage. Choose a three piece suite on hire purchase in a range of fucking fabrics. Choose DIY and wondering who the fuck you are on a Sunday morning. Choose sitting on that couch watching mind-numbing spirit-crushing game shows, stuffing fucking junk food into your mouth. Choose rotting away at the end of it all, pissing your last in a miserable home, nothing more than an embarrassment to the selfish, fucked-up brats you have spawned to replace yourselves. Choose your future. Choose life.

Renton chooses heroin instead, but in his nihilistic fury and cynicism he is opening the possibility that other choices might be possible, other options which preserve hope but reject this present and the choices that we are presented with.

A radical understanding of 'choice' as a refusal of here and now is what leads me and plenty of others to have practical daydreams about an alternative future. There are a variety of ways in which this hope might be understood, but the one I want to bet on here is one in which a variety of 'post-capitalist' forms of organizing produce difference (Gibson-Graham, 1996, 2006). Like the postmodernists, I doubt whether one principle can bear the weight of all our different intentions, but I don't think that lets us off the hook of positing different sorts of future. My gamble is on a bestiary of forms, on an irreducible pluralism which generates resilient and distinct economies. I think that this means that there will be a tendency towards the small, the local, partly because giganticism erases distinctiveness when it swallows it, but also because shorter low-carbon supply chains and meaningful senses of responsibility to human and non-human others require proximity. Most importantly though, I think that we must assume that organizing is various, and that there are no best ways. This is a radical contingency theory of organizing, in which every feature of organizing can become a variable. Just as we might travel to other places and discover different flora, fauna and landscape, so would I like to think that we could discover organizational variety in different places too. We should be suspicious of utopia, but enthusiastic utopians.

Human beings are organizing animals. Through language and socio-technical arrangements, they build worlds to live in, and the baroque complexity and variety of these creations are what distinguish them from the other creatures on earth. What we know of human history and physical and social anthropology tells us that the variety of these human-made worlds has been spectacular. Empires that stretch across maps, communes and monasteries that refuse the world, secret organizations that hide their very existence, kings with the power to erase life with the flick of a pen, circles of gift giving with sea shells across chains of islands, nomads following migrations of animals, glittering cities with towers that reach the clouds, pirates and smugglers who share their plunder, and small ceremonies involving particular sorts of food prepared and served quietly in houses made from paper. A science fiction catalogue of permutations, of fantastic worlds known and unknown, of teeming forms of life which endlessly mutate into shades of horror and violence, as well as beauty and generosity.

This sort of recognition of variety, of radical diversity, suggests two things. One is that accounts of the future that totalize, extending the implications of a particular social relation or technological principle, are insufficient to describe (or even imagine) a future which is highly varied. Futurologists tend to extend the present one-dimensionally, actually restricting imagination rather than encouraging it.[6] Second, what I have characterized as 'post-hope' critique is often paralysed when it comes to the future because it spends so much time undoing the present and naming its many injustices and partialities. As I said, I do think that this is a crucial move, an unsettling which allows hegemonic common sense to be seen as provisional and potentially replaceable, but it is only the first move, because the second requires hopeful descriptions of different worlds. It requires, and this is not very cool, making some suggestions about desired forms of policy, finance, regulation and other dull matters.[7]

Even in the most mundane of terms, it is not hard to question the logic that supports the boring inevitability of global capitalism and its mesh-work of gigantic corporations. In fact, the corporation is only one form of organizing amongst many, many others, because there are lots of different forms of actually existing organization: producer co-ops, employee-owned trusts, communes, local exchange trading systems, community interest companies, industrial democracies, partnerships, open source organizing, collectives, worker self-management, intentional communities, bartering, feminist separatist groups, anarchists, fair trade, the social economy, B-corps, community currencies, complementary currencies, bioregional-ism, self-provisioning, syndicalism, slow food, transition towns, time banks, gift relations, social accounting, the commons, recycling, com-munity energy, permaculture, appropriate technology, city-states, com-munitarianism, credit unions, ecovillages, consumer co-ops, trade unions, the sharing economy, mutualism, microfinance, fair trade, Islamic finance, syndicalism, social enterprise, bartering and so on and so on (Parker et al., 2007). This is a list that, once started, is hard to bring to a stop, just as (for Bloch) imagination is a feature of the 'not-yet', the unfinished, an ontology of the human that is anticipatory and open-ended (Geoghegan, 1996).

Hope, to paraphrase Hebrews 6:19, is an anchor which allows the pos-sibility of disclosing a radically different future. Without hope, swept away by the present, there are only the dull futures of serious futurologists, and the cool critiques of post-hope theorists. So it might be uncool, perhaps a bit evangelical, but I think we have to bet on hope. This means pushing against the entropy that market managerialism routinely generates on a global level. The same shouty global brands and celebrities, the same foods and products moved around in shipping containers, and even the same language. This is boring because it seems to suggest that our collective future is one which everywhere and for everyone will be the same. (And all the while, the planet warms.) For me, hope is the whisper of the strange, of existence and experience which are not a marketed cliché, the flight of a thing with feathers.[8]

NOTES

1. Some small parts of this chapter are edited from M. Parker (2016). Thanks to the editors and reviewers for their comments on an earlier version of the chapter.
2. To which sophisticates might add Cartesian dualism, logocentricism, essentialism, humanism and so on.
3. And, yes, I'm one of them too.
4. Unless, and this would be most uncharitable, the critique is merely deployed in order to claim a valued identity or, worse, to add a performative publication to a curriculum vitae.
5. Which is in itself a pretty comfortable position to be in, suggesting that even boredom would be a luxury for some.
6. Though, in case I am misunderstood, I am not arguing that this is always true of writers of science fiction, particularly those who present radical futures.
7. Something that most critical theorists, even those who recognize the importance of utopianism in critical thinking (such as Benhabib, 1986), ultimately keep at arm's length with suggestive but vague phrases about polities, or communities of rights and responsibilities.
8. A poem by Emily Dickinson (1999).

3. The utopian quest for an alternative[1]

Roland Paulsen

Some time ago I met a great social critic at a restaurant. She had just won a prize – because she was such a great social critic – and she told me that she had noticed something strange about herself. Thinking about the climate crisis and social disasters did not make her as sad any more. No, it was almost the opposite. Now, reading about how a country's economy was being damaged or how cartographers were forced to draw new coastlines on the maps of the world, she experienced a secret joy in the midst of all the horror. Soon it would not be possible to go on like this any longer. Soon we would be forced to change.

Like the good Marxist she was, she had no problems with intellectualizing her feelings of joy. The hope of socialism has long rested on the inner contradictions of capitalism – for Marx said so. And in terms of dialectics it was also easy to understand: for the pendulum to swing, it must first reach its extreme position, and so on. Nevertheless, she wondered: weren't her feelings a bit perverse?

Although I could easily recognize some of myself in her confession, I immediately began to moralize. Yes, that was too extreme, I said. It was as though she was stuck in the negation. She knew everything one needed to know in order to criticize capitalism point by point, but she never came up with an alternative – and she never revealed what type of society she preferred to the capitalist one. In this respect, it was quite likely that she contributed to a general longing for the apocalypse, I admonished her.

The great social critic, who is a very sincere person, said she thought that was all such a shame. Whenever she was lecturing, the question would pop up: 'What is the alternative and how do we get there?' Her standard response to this, 'We have to create a different economic system', was no real response, she admitted. She did not even know what that meant. At the same time, she did not accept the conditions. Just because you criticize something, it does not mean that you must have a complete answer as to what the alternative should look like. Criticism would die out if it were the case that for every wrongdoing we address we have to come up with a righteous solution.

I went home, and I thought that she was right.

THE RETURN OF UTOPIA

One can, of course, say that something is wrong without having a ready plan of action. In political discourse, however, especially when the precariously amorphous mega-categories of 'capitalism' and 'socialism' are set in opposition to each other, it is difficult to avoid the feeling that the lack of concrete alternatives makes the real contradictions hard to distinguish.

As for myself, I sense that the ideological debates I have ended up in rarely concern concrete facts. Socialists, liberals and others usually do not have any great difficulty agreeing with one another that the climate threat is real, that our current means of production are ecologically unsustainable, that the world's inequality is too high, that the financial sector dominates society too much, and so on.

It is not in the analysis that the major differences of opinion exist; the dissension arises in relation to the question of whether there are any workable societal alternatives.

For a long time the fatalist left – surely confident that history is on their side – and the neoliberal right have helped each other to bury this question. Margaret Thatcher even found an acronym to dismiss it: TINA. *There is no alternative!*

In recent years, though, more and more social scientists have become interested in providing an empirically grounded answer to the question of what an alternative might look like. For example, could cooperative companies offer a model for economic democracy? Could the 3D printer lead to the people's appropriation of the means of production? And what happens if one provides a basic income to people on a smaller scale, say a few thousand people, as they have done in Finland?

In the shadow of the apocalypse, we simply witness the return of the utopias.

'CAN'T YOU JUST GIVE MONEY TO EVERYONE?'

According to British sociologist Ruth Levitas (2013), utopian thought is based on an understanding of society as an ongoing movement. The 'non-place' etymologically indicated as the origination of the word 'utopia' can therefore never be a 'good society' at all times. In *Utopia as Method*,

Levitas (2013) rather describes utopia as a provisional attempt to map out a dormant potential. And this we do all the time – more or less. It is impossible to regard society as it is without at the same time relating it to what it should be, writes Levitas. Utopian thought exists within each one of us, but we are bad at utopian thinking. We are simply untrained.

As society is constantly moving, our openness to different kinds of utopias also seems to vary over time. The first utopia I met was both simple and ingenious. Still, it took a long time before it got any major public attention.

'Can't you just give money to everyone?' someone asked during a classroom discussion on world poverty, in secondary school. With surprise in our eyes we turned to our teacher, and for a second we were in Utopia. 'Inflation', was the answer. And soon I remembered the belief that had been drilled into us, children of the 1980s, even in the Donald Duck comics: if you give away money just like that, then money will be worthless. And then everyone will be very poor. And then it will eventually turn into a world war.

Today, the idea of a 'guaranteed basic income' or 'citizen wage', as it is called in the adult world, is spreading across the world. Among the advocates, we find eight Nobel laureates in economics (most recently, Joseph Stiglitz) and a number of social scientists like David Graeber, Guy Standing and Yanis Varoufakis. In the primary election of the French Socialist Party in 2017, basic income was at the top of the agenda, and it seems to have contributed to the victory of Benoît Hamon, an active proponent of the basic income. In June 2017, almost a quarter of Swiss voters said yes to a shockingly high base income (equivalent to 2000 euros a month), which, if realized, would have meant a revolution.

The most interesting thing about the basic income is that it is already under investigation in Finland, Utrecht and Kenya. In Kenya, for example, a ten-year experiment funded by various actors from Silicon Valley will soon be launched with approximately 6000 recipients. Experiments are also planned on a regional level in, for example, Uganda, Italy, Scotland, Canada and the United States. One purpose of these experiments is to measure how health, well-being and zeal are affected by a reduced pressure to work. In utopian terms, however, an important aspect to consider is the widening of the window of opportunity that presents itself as the hitherto improbable suddenly occurs.

UTOPIAN THINKING GONE HAYWIRE

The will to turn utopian ideas into concrete practice has, as few know, existed among utopians since the late 19th century, when utopian thought, with Henri de Saint-Simon at the head, gained momentum, fuelled by industrialization. Even though the early utopians did not hesitate to embrace wild and grandiose ideas in their writings, they were keen to implement their ideas as soon as possible, albeit on a limited scale. The brightest shining example of this is Robert Owen, who, as a capitalist, made the New Lanark production plant outside Glasgow into a socialist experimental workshop, with shortened hours of work for the factory workers, a day nursery school for the employees' children and the prohibition of both child labour and child chastisement. In 1810 these were radical ideas that spread quickly.

Although Marx and Engels did not accomplish half of what Owen did during their lifetimes, they dismissed the utopians of the early industrialization as idealist. In Engels's historiography all socialism before Marx's was considered to be 'utopian socialism', whereas Marx's ideas were described as representing 'scientific socialism'. Not for nothing, 'utopia' was for a long time a controversial word in the Marxist vocabulary. In recent years, however, Marxists have become more open to and benign about the concept.

An example of such a Marxist is Fredric Jameson, whose book *An American Utopia* was published in 2016. Jameson is the author of the widespread quotation that we live in a time where 'it is easier to imagine the end of the world than to imagine the end of capitalism' (Jameson, 1994, p. xii). According to Jameson (2016), the fatalist left – who avoid the question of what the alternatives to capitalism might mean – are accomplices to the degeneration of utopian thinking. The Marxist analysis that followed in the wake of the financial crisis remains, he writes, 'oddly fixated on an impossible present without any visible historical future, save catastrophe' (p. 71).

However, as Jameson himself is fantasizing about the future, everything goes haywire. Jameson imagines that a people's 'universal army' could form the basis of a growing organism that ultimately puts the capitalist state apparatus out of business and introduces full employment, free wifi for all, 'popular control of the media', 'the prohibition of the most noxious right-wing propaganda' and so on and so forth (2016, p. 8). It is both a confused and an extinct utopia, but above all a sad example of how authoritarian socialists still can choose not to relate to the totalitarianism of earlier attempts to invoke state socialism.

REVOLUTIONARY REFORMS – OR TINA PRESERVATIVES?

The now-living utopian who has developed the most systematic analysis of different alternatives, the sociologist Erik Olin Wright, is also a Marxist but significantly more liberal than many others. In *Envisioning Real Utopias* (2010), Wright describes how one can, besides discussing the desirability of a specific utopia, study its effects and feasibility by looking at the utopia in its existing forms.

For example, Wright analyses the utopia of direct democracy from the perspective of the participatory budget system developed in Porto Alegre. He addresses the utopia of economic democracy in light of the problems and advances that Mondragon – the world's largest cooperative, with industrial manufacturing, its own bank, its own university and over 70 000 members – has encountered during its 60-year-long history. As president of the American Sociological Association (the stronghold of sociology), Wright has launched several utopian research projects, and his ideas have been particularly influential in the aforementioned research on basic income. Wright, however, also belongs to those who have criticized the basic income project in its more diluted forms.

And this is a telling problem: the closer the idea of a basic income gets to realpolitik, the thinner it gets. The amounts that are currently being tested are very small (in Finland, the amount is 560 euros per month, in Utrecht 960 euros), and, strikingly, often the experiments are legitimated with assurances that people will continue to work as before.

When I talk about basic income, I usually try *not* to pacify the 'responsible' citizens who want everything to continue as before. Asked whether people with a basic income really will be as motivated to work as they are today, I answer 'Hopefully not.' Asked about who will want to carry out the 'dirty jobs', I answer 'Probably no one.' If everyone had 'go-to-hell' money, it would probably be more difficult for employers to recruit, and then they would have to offer sufficiently appealing employment conditions in order to attract people of their own free will.

Many companies would most likely have to shut down their operations, and thus total production would be reduced in an ecologically sustainable direction – which in turn would require that the taxation base would be broadened from labour to the entire production system. It would require a giant transformation – which is the reason why French philosopher André Gorz (1969) labelled the idea of a basic income a 'revolutionary reform'.

When other proponents of basic income depict basic income as a way to mitigate the consequences of automation, slim welfare to a minimum and subsidize minimum-wage jobs, it seems that the utopian idea of a society without compulsory work is distorted into a preservative TINA institution in the spirit of Thatcher. It is both bizarre and depressing to think that we should be part of the very same movement.

A QUEST FOR A 'GOOD SOCIETY'?

This dialectic, of how surprisingly easily utopia can be inverted, is a recurring theme in the utopian science fiction literature. It was not, however, until I read Ursula Le Guin's (1974) novel *The Dispossessed*, in which the anarchist planet Anarres is portrayed, that I could understand, and to some extent embrace, the intrinsic fragility of all utopias.

Like no other science fiction writer (possibly with the exception of Kim Stanley Robinson), Le Guin manages to describe utopia as a painful process, where the risk of failure remains imminent, and unintended consequences lead to new utopias. The novel's subtitle – *An Ambiguous Utopia* – is explained in the very first pages.

On Anarres there is no capital to accumulate. Money has been abolished, children are raised to refrain from wanting things, hierarchies are gone, sexual equality prevails and work is voluntary and disconnected from issues such as having food on the table and somewhere to live. Yet, at the same time, the narrative revolves around the characters' frustrations: the material scarcity; the slow decision-making of the syndicates; the normative pressure to adapt and to contribute to the collective. The drones that choose not to work – the so-called 'nuchnibis' – have indeed the right to the same standard of living as all the others on the planet, but they are not well liked.

In particular, Le Guin takes an interest in the informal power structures that the protagonist is forced to submit to, power structures that, just because they are covert and intertwined with ties of kinship, are difficult to complain about – and challenge.

The peculiar thing about Le Guin's writing is that, by focusing upon the dark side of an anarchist utopia, she makes it so much more alive and – what is truly paradoxical – more appealing. In this sense, Le Guin's novel proffers important insights for all those who engage in political debates on utopian alternatives: the very notion of a permanent 'good society' is both dangerous and unrealistic. Those who honestly want to argue for an alternative must be able to convince their opponents that all its costs, problems and unintended consequences are preferable to the existing society. The utopian endeavour is therefore something other than a project of opposition (with social criticism as an end in itself). It is a challenging quest, an appeal to hope, weighted by an impossible burden of proof.

Perhaps this quest is the only thing we can with certainty attribute to a 'good society'. This is at least what the Polish sociologist and basic income advocate Zygmunt Bauman once suggested:

> A good society is a society that thinks it's not good enough. A democratic society is a society that does not believe it is democratic enough. A righteous society is a society that does not believe it is righteous enough. The worst possible society is a society that considers itself to be sufficiently good, democratic, and righteous – a society that believes it has reached the limits of the possible. (Quoted in Sigrún, 2003)

NOTE

1. This text was originally published in *Dagens Nyheter* on 2 April 2017, and is here reprinted by permission of the publisher. The text is translated from Swedish and slightly adapted by Daniel Ericsson.

4. Epimethean hope or Promethean expectation? The role of organisational behaviour

John Vaughan

INTRODUCTION

> If ... only one person were of the contrary opinion, mankind would be no more justified in silencing that one person than he, if he had the power, would be justified in silencing mankind. (Mill, 1978, p. 16)

The chapter is an invitation to business school faculty. The thesis says we need to cultivate democracy and free speech along with human rights and intelligent decision making, and one of the most effective places to do this is the business school. The chapter is a distillation of personal experience from my four decades in world-rated business schools, and the aim is to pass on some of what I have learnt and invite readers to adopt some of my conclusions. In this sense the work is ideographic, but within that there is a deconstruction of several authors' work along with a personal comment as to why I think the piece of work deserves more consideration. The chapter uses 'we' to indicate joint consideration between author and reader and 'I' when it refers to my own experience.

Illich (1970, p. 105) distinguishes between Epimethean 'hope' and Promethean 'expectation'. 'Hope ... means trusting in the goodness of nature', while expectation means we plan and expect results. This chapter intends to focus on the more practical 'expectation' but sees the two as linked. Bauman (2007, p. 99) refers to an innocent time of hope as a time of the 'gamekeeper' where everything developed well when 'not tinkered with' and our job was merely to trim things. Our current predicament, however, says Bauman (2007, p. 98), is that we live in the age of 'the hunter who could not care less' (2007, p. 101). In Bauman's view, we need to get back to an intermediate age, that of the 'gardener' who assumes order comes from 'his constant attention and effort' (2007, p. 99). This chapter will focus, therefore, on how we act as 'gardeners' within business schools.

The chapter follows five themes, focusing on authors whose work has become significant to me. First, we examine problems that exist in the modern, 'hunter's', world through Bauman's critique of neoliberalism. Second, we look at the way 'thinking' can be encouraged, based on Dewey's (1997) ideas. The ability to think critically is seen as the key underpinning to the values mentioned above. The third theme is to recommend the adoption of a more ideographic methodology (Gill and Johnson, 1997) in organisational research. Fourth, we look at a view of organisational behaviour (OB) and recommend it in the curriculum of the business school. Finally, there are reflections on practice for educationalists to consider, with reference to multi-cultural group learning. All of the authors mentioned are both critical and thoughtful, and these two elements link their ideas. The reader is invited not only to teach the ideas of the authors but also to use their ideas and models practically in the classroom.

LIQUID TIMES

> As long as [personal freedom] remains a phantom, the pain of hopelessness will be topped by the humiliation of haplessness. (Bauman, 2007, p. 65)

We open with Bauman's (2007) critique of neoliberalism. He says we face challenges that previous generations have not had as a consequence of the 'liquid world' in which we have come to live. First, there is the idea that social forms are no longer concrete but have become fluid and impermanent. Second, the nation state has less power today, compared to the forces and powers acting globally. Third, there is the 'curtailment of communal, state-endorsed insurance' (2007, p. 2) against individual life mishaps. Fourth, there has been a 'collapse of long-term thinking, planning and acting' (2007, p. 3). Finally, the responsibility for remedying these issues has been moved to the individual, away from larger social forms.

Because of these issues, Bauman asserts, the world has become inhabited by 'citizens–sheep being protected from wolves–criminals, by sheepdogs–police' (2007, p. 13). People become more insecure but, paradoxically, seek less freedom. The recent success of the hard men in politics (Duterte, Trump, Orban, Bolsonaro) may bear this out. People think they are seeking safety, but they are just following the pretence of safety, and governments use this fear factor as a source of continuing in power. Bauman refers to all of this as a 'strategy of capitalizing on fear going back into the early years of the neoliberal assault on the social state' (2007, p. 17).

Bauman claims to have no answers: 'all answers would be peremptory, premature and potentially misleading' (2007, p. 4), but there are hints. For example, 'The demon of fear won't be exorcized until we find (or more precisely construct) such tools' (2007, p. 26) as will give us the power to regain control over our lives. This marries with the idea that Promethean 'expectation' should take precedence over Epimethean 'hope'. The problems of neoliberalism, says Bauman, are that it strips assets, feeds off non-capitalist organisations and creates wasted lives among refugees and immigrants who are then demonised by the society in which they seek protection. The real issue, says Bauman, is one of the 'individualisation' of society in which social ties and communication break down. Paradoxically, this goes against Mill's veneration of private, contradictory thought.

Individualism, in turn, brings the problems of the large city where the wealthy build ghettos for themselves to keep away from the underclass. People seek 'a community of sameness' (Bauman, 2007, p. 87) without realising that such action is merely palliative, providing no real solution. Bauman's idea, mentioned above, is that we live in the world of the 'hunter'. In such a world, you should apply yourself to the system which has emerged, and if this means taking four low-paid jobs at unsocial hours in the 'gig economy' then so be it! The neoliberal rationale says it is all for the good, argues Bauman. However, if for some 'human' reason you do not want to be a hunter, then, says Bauman, you risk becoming one of the hunted.

THE TRAINING OF THOUGHT

> The feeling that ... facts, facts produces a narrow Gradgrind, is justified because facts are dealt out as ready-made articles to leave no room for imagination. (Dewey, 1997, pp. 223–224)

The chapter now moves on to Dewey's (1997) work, which extols the virtues of the scientific mind, shunning the idea of accepting concepts without evidence. The rationale for its inclusion here is that a thoughtful, imaginative approach to life's problems should enable us to address those problems. Dewey's writing promotes an ideographic direction as seen in the quote above, and his contribution begins with a summary of 'typical forms of wrong belief' (1997, p. 22) where he notes that some people do not really think at all but just take as given what their parents, teachers or society tells them. Dewey complains that such people are lazy, refusing to use the mental capacities they have been blessed with.

The second mode of wrong thought is amongst those who only believe what they think serves their own best interests, ignoring contrary evidence or evidence which supports the claims of others' interests. The third type of wrong thinkers, says Dewey, are those who try to follow reason but, because they only converse with one type of person, remain 'in some little creek . . . but will not venture out into the great ocean of knowledge' (1997, p. 23). Dewey says the good news is that curiosity is natural to a human. He describes it as an 'eagerness for a larger acquaintance with the mysterious world in which [we are] placed' (1997, p. 32), and when we are curious we ask questions and suggest answers.

A simple solution may be correct but it 'will not possess the fullness and richness of one arrived at after comparison with a greater variety of alternative suggestions', says Dewey (1997, p. 36), and it is the attention to the depth and breadth of thinking which Dewey feels should be paramount in education. It is important that any student be taught how to suspend conclusions until a wide range of possibilities are in. Here, Dewey's ideas match those of Wood and Mintzberg to come, implying the importance of an approach which does not seek simple hypotheses. 'Thinking is specific in that different things suggest their own appropriate meanings, tell their own unique stories, and that they do this in very different ways with different persons' (1997, p. 39).

Dewey is mainly talking with regard to natural science and the discovery of facts and laws. Nonetheless, his main point is to say that all problem solving begins with the development of many hypotheses 'or conditional principles of explanation' (1997, p. 82). Along with this Dewey stresses the need for the search for negative cases, or those which disconfirm our natural biases. This is how we find a more nuanced theory and not a perfunctory one. Dewey also focuses on the importance of intuition and shows the importance of the skill some researchers have in interpreting better than others, something 'we call a knack, tact, cleverness; in more important affairs, "insight", "discernment"'. This can be instinctive, says Dewey, but also it could be the 'outcome of long familiarity with like outcomes in the past' (1997, p. 104).

Dewey's wrong modes of thought, along with his words on the nature of problem solving and intuition, preface Mintzberg's words below on the need for 'intellectual rigour' to take precedence over academic rigour. We also need to take a holistic, cross-fertilising approach, according to Dewey, as without one 'there is a lack of intellectual context' (1997, p. 117).

WHY IDEOGRAPHY?

> Managing is mostly about nuances, while the popular works mostly provide formulas – painting by numbers so to speak. (Mintzberg, 2004, p. 398)

Henry Mintzberg rose to prominence in the late 1970s and is perhaps the best-known and most highly regarded professor of management amongst practising managers. He is also widely known in business schools but, in my experience, does not have the status that he has amongst practitioners, and my reflections suggest that it is his inductive/ideographic methodological approach which might be the issue. As we will see, Mintzberg pleads for 'intellectual rigour' to take precedence over 'methodological rigour', and these and other facets of his approach I wish to develop for the consideration of the reader.

Gill and Johnson (1997) describe ideography as focusing on qualitative data, induction and problem solving. Mintzberg (2004) describes his approach as inductive, but, for the purposes of this chapter, induction and ideography will be treated as the same thing, since induction comes under the above definition. The core of Mintzberg's (2004) analysis is the idea that researchers focus too much on methodological rigour. The idea of a 'gap in the literature' is not of much importance to Mintzberg, compared to the glaring problems within organisation and society, in our case, according to Bauman, neoliberalism. The 'gap in the literature approach' leads to decreasing circles which become ever more specialised and ignore larger issues. 'The library is the worst place to find a research topic', says Mintzberg (2004, p. 402).

The problems of the 'gap in the literature', deductive approach is that it leads to 'narrow concepts', 'a closed shop' and researchers talking only to each other without engaging with practitioners and the wider community. The point to note is that Mintzberg reads widely and cites other researchers extensively, but he does not start with the reading. He makes much of the need to engage with practising managers instead of only dealing with other academics, and this is what he considers 'intellectual'. Perhaps the recent focus on 'impact' and collaboration in business schools are showing Mintzberg's ideas coming into fashion, and his comments do not decry any particular work using a deductive approach; he just wishes to move researchers away from that emphasis and invite them to look at wider, more holistic issues.

Good research ideas 'come from quirky sources' which 'violate conventional wisdom', says Mintzberg (2004, p. 395). He goes on to show the difference between organisational research and research in the natural sciences by showing that organisational researchers look at 'the subjects of everyday life' (2004, p. 396), not nuclear fission, and this leads us to recognise our involvement with the subjects we study in a way which is both ontologically and epistemologically different (Packard, 2018, p. 40) from that of our colleagues in the natural sciences.

Finishing with Mintzberg (2004), he complains that a deductive approach is 'taken as an article of faith' (2004, p. 399) that 'factor[s] out the human dimension' and demands 'citation, definition and tightness' not 'description, insight and speculation'. A colleague of Mintzberg is quoted: 'it is like an art critic saying that, if the Sistine chapel ceiling were one foot higher and the index fingers of God and Adam one inch further apart, the impact would be two per cent less' (2004, p. 397). This same point is made by Kuhn (2009, p. 101), who points to the 'revealing logical lacuna in the positivist's argument', meaning that a subjective statement claiming the importance of objectivity is illogical. Readers may prefer the same point made by a poet, e.e. cummings (2019): 'While you and I have lips and voices which are for kissing and to sing with who cares if some oneeyed son of a bitch invents an instrument to measure spring with?' Research is subjective; it is what humans do!

Reading through Mintzberg's work, one is overwhelmed by the importance he attaches to the human drivers of research, values in fact. Ideography, by focusing on the 'Id' or individual, gets away from the approach of aggregating and generalising about people. We may indeed see similarities and remark upon them, but also we should look for uniqueness, which may enable us to learn from those who are different. Mintzberg also regularly points out the illogicalities of those who claim to be rationalists, as Kuhn did above. Finally, readers may like to consider what Mintzberg says about 'gatekeepers' such as journal reviewers, book editors and promotion panels. If you are, indeed, always looking for academic rigour, do not be surprised if the intellectual side is neglected. Business school faculty, in my experience, have both abilities, but it is only in private conversations and at conferences that their intellectual sides seem to be allowed to come out.

WHAT IS ORGANISATIONAL BEHAVIOUR?

> A working sensitivity to the rational, non-rational and irrational behaviours in organisations can make us better managers and, perhaps more importantly, wiser individuals. (Wood, 1997, p. 223)

We now look at a view of organisational behaviour (OB) as a means to replace inactive hope with active planning and expectation of results, a Promethean view perhaps. These results were alluded to in the introduction to the chapter as democracy, free speech and intelligent decision making. Although Wood says OB does not exclude any particular research approach, it is clear from his writing that he concurs with the views of Mintzberg expressed above.

This view defines OB thus: 'It is a loosely related set of theories, methods and topics drawn from a variety of independent thought and research in the social and natural sciences, the humanities and the arts' (Wood, 1997, p. 217), and its definition might provide the answer to Bauman's question: how do we get back to the world of the gardener? What Wood is saying is that OB is anything relating to organisations and the humans who inhabit them. A deconstruction of the definition allows us to expand our thoughts. The first concept is the idea of being 'loosely related', implying that what is to come is not a 'concrete' set of connected things. These loosely related things are 'theories, methods and topics', implying it is not just theory in which OB is interested. The final part of Wood's definition includes 'social sciences', 'natural sciences', 'humanities' and 'arts', i.e. anything human!

Of particular note here are the loose connections, in recognition of a synthetic approach to study rather than the dominant analytic approach of a traditional business school. Going on from this is the insight that all other business school areas emphasise a functional aspect of the neoliberal organisation: marketing, finance, accounting, production or operations, for example. Wood contrasts OB with human resource (HM) management in that both look at topics such as personality, recruitment, training and teamwork, but the language uncovers the neoliberal clue. How can humans be a resource when they are complex creatures combining 'rational, non-rational and irrational behaviours' (Wood, 1997, p. 223). And why do they need to be managed? The word 'management' re-emphasises the idea that people are to be controlled, not understood or respected: a managerialist view.

The neoliberal, HR, view matches Wood's definition of bad OB as 'an apologist for entrenched social, economic and political interests' (1997, p. 217). Evidence for the view that too much of recent university life has been of this negative sort comes from the report on 'bullying in higher education' (John, 2014), which found three key problems: first, the idea that leaders were putting money before learning, people and values; second, that HR exists to support management decisions, ignoring the 'hurt that staff routinely experience'; and, finally, that universities feel they are untouchable owing to the power they wield and the nervousness of intimidated staff. Readers might ponder how we can encourage a better approach to OB, both as a study and as a tool which 'penetrates beneath the myopic and conventional wisdom' (Wood, 1997, p. 223) implicit in John's critique. Any creative solutions generated might improve the conditions of the readers of this chapter, and, again, Promethean action would take precedence over the hope that things will get better.

Wood's ideas focus heavily on the notions of multi-disciplinary learning and an approach to triangulation which seeks to uncover nuances rather than find an ultimate truth. He emphasises the idea that OB is a 'hodge-podge of various subjects' which help to bring the 'collective wisdom of human history into the decision-making calculus of developing managers' (1997, p. 217). For this chapter's emphasis, his ideas are crucial, because he consistently focuses on the fact that OB is not 'soft' but the hardest part of the job of the organisational manager and this poorly understood behavioural 'stuff' is vital if we are to hope that organisations can drive solutions for the human-made problems of the planet. 'The failure of organisations cannot be laid at the feet of workers or shifting markets; organisational failure is a failure of management' (1997, p. 223).

We finish with Wood by commenting on two of his insights, interpretations which can only be made by a creative mind. One is his focus on the importance of the rational, non-rational and irrational in OB. The rational, perhaps the realm of the traditional business school, suggests we collect all available measurable data and then make a decision based on the self-evidence of that data. The non-rational is the realisation that intuition plays a large part in organisational decision making, while the irrational makes us see that not all people behave in the way the data suggests.

A second key insight is Wood's concept of 'levels of analytic abstraction' (1997, p. 220), where he points to the idea that most people give explanations which do not go much beyond the personal. Wood suggests we need to look at further levels of abstraction such as the group, inter-group, organisational and societal. 'We could of course add . . . the international and global levels, as well as . . . a historical approach' (1997, p. 222). The inclusion of such considerations can promote the levels of thought and intellectualism promoted by Dewey and Mintzberg and has led to the development of the practical ideas contained in the next section.

A PRACTICAL APPROACH FOR EDUCATIONALISTS: THE MULTI-CULTURAL LEARNING GROUP

Thoughtful reflection on experience in the light of conceptual ideas is the key to management learning. (Mintzberg, 2004, p. 253)

Mintzberg says that management courses should only be for those with experience and who are currently practising. Here I part company with Mintzberg, because there is a huge market around the world for courses for people with little work experience, and one of the key motivations for non-English speakers is the realisation that they feel they will improve their language skills and their general communication strategies as well as their understanding of organisational theory. All adults also have experience of organisation, whether it be family, school, synagogue, youth group or wherever. Nonetheless, whether course participants are young people with little work experience or practising managers, the key rationale of the 'multi-cultural learning group' (MCLG) (Vaughan, 2015a, 2015b) can help as a source of learning based on, but also to develop, the ideas of the authors mentioned above.

This model developed because a higher level of abstraction was applied to the issue of management education, delivered largely in a second language at master's level. It evolved because of a Deweyan attitude to thought and a Mintzbergian approach to research, treating the classroom as a laboratory where constant experimentation took place. Like all theory involving humans, it cannot be said ever to be complete, but some of the key insights are given below. Readers are invited not to copy what is said but to experiment themselves using the key basic principle that most good learning happens in groups and the members of the groups have a wealth of organisational experience to discuss and pass on while discussing concepts presented by the tutor as mentioned in the Mintzberg quote at the beginning of this section.

The MCLG consists of five or six students, and practising management educators do not need influence at the highest levels of institutions to use the model. It can be adapted to virtually any extant module as detailed here. The first and most important driver for this model is that it follows the ethos of all that has been said above by Wood, Mintzberg and Dewey. It aims not to have subject experts delivering 'facts' that can be easily attained online but to allow course participants to look at chosen models in a group setting which takes advantage of the diversity found in the class amongst these participants. Of course, the class facilitator is key in forming the groups, directing procedures and commenting, where appropriate, with an 'expert' view. Facilitation, allied with lecturing skill, is seen as crucial.

The key benefits of this approach are that: first, it develops the training of thought as recommended by Dewey; second, it encourages a diversity of ideas and perspectives based on the diverse backgrounds of those taking part; and, finally, it develops the communicative arts of exposition and listening to the views of those one might consider to be 'other' than oneself. In a typical master's class, but also more and more with undergraduates, this develops the ability of non-native English speakers in this, their second or other language. The 'otherness' mixed in the group may be gender, religion, provenance, ethnicity or political leaning to name but a few.

The facilitator's first job is to set the groups up. This is done by asking participants to fill out a form containing all the relevant details of gender and so on mentioned above. Once the facilitator has all the filled-out forms, s/he can form the groups, first by dividing the participants into five or six groups and then perhaps placing one Chinese person into each of the groups (as Chinese is usually the most represented ethnicity). Experience in several business schools suggests that the facilitator might then put another Chinese person, of another gender or geographical region, into each group. The facilitator continues so that there is a good mix of prov-enances and as much equality of gender as possible. Ideally, participants will have done the Belbin (1993) team role assessment, and the results can be used to get a good mix of behaviours, cerebral attributes, action and people. Once learning begins, a tutor can choose basic OB models to help develop the skills mentioned above.

A good starting point for such a course is the Johari window, which encourages students to work more effectively together. A key role in the Belbin assessment is that of the co-ordinator, and the tutor can appoint someone in each group to take on this role during the first week. For future lessons, other students can take on the role on whatever timescale is appro-priate. At the end of the co-ordinator's period in charge, s/he sends the tutor a brief report on the other participants and the quality of the learn-ing taking place. Students seeing these models for the first time may be said to be 'being taught', but the key for their inclusion is for their usefulness to the group learning process not the fact that they are being taught.

Another key part here is that the tutor only speaks in short bursts, setting up the model and providing feedback when students have finished their discussion. During the discussions, the tutor visits the groups, throwing in comments for clarification or simply building a networked, communal classroom. The tutor's visits to the groups enables her/him to learn names and nuances and ensure that the classroom practice succeeds. As the cliché says, it is only through use that understanding comes. These discussions give non-native speakers regular and consistent practice using English, and native speakers, with the right attitude, can develop their leadership and co-ordination skills in a non-threatening environment.

We looked at OB models for course content, but anything intellectual is worthy of consideration, as will be seen in the final words below referring to Diamond's (1999) *Guns, Germs and Steel*. Certain students will wonder why they are studying such things on a management programme, and those who support what Wood called 'poor OB' and nomothetic methods will turn their noses up, but it is important, following Dewey, for student intellectual development and imagination, and the skills developed can be sold at any job interview. For the purposes of Epimethean 'hope' and Promethean 'expectation', it is also important, as some students will be unaware of basic models and issues relating to human rights, a scientific mind and the notion of democracy.

This brings us on to the form of assessment, where a 'critical incident' essay is recommended, and once again this is a key part of the learning to be had in a multi-cultural group situation. It develops the skill of writing, in English, something of 'report' length, while requiring basic academic and referencing skills. One thousand words is perfect and a great skill for the students to develop. It enables them to use observations, reflect and then comment on those observations while referring to academic models for back-up, and an example is now given from the final essay of a young Nigerian male:

> I had felt cheated and not proud to be African which resulted in low self-esteem. However, by the end of the class sessions on Diamond's (1999) research, I discovered that these differences are the result of natural and geographical factors rather than intellectual differences between Europe and Africa as I had previously been made to believe. As a result, the feeling of inferiority I once had has disappeared and I am now proud to be African knowing that the differences are nature's way of making the world beautiful in diversity.

I know that not all readers will be affected by those words as I was, but I would ask you to consider the view that the level of learning expressed, life-changing perhaps, is of a different dimension to that experienced when encountering 'return on capital employed', and such learning can only be experienced when students are thoroughly engaged within the models, not just viewing from the outside. Earlier mention was made of the customer base, largely global master's students studying in English-speaking contexts. The MCLG provides an environment for much more innovative learning using this context, particularly outside the classroom. Readers will no doubt already have their own ideas and practices.

FINAL WORDS

This chapter has been about democracy and the development of 'thinking' in education. It is a repudiation of norms and averages and a celebration of diversity and humanness. It is based on certain values which, hopefully, come through in the writing. The author hopes, or perhaps expects (Prometheus again), that it has provoked some thinking amongst business school teachers and researchers. The expectation is that it demonstrates the utility of the ideas expressed in the intellectual development of thinking and enables some to consider the rationale for the way they do research.

In my view, there is a marked contrast between a working subservience to neoliberalism that goes on in some business schools and the thoughtful, insightful, intellectual views one might encounter at conferences such as the British Academy of Management. This gives me hope. The business school has such a massive influence in the world that those intellectuals of whom I speak, if they really want to influence the world and create a problem-solving collaboration based on democratic values, must try to influence a change of direction wherever they can. The hope of possibility joins the expectation of success! Epimetheus and Prometheus together.

5. Transforming work into "play": Genuine conversations as hope for meaningful organizational change

John G. McClellan

The discourses associated with contemporary work life position those working in organizations as actively pursuing their own self-interests and purposely seeking self-fulfillment. However, careful examination of these ways of talking about work reveals how anxiety, uncertainty, and a constant inability to be content in the workplace are (re)produced. As organizational participants become increasingly disengaged and unresponsive to others, unhappiness at work becomes framed as an individual problem and hope for meaningful change fades. In this chapter, I review three prominent discourses that permeate contemporary work life and expose how the alignment of these discourses produces a constellation of meaning that leads to self-subordination and self-alienation, resulting in a profound sense of emptiness. However, inspired by Gadamer's (2004) notion of genuine conversation as play(ful) interaction with others, I find hope for meaningful organizational change in responsive dialogue about the discontent with work that expands possibilities, shapes new identities, and carries contemporary work life beyond interregnum.

CONTEMPORARY DISCOURSES OF WORK AND SELF

I use the term "discourse" to refer to systems of meaning, produced and maintained through talk, texts, and the practices of everyday life. These discourses are inherited from the past and provide a vocabulary constituting contemporary understandings of the world and the self in relation to the world (McClellan, 2011; McClellan and Deetz, 2012). Embracing Foucault's (1972, 1980) notion of discursive formations, when particular discourses align in mutual support, larger constellations of meaning become naturalized ways of knowing and being (Deetz, 1992; Deetz and

McClellan, 2009). Such discursive constellations, or large-scale organized systems of meaning, emerge when particular logics, vocabularies, and assumptions are mutually reinforced in everyday talk to "order and naturalize the world in particular ways" (Fairhurst and Putnam, 2004, p. 8). Further, as individuals assume subject positions within such discursive constellations, they become subjected to normalized power relations and other discursive regulations (Weedon, 1997). However, hope of change resides in recognizing that these organized systems of meaning are always arbitrary, partial, and incomplete and can be transformed through reclaiming conflicts of meaning in conversations with others (McClellan, 2011).

With a concern for the increasing discontent with work in the "new economy," this perspective directs attention to the contemporary discourses of work and how particular vocabularies, inherited from the conditions and experiences of late capitalism (Gabriel, 2005; Alvesson, 2014), form constellations of meaning that lead to unhappiness at work. Specifically, work in the 21st century is often talked about in terms of constant change, heightened consumption, and freedom of choice. When these discourses align in mutual support, a discursive constellation is constituted that positions organizational participants in a cycle of continued anxiety, consumption, pursuit of perceived self-interests—and emptiness abounds.

CONSTANT CHANGE

In the 20th century, work life was marked by stable organizations, legal-rational authority, and the perceived ability to steadily progress "up" a career ladder. Patriarchal forms of organization, bolstered by the Protestant work ethic and bureaucratic forms of organization, offered employees a stable self-narrative (Gabriel, 2005). And one's work identity was shaped by years of working in a particular industry, company, or profession. However, in the 21st century, work life has changed. The dominant and most celebrated narrative of contemporary work is one of constant change. As contemporary work is marked by talk of flexibility and transformation, organizational participants are required to be readily adaptable to a variety of work roles. Employees often move from one job or career to another and work for several organizations during their working life. This discourse contributes to an understanding of work life as tenuous and uncertain. As Gabriel (2005) explains, "Western society has moved from a society of massive, concrete buildings and massive, concrete organizations to one of flexible but fragile work arrangements and flexible but fragile organization" (p. 10).

The discourse of constant change makes new demands on organizational participants. The flexible workplace requires malleable employees constantly able to adapt to uncertainty. Employees are positioned to enact what Gabriel (2005) refers to as a "chameleon-like proclivity" in which they are required to "adapt to different work environments, to play any game and to be constantly on the lookout for better opportunities and better prospects" (p. 23). Further, as work become less visible and tangible, workers become more adept at generating "a positive—if somewhat superficial—well-polished and status-enhancing image" (Alvesson, 2014, p. 8). Managers and employees alike become preoccupied with promoting the hype and spectacle of their efforts as they constantly perform a readiness to become anything that is needed. The discourse of constant change contributes to a workplace in which "insecurity and fear are endemic; careers become spasmodic and fragmented, their different steps failing to generate cohesive or integrated life-stories" (Gabriel, 2005, p. 15). As a consequence, the discourse of constant change constitutes a deep insecurity about the ability to succeed and skewed work efforts toward displaying positive, status-enhancing images of the self to overcome these insecurities.

HEIGHTENED CONSUMPTION

Aligned with the discourse of constant change, work life in the new economy is also talked about in terms of heighted consumption (Bauman, 1998; Alvesson, 2014). While the last century was driven by increased mechanization and tangible production, the new economy is "preoccupied with spectacle, image and consumption" (Gabriel, 2005, p. 10). As the discourse of constant change generates insecurities, consumption becomes the opiate by which organizational participants attempt to satisfy individual needs and fulfill desires for gratification. In other words, as fluid and flexible work arrangements generate anxiety, workers consume to find meaning, pleasure, and identity (Ritzer, 1999; Gabriel, 2005). This powerful consumption orientation in the new economy saturates and overcomes relationships, perceptions, and images of the self. No matter what desirable qualities employees seek, whether happiness, satisfying relationships, or self-fulfillment, there always seems a commodity somewhere to provide it (Gabriel, 2005; Alvesson, 2014). As Alvesson (2014) explains, it is through consumption that people "adopt the template of a natural, normal, and desirable person" (p. 35). And, as management practices embrace the worker as "fantasizing consumer" (Ritzer, 1999; Gabriel, 2005), consumption becomes both the source of meaning about work and an outlet for discontent. However, the fantasies and promises of consumption fail to resolve the anxieties generated by an ever-changing and flexible workplace.

In fact, employees are left with "a very similar feeling as a consumer—one never has enough and what one has is never good enough" (Gabriel, 2005, p. 24). As a consequence, workers in the new economy become discursively positioned as "constant consumers," disappointed with work yet actively attempting to pursue fulfillment through consumption.

FREEDOM OF CHOICE

As the discourses of constant change and heightened consumerism align, the concrete and stable structures of the last century dissipate, and the guilt associated with the Protestant work ethic is replaced by the fantasy of consumerism. What emerges is a new sense of freedom in everyday work. Specifically, as the precarious and uneasy sense of identity presented in a discourse of constant change aligns with the promise of instant gratification in consumption, a new discourse of "free and unencumbered pursuit of freedom and choice" emerges (Gabriel, 2005, p. 21). Becoming a hallmark of work in the new economy, this sense of freedom emerges in the *perception* of having unencumbered access to "the act of choosing what to buy and consume and the act of choosing how we spend our time and what work we do" (Gabriel, 2005, p. 15).

However, this perception of freedom is imaginary and contributes to an ongoing cycle of discontent. As organizational participants consume to overcome the anxieties of a fluid and flexible workplace, they are only able to choose from among prepackaged identities offered to consumers. The unfulfilled promises of consumption leave employees perpetually disappointed and longing for more; and the cycle persists. As Alvesson (2014) explains, "individuals lock themselves and others in a high-consumption existence and, ironically, this is often referred to as 'freedom'" (p. 45). As a consequence, the alignment of discourses positions workers in an ongoing cycle of overcoming anxiety through consumption, which ironically requires continued work to maintain the imagined freedom to choose what one does and who one becomes.

SELF-SUBORDINATION AND SELF-ALIENATION

As the discourses of the 21st-century workplace align, they produce a normalized, taken-for-granted understanding of work that limits options and distorts possibilities. As Gabriel (2005) explains, in contemporary work "ambivalence, confusion and anxiety become associated with new, different forms of entrapment" (p. 25). Specifically, as the discourses of contemporary work align in mutual support, a constellation of meaning is created that constitutes practices of self-subordination and self-alienation. Organizational participants become disconnected from others, blamed for their own discontent, and left with a profound sense of emptiness.

Self-subordination arises in the active pursuit of fulfilling a particular work identity. As workers engage in the perceived freedom of choice through consumption, identities are defined in terms of organizational interests. Both managers and employees self-monitor to fulfill what they perceive the "good worker" to be. Efforts to work late, submit positive self-evaluations, and engage in other forms of displaying the value of one's work (and of one's self) define the normal way of being at work. As Deetz (1998) explains, employees consent to a particular "discursive formation through strategizing their own subordination and engaged in active self-surveillance and self-control" (p. 153). Often described in terms of "unobtrusive control," these mechanisms are subtle yet powerful means of control that emerge when the discourses of constant change, increased consumption, and perception of freedom align to position workers as "freely" pursuing their identity and perceived self-interests. These mechanisms of control operate by taking advantage of the anxieties of the changing workplace, the fantasy of consumption, and perceptions of freedom by positioning individuals as in control of their own actions to the benefit of the organization. Thus, through the perceived freedom to choose, people at work actively make decisions fulfilling their self-interests and constraining possible responsive options.

Self-alienation then arises from attempts to resist particular work identities. As forms of control extend into the realm of identity, some workers seek to distance or protect certain aspects of their personhood from the reach of the organization. In a process referred to as "dis-identification," employees often strive to create or preserve a more "authentic" self outside organizational meaning systems (Costas and Fleming, 2009). However, as employees are continually put on display and managerial efforts target employee selves as strategic resources, the "boundary between the narrated imaginary of authenticity and corporate defined identity is difficult to sustain" (p. 360). As a result, self-alienation emerges as "a kind of unhappy consciousness" (p. 374) arising in "those reflexive moments when actors recognize that 'who they really are' is in fact the unwanted corporate self" (2009, p. 354). As a result, workers experience an increasing disconnect from others and an overwhelming feeling of emptiness.

As the discourses of constant change, heightened consumption, and perceived freedom to choose align and permeate across workplaces, self-subordination and self-alienation become sedimented, fixed, and taken-for-granted qualities of work life. As a consequence, everyday communication about the self at work becomes increasingly distorted by the discourses of new capitalism. Managers and employees, focusing on their own self-fulfillment, become less responsive to others and incapable of challenging and disrupting the dominant discourses guiding work. As work life becomes distorted into a cycle of self-interest, display, and consumption, attaining happiness with work becomes framed as an *individual* task that, ironically, when pursued generates more discontent. When workers become "entrepreneurs of the self," any dissatisfaction with work is perceived an individual failure rather than a collective responsibility, and employees become further disconnected, unresponsive to others, and subsequently blamed for their unhappiness at work.

HOPE IN GENUINE CONVERSATIONS

Hope for generating more positive workplaces requires reconnecting with others and talking about the discontent and unhappiness of work. Embracing Courpasson's (2017) notion of an "activist sense of everyday life," the workplace can become the place where individuals challenge and disrupt the taken-for-granted meanings of work that constrain and preclude more mutually responsible ways of knowing the self at work from emerging. Hope is not redeemed, however, through the actions of individual workers. Hope for change requires a responsiveness to others and a willingness to participate in conversations with others that reclaim alternative meanings and reveal a horizon of possibilities for happiness and fulfillment. Gadamer (2004) provides such hope in the practice of genuine conversation.

Gadamer's *Truth and Method* (2004) offers a treatise on philosophical hermeneutics in which he develops an understanding of how we come to our essential way of being in the world. In this work, Gadamer explains the "hermeneutic experience" as a practice that can expand our "horizons of understanding" as we encounter new situations in conversation with others. Recognizing consciousness as influenced by history, he argues that contemporary individuals have become largely unaware of the tradition that shapes particular ways of knowing. However, if people remain open to the notion that all things are always much more than language can describe and are able to talk with others about their experiences in the world, they can become more aware of their traditions and expand everyday ways of knowing. In this way, Gadamer offers a process of mutual engagement within which people can expand traditions and transform understandings of the self through open and "playful" interactions with others.

Gadamer (2004) begins by explaining how people come to understand texts, such as a piece literature or a great work of art. He argues that meanings of texts are not determined by the actual or imagined intentions of the author. Instead, understanding involves "a dialogic and reciprocal experience of questioning texts and remaining open to being questioned by them" (Anderson et al., 2004, p. 3). In other words, understanding a text requires an openness to allow the subject matter of the text to question one's tradition, or assumptions about the everyday world and ways of knowing the self. As Deetz (1992) explains, "the imaginary self and world produced in discourse is challenged by the excess of what the discourse is about over the description of it" (p. 165). For Gadamer (2004), the hermeneutic experience is about reclaiming conflicts of meaning to expand possibilities and transform tradition(s). If we participate in the world this way, when we encounter new situations that violate some of our traditional assumptions "our awareness expands and our understanding of the tradition evolves" (Craig and Muller, 2007, p. 220).

Gadamer (2004) extends this idea of understanding texts to include other people. He explains that, because we encounter tradition in the form of language, our tradition speaks to us. And, because we experience the world and others in language, all subject matter of the world as well as all "others" can be a part of the hermeneutic experience. Gadamer emphasizes that the object of discussion is what connects people in dialogue. He explains that, when there is mutual engagement with others on the object of discussion, and both interactants are genuinely trying to understand this subject matter from differing traditions (inherited by each individual), then new understandings or ways of knowing can arise. This form of mutual engagement is referred to as "genuine conversation."

Gadamer (2004) argues that a conversation is "genuine" when it fulfills two important qualities. First, genuine conversation requires openness to expand horizons. Participants must sincerely want to know what they don't know and be open to having their tradition questioned by the other. According to Gadamer, this process "involves recognizing the I myself must accept some things that are against me, even though no one else forces me to do so" (p. 355). This type of experience demands vulnerability—a recognition that one does not know everything about something—and openness to different ways of knowing the same thing. Second, genuine conversation requires dialectical engagement. Gadamer explains that the process of understanding unfolds in a tension-filled to-and-fro process that "proceeds by way of question and answer" (p. 357). When those participating in conversation have a genuine desire to know what the other thinks about the subject matter, questions will arise with the purpose of knowing more than what one already knows—and this requires a responsive other to do the same.

Gadamer (2004) describes genuine conversation using the metaphor of "play." Specifically, he explains the tension-filled experience of conversation as a "movement to-and-fro" (2004, p. 106) that necessarily requires another "player" and an object of play (or subject matter) that demands responses to the "moves" made by each player. Genuine conversation is thus an act in itself, a process that is embodied and literally played with others. It is something that cannot be planned, scripted, or predetermined. As Stewart et al. (2004) explain, genuine conversations "have the structure of play, a patterned-yet-always-new dynamic that people enter, influence, and are subject to and guided by" (p. 29). When engaged as play, a conversation flows freely and "because the participants do not guide it according to any preconceived plan. They follow the subject matter wherever it goes in a common search for truth, with each comment raising some challenge to understanding that leads to the next" (Craig and Muller, 2007, p. 221).

According to Gadamer (2004), participating in the play of genuine conversation is fundamentally transformative. This form of communicative understanding "is less a matter of reproducing or apprehending prior meanings than it is a process of producing new and fresh meanings" (Anderson et al., 2004, p. 3). As individuals engage in open, responsive conversations with others about their experiences in the world, the differing perspectives of others expand the horizon of possibility for knowing the world. Further, this process of playful, dialectical interaction transforms ways of knowing the self in relation to the world. Gadamer (2004) explains that reaching an understanding with others "is not a matter of putting oneself forward and successfully asserting one's own point of view, but being transformed into communion in which we do not remain what we were" (p. 371). In this way, genuine conversation "becomes an experience that changes the person who experiences it" (Gadamer, 2004, p. 103). As Deetz and Simpson (2004) explain, this form of interaction is "aimed less at self-expression and more at self-destruction" (p. 143). As such, embodied participation in responsive, mutual engagement with others is transformative in the sense that participants can no longer be who they were prior to the conversation.

TRANSFORMING WORK INTO PLAY

Gadamer's (2004) notion of genuine conversation offers hope of transforming understandings of work life in the new economy. Contemporary understanding of work (and the self at work) can be recognized as a taken-for-granted tradition, inherited from the dominant discourses of late capitalism, and actively (re)constituted in the everyday talk, texts, and practices of work. Transforming everyday work into play, however, offers hope of expanding this tradition and generating new understandings of work and self through responsive interactions with others. Specifically, if organizational participants can mutually engage each other in the "play" of genuine conversation about the discontent of work, the discourses of contemporary work life can generate more mutually satisfying workplaces and subjectivities.

Each encounter with others at work becomes a choice or, as Deetz and Simpson (2004) explain, every interaction "holds both the possibility of closure or new meanings" (p. 143). Thus, every engagement with others at work can result in a reproduction of the dominant socially projected realities or become a responsive interaction that offers the possibility of producing new discourses guiding work in the 21st century. In this way, overcoming the anxiety and emptiness of contemporary work life is not found in the individual pursuit of self-interests, but in reconnecting with others. Conversation, not consumption, becomes the process for meaningful organizational change.

Guided by genuine conversation, transforming practices of everyday work into "play" requires openness to not knowing and actively engaging others in sincere questioning and reciprocity. If managers and employees turn to the other about the discontent of work and engage in conversations about anxiety and emptiness with a sincere desire to learn from others' perspectives, it can generate new understandings of work and the self. As people become more open to the indeterminacy of work and invite conversations about discontentedness at work, it could reclaim conflicts of meaning and expand horizons of possibility. In this way, transforming work into "play" offers hope of replacing emptiness with openness and self-improvement with responsive engagement.

In this way, hope for change emerges when the subject matter of genuine conversation includes the very problematic understandings of work, the workplace, and the self at work that result in emptiness and unhappiness. For instance, what if the discourse of constant change became the subject matter of conversation? Consider if a manager working at an organization experiencing rapid growth, a merger, or downsizing facilitated a discussion among employees about the changes taking place and focused the conversation on current practices or roles that work well and should be maintained. Imagine what might be possible if those faced with constant change and uncertainty engaged in genuine conversation about the things that should stay constant. If employees did not talk about what is changing, but asked questions of each other about what should remain the same and responded to each other with a sense of genuinely wanting to know what is valued and appreciated by others, it could lead to more gratitude and satisfaction with work. And what might happen if conversations focused on the challenges of being a flexible worker in an ever-changing workplace? Consider if a workgroup with members at different locations across the globe or who work from home took moments to engage in conversations about the uncertainties associated with their flexible work arrangements and focused on activities that promoted support and collaboration. If employees talked openly and "playfully" about their lived experiences at work, it could transform individual efforts from presenting positive self-images toward collective efforts to ameliorate anxieties and generate more optimistic and supportive work experiences. These types of conversations could reveal new ways to know work and present new forms of contentment with one's self at work.

Similarly, hope arises in "playful" conversations about finding happiness and fulfillment at work. Rather than turning to the fantasy of consumption, what if employees turned to each other and engaged in mutually responsive conversations about what is most fulfilling and exciting about work? Consider if a group of colleagues periodically met to celebrate working together and participated in discussions highlighting the moments they felt happiest at work and talked about what was most exciting for the future. Engaging in such conversations can underscore work experiences that offer joy and reveal hidden and not yet able to be articulated possibilities for workers' identities. If employees could talk with others about who they are and what they might wish to become, they could collectively shape more fulfilling and mutually supportive self-narratives.

Additionally, hope appears when the freedom to choose includes a desire to talk with others about opportunities and mutually supportive choices at work. What might emerge if managers and employees could openly and responsively discuss options available that would make work less anxious and more content? Consider if a leadership team, contemplating a new initiative, invited representative stakeholders across the organization to talk through possibilities, collectively envision a potential end state, and discuss varied mechanisms for implementing the program so everyone knew what to expect. These conversations could reveal ideas not currently seen or known and lead to new possibilities and innovative ways of working together. Similarly, what if decisions were not individually made, but were approached collectively in conversation that considered options that worked for everyone? Consider if a manager, charged with making a decision affecting an entire workgroup, invited a series of conversation asking for everyone's unique view and then talked through viable options that ensured all voices were heard and everyone's interests were considered. If managers are open to understanding others' perspectives about what could be done or accomplished, it could free employees from the cycle of being perpetually disappointed. Talking about what is really possible invites opportunities for working together and engaging in choices that are informed by multiple voices—constituting working conditions that are supportive of many differing perspectives. These types of conversations could promote new meanings about organizational goals and how workers, together, might best achieve these aims. Further, what if the many identities lived by employees were celebrated in conversations at work? Consider if a supervisor needing to coordinate schedules invited a discussion that allowed employees to coordinate their schedules in relation to their "other" ways of being, such as the parent needing afternoons to pick up children from school, a volunteer who spends Fridays at a non-profit organization, or the athlete with a morning training routine. Being open to difference can generate the possibility for individuals to be seen as more than just "workers" and feel supported at work for their many life pursuits, experiences, and identities.

Overall, hope for change requires choosing to engage with others in responsive and caring ways. Appreciating different perspectives and inviting others to engage in open, tension-filled conversations about the real discontents of work can transform the contemporary discourses of work, constituting mutual support rather than self-promotion. Transforming work into "play" can overcome the emptiness of contemporary work life through responsive engagement with others. Rather than pursuing self-interests and manipulating images of work, workers can engage in conversations about these concerns with others. Rather than overcoming anxiety of the ever-changing workplace by seeking happiness in consumption, employees can talk with others about opportunities for finding fulfillment at work. Rather than pursuing a mythical sense of freedom, individuals can freely question the meanings of work and discuss real possibilities for a better workplace. Combined, hope emerges when self-subordination is transformed into mutual engagement and self-alienation into mutual support.

AN INVITATION FOR CHANGE

Meaningful transformation of the contemporary workplace through genuine conversation demands organizational participants embrace the "otherness of the other" and be open to different meanings (re)generated in conversation with others. This is a challenging task when contemporary discourses of work distort and limit horizons of possibility. Inviting others to participate in genuine conversations can, however, make visible a horizon of alternatives that often remain hidden beyond the dominant constellations of meaning. Thus, transforming the meaning of work in the new economy requires inviting others to participate in genuine conversation and making a commitment to participate in the tension-filled "play" of to-and-fro questioning and responsive engagement. Inviting others to participate in responsive conversations about the emptiness of work can transform the discursive constellation of work in the new economy.

Specifically, the self-awareness generated in playful dialogue with others offers hope of challenging the discursive constellations of contemporary work that privilege the self and disconnect individuals from each other. As Deetz and Simpson (2004) explain, there is a productive potential in the self-awareness generated in dialogue when "understanding reopens the things of our world to redetermination" (p. 145). In this way, contemporary understandings of work can be transformed not through some new-found self-determination but on the recovery of the demand of the "subject matter" in conversation with others. Moving contemporary workplaces beyond interregnum requires reclaiming happiness at work as a collective responsibility enacted in responsive communicative practices that promote mutual appreciation and collaborative engagement.

6. Hope in business organizing for societal progress: Three narratives[1]

Stewart Clegg, Ace Volkmann Simpson, Miguel Pina e Cunha, and Arménio Rego

INTRODUCTION

This chapter explores the role of capitalist organizations in providing hope for the betterment of society. At the individual level, Snyder has defined hope 'as the perceived capability to derive pathways to desired goals, and motivate oneself via agency thinking to use those pathways' (Snyder, 2002, p. 249). Yet we are concerned with hope at the broader societal level. Accordingly, we draw upon Braithwaite's (2004) sociological definition of collective hope as 'a shared desire for a better society, articulated through a broad set of agreed-upon goals and principles, developed and elaborated through socially inclusive dialogue' (p. 146). The impact of business organizations on social and other relations is significant. Capitalistic organizations have a fundamental role in the betterment of society through the widely agreed-upon objectives of fostering prosperity, wealth creation and innovation. Unfortunately, they also tend to breach their social licence by additionally fostering exploitation, degradation and domination. Our emphasis is nonetheless hopeful, concerned with questioning the conditions under which business organizations contribute towards social well-being. Towards this end, as we summarize in Table 6.1, we organize the material using a framework with three areas of analysis or narratives: 1) ethical; 2) empirical; and 3) prudential (Riemer et al., 2013).

Our *ethical* analysis is concerned with the question: 'What ought to

Table 6.1 Three narratives

Narrative	Basis	Question	Discipline
Ethical	Values	What ought to be?	Philosophy
Empirical	Facts	What is?	Science
Prudential	Judgement	What can be?	Policy

be?' The focus here is on values, with philosophy as the foundation. This domain is normative in prescribing, within the context of this chapter, that business activity ought to promote social well-being. Our review of the literature will touch on more than 2000 years of Western thought on wealth generation, from the classical Greek philosopher Socrates, to the medieval Church, to the philosophers of the Enlightenment. This broad philosophical review will introduce us to some of the most influential thinking that has formed the foundational bedrock of Western civilization through the ages to the current day.

An *empirical* analysis provides a descriptive understanding of the relationship between business activity and society, focusing on the question: 'What is?' Here we draw on scientific observation as our foundation in considering economic data collected over centuries. The analysis will demonstrate that the organization of business activity has both positive and negative social effects, both inspiring and discouraging hope. If the question is how to promote social betterment while inhibiting social harm we conclude that this is always a matter of judgement.

The *prudential* analysis will therefore consider how judgement influences the contingencies whereby business organizations can generate profits while reducing social harm and fostering social betterment (or not). Our primary question here is: 'What can be?' We address this question by considering the role of policy and values in informing capitalist organizational practices that have a goal of contributing to the good of society. We analyse practical pathways organizations can take and are taking to be a force for good in the world using models such as corporate social responsibility, creating shared value, stakeholder theory, conscious capitalism and sustainability. While considering these different models, we will also note their limitations – which leads us to conclude by reflecting on the vital role of the democratic governance of society; more radically we consider the design of organizations around inclusive, participatory democratic values as a safeguard of hope.

THE ETHICAL NARRATIVE

A widely held assumption of our time is that business organizations drive societal progress by creating jobs, products and services, and investment in innovative technologies that solve human problems. This is a relatively recent view, emerging in the seventeenth and eighteenth centuries with the twin innovations of the Enlightenment and the advent of industrial capitalism, and best captured by Adam Smith (1776) in *An Inquiry into the Nature and Causes of the Wealth of Nations*. New social constructions emerged as an unanticipated result of ultimate ethical and religious values (Weber, 1930) that kick-started the process Smith referred to as 'primitive accumulation'. Calvinism generated not only a work ethic but also, in consequence, capital. We can gain insight into this social construction by contrasting it with past constructions.

Through much of history, philosophers, Church leaders and rulers were less than hopeful of the social benefits of commerce, viewing merchant and business activity as socially subordinate if not malignant. Aristotle distrusted merchants. He emphasized a state governed by a virtuous middle class of free men (women were not included) heading self-sufficient households, where independent craftsmen or slaves deemed unworthy of citizenship provide material needs. The possession of sufficient wealth was necessary for civic engagement (voting in the agora and the military duty to defend the city) and the exercise of virtuous liberality and magnanimity in sacrificing for the common good. The active pursuit of wealth through trade was regarded as morally hazardous – 'the trafficking in goods' through commerce where wealth is the means and objective of exchange was viewed as counter to not only political virtue but also individual moral well-being: 'the citizens should not live a vulgar . . . or a merchant's way of life', Aristotle wrote, 'for this sort of way of life is ignoble and contrary to virtue' (2013, p. 202). Athenian bankers, merchants and moneylenders were even denied citizenship (Millett, 2002).

The Christian Gospels and early Church Fathers were similarly suspicious of and even hostile towards merchants and trade. According to the Apostle Mark, Jesus drove out all of those 'that sold and bought in the temple', as he 'overthrew the tables of the moneychangers, and the seats of them that sold doves' (Bible, 1997, Mark 12:15–16). The Apostle Matthew reports that, in his Sermon on the Mount, Jesus preached 'For where your treasure is, there will your heart be also' and 'Ye cannot serve God and mammon' (Bible, 1997, Matthew 6:21, 6:24). The *Decretum*, a collection of canon law from the middle of the twelfth century, referenced these passages declaring: 'The man who buys in order that he may gain by selling it again unchanged as he bought it, that man is of the buyers and sellers who are cast forth from God's temple' (cited in Tawney, 1926, p. 35).

In the late Middle Ages, a more urban economy arose with the development of cities and new financial instruments as the bonds of feudalism were increasingly weakened by peasant revolt, bubonic plague and pestilence, the latter caused by calorific shortfalls because of the exhaustion of available land using the existing technology in the face of diminishing yields for an increasing population (Anderson, 1974). The Scholastic theologians headed by Thomas Aquinas presented a more hopeful reconsidered Church position on commerce, one that reconciled the Church with the views of the texts of the newly rediscovered Aristotle (Muller, 2003). Private property was held to be legitimate, as it was the basis for the family and social order, where division of labour 'naturally' led to the hierarchy of estates (status groups). Economic activity was necessary for family heads to be able to support their dependants appropriately to the standards of their estates.

Through a rhetorical process of paradiastole, Enlightenment philosophers redistributed virtues and vices and vice versa (Skinner, 1996). Mandeville's (1670–1733) *The Fable of the Bees: Or, Private Vices, Publick Benefits* (1714) makes the case that individual self-interested character dispositions of pride, vanity and ambition, long stigmatized as vices, were in fact necessary conditions for social prosperity. Mandeville's insistence that economic prosperity would cease without individual ambition for luxury and pride was echoed in the century that followed both by proponents such as Voltaire and Adam Smith and by critics such as Karl Marx. The latter agreed with Mandeville's analysis of the vicious basis for commerce but did not share his admiration for the private accumulation of affluence (Muller, 2003). Adam Smith (1723–1790) developed arguments supporting individual self-interest as the basis for social order in *An Inquiry into the Nature and Causes of the Wealth of Nations* (1776). Smith reasoned that a liberal capitalist market economy, where people have the freedom to compete in pursuing their own self-interest, is the best vehicle for improving the standard of living of the greatest majority of the population, leading to what Smith termed 'universal opulence'.

Smith was well aware of the need for a moral order as well (Smith, 2010). Smith's 'commercial society' was referred to pejoratively by Marx (1818–1883), its critic, as 'capitalism' (Marx, 2015), a term now embraced positively even by the market's fiercest advocates. Marx saw market competition as inherently a morally abhorrent system of exploitation, inequality and political instability that systematically alienated skilled workers from the products they produce. The effect was to turn artisans into paid labourers, doing routine tasks in assembly lines 'as living appendages' of the machines they operated. The above historical overview of Western thought is ambivalent in providing hope concerning the relationship between the organization of wealth generation and the betterment of society, but also mostly theoretical. What does the empirical evidence tell us about the relationship between organizations, specifically financial organizations, and social well-being? Is there support for Voltaire and Adam Smith's arguments that trade provides a common platform for inclusive dialogue supporting peace and prosperity among trading nations?

THE EMPIRICAL NARRATIVE

While Voltaire regarded the London Stock Exchange as the embodiment of how trade achieves the objective of international collaboration and peace, there is evidence of business organizations contributing to violent social conflict through collusion with authoritarian state authorities, through assuming the role of government, and through various forms of human rights abuse or neglect of people's working conditions (Banerjee, 2008; Reinecke and Donaghey, 2015).

The part played by the British East India Company, described as one of the world's first multinational organizations (Clegg, 2016), in expanding the British Empire as one based on commerce provides one such negative example. With the support of its private army, the Company came to rule most of India. Tax revenue eventually eclipsed profits from trade as the greater source of shareholder dividends (Robins, 2007). The British South Africa Company similarly employed a private military that was engaged in capturing African diamond mines, furthering the interests of both the firm and the British state (Thomas, 1996).

It may be objected that these examples of profit-seeking organizations colluding with state authorities in undermining the security and rights of sovereign populations are confined to a past historical era of colonialism. There are, however, numerous cases that are more recent. One high-profile example of doing business with a dictatorial regime is that of IBM maintaining computational machines used in the Nazi concentration camps during the Second World War (Wilson, 1993). Ikea's collusion with the oppressive Communist East German government by contracting prison labour in the 1970s and 1980s to manufacture its furniture (Connolly, 2012) is another case. Shell has also been criticized for collusion with dictatorial regimes and complicity in human rights abuses associated with its Nigerian subsidiary and the Nigerian government in the 1990s (Wheeler et al., 2002). Despite millions of dollars of royalties being generated, local communities affected by company operations remained hopelessly impoverished as traditional livelihoods were eroded.

It is increasingly typical for multinational mining companies operating in developing countries to employ transnational private armies to protect their interests from violent conflicts that arise between indigenous communities, governments and the multinational organizations (Mbembe, 2008). Banerjee describes such destructive business practices that involve dispossession, infra-human working conditions and even death as necrocapitalism, defined as 'contemporary forms of organizational accumulation that involve dispossession and the subjugation of life to the power of death' (Banerjee, 2008, p. 1541).

There are, however, more hopeful alternative examples of business organizations operating in a manner that promotes social well-being in terms of security, peace and prosperity (Kanter, 2011, p. 66, wrote about how 'great companies . . . instead of being mere money-generating machines . . . combine financial and social logic to build enduring success'). Economists note that, with the arrival of capitalistic business organizations, economic growth, as measured by gross domestic product (GDP), has triggered a significant rise in the world's wealth. The world's economy was stagnant for 820 years from the year 1000 up until 1820, during which time it grew just six-fold (Wolf, 2004). With the arrival of capitalism and the industrial revolution, in the 178-year period between 1820 to 1998, the world economy grew 50-fold, at a rate faster than population growth, with an average nine-fold increase in individual incomes. More important for the objective of enhanced social well-being, these GDP increases translated into an improved standard of living with increased availability of food, clothing, shelter and health care (Easterlin and Angelescu, 2012) and decreases in average weekly working hours and work by children and the elderly (Barro, 1997).

Can business organizations contribute to peace? This is the question Spreitzer (2007) sought to answer empirically in a novel manner – using cross-country data from existing international databases. Spreitzer found that, in countries where the leadership of business organizations is more participative and where employees have greater agency and decision-making authority, there is significantly less corruption and unrest. The causation of this association can, of course, flow in the opposite direction, where more democratic countries lead to more participatory business organizations. Democracy is a topic we will return to at the end of this chapter.

THE PRUDENTIAL NARRATIVE

Having completed a review of ambivalent ethical prescriptions for the relationship between business organizations and society, as well as mixed empirical evidence describing positive and negative effects of this relationship, we now consider the prudential implications of managerial judgement in fostering potential social benefits and minimizing negative effects. It is here, more than anywhere else, that one can identify cause for hope. Braithwaite (2004, p. 146) holds that the process of collective hope requires three elements to work in concert: 'commitment to shared goals, collective efficacy through democratic participation and a sense of group membership, and trust in institutional pathways for implementation'.

Management is often taught as a value-neutral science based purely upon the objective reading of factual data (Ghoshal, 2005), but the centrality of goals and agency means that managing is always interpreted through the filter of values. Every decision incorporates values based upon deeper philosophical assumptions: some values strive for narrow benefit; others strive more widely.

Corporate social responsibility (CSR) conveys the notion of business organizations self-regulating through the voluntary uptake of socially responsible practices above and beyond what is required by the letter of the law as a demonstration of corporate citizenship or corporate conscience (Ghoshal, 2005). Organizations that act, as would any good citizen, in a fair and responsible manner, doing the right thing by others, are admired more than their rapacious counterparts. For some, however, the ideas of Voltaire and Smith about self-interest providing a social benefit are taken to the extreme in arguing that the sole responsibility of business is to maximize profits for shareholders (Friedman, 1970). In contrast, there is increasing recognition that it is essential for organizations to operate in a socially responsible matter beyond what is required by the law, as many legal activities are socially reprehensible.

Key practices for implementing CSR within business organizations include appointing directors or managers responsible for CSR, developing and publicizing CSR statements and ethical codes of practice, donating to charities and supporting social and environmental causes, enrolling as members of public forums or environmental groups, and publicizing a record of socially responsible practices. Claims of CSR practices made by organizations, however, are not necessarily legitimate. Organizations are often accused of adopting CSR merely to engender public and share-holder trust and reduce legal risk, as a cynical public relations exercise in 'window-dressing' designed to pre-empt the government's role as social watch-dog (Henderson, 2001). Business organizations also sometimes use CSR to deflect public attention away from harmful aspects of their business practices. Cynicism towards CSR, both by business executives and by critics, places business organizations in an absurd situation where they are damned if they ignore the negative social impacts of organizational operations but also criticized for trying to do something about it (Morsing et al., 2008). At the end of the day, it is better to be damned for trying to do what is right than for acting as a 'social parasite' (Hanlon and Fleming, 2009, p. 944).

Creating shared value (CSV) is a concept which builds upon the notion of CSR introduced by Porter and Kramer (2006). These authors challenge the idea that the activities of business organizations and the well-being of society necessarily conflict with each other. Rather, they argue, the success of both business and the community are mutually interdependent. Business organizations therefore should identify and enact policy that leverages the natural links between their strategies and CSR, by shifting their focus away from responsibilities, towards a focus on value creation. They portray CSR as often reactionary, driven by external pressures and reputation management and constrained by budgetary limitations. The interests of society are pitted against the interests of the business organization, highlighting the costs of complying with externally enforced social requirements. CSV in contrast is proactive and driven internally by strategic opportunities that provide benefit for both the organization and society. Here the focus is on opportunities for competitive advantage through incorporation of a social value proposition within the organizational strategy. CSV represents a significant shift in paradigm from the traditional role of how business organizations see their role in society, as well as themselves.

Stakeholder theory is another approach that seeks to address the limitations of CSR. Stakeholder theory argues that the numerous groups impacted by organizational practices have a legitimate voice that needs to be acknowledged in organizational policy and decision-making. Originally articulated by R.E. Freeman (1984), stakeholder theory defines a stakeholder as 'any group or individual who can affect or is affected by the achievement of the organization's objectives' (1984, p. 46). Stakeholder theory has been further developed by Mackey and Sisodia (2013) as conscious capitalism, which has become a worldwide movement. These authors argue that capitalism correctly practised has essential qualities of goodness, ethicality, nobility and heroism. Its goodness springs from its ability to create value for stakeholders, its ethicality rests on its foundation of free voluntary exchange, while its noble heroism derives from the power to alleviate human poverty and drive economic prosperity.

Sustainability scholars emphasize the interactional relations between the environment and socio-economic activity. Hence there is a trifurcation of social, environmental and economic considerations, usually qualified as 'the 3 Ps' (people, planet, profit). The pathways of CSR, CSV and stakeholder orientations through which business organizations demonstrate 'commitment to shared goals . . . and a sense of group membership' (Braithwaite, 2004, p. 146) in contributing towards the public good provide a source of collective hope. Nonetheless, we see the need for one more piece in this puzzle: the safeguarding of these pathways through 'democratic participation . . . and trust in institutional pathways for implementation' (Braithwaite, 2004, p. 146).

THE DEMOCRATIC SAFEGUARD

The best antidote to unscrupulous behaviour and safeguarding the public good is democracy, both societal and organizational. For much of the twentieth century, especially in Scandinavia, the dominant feature in organization design was the implementation of the principles of industrial democracy. Scandinavian industrial democracy was partly based on socio-technic systems theory, which began in the London-based Tavistock Institute in the post-war period but had its most notable take-up in Scandinavia, initially in Norway (Klemsdal et al., 2017). Socio-technical systems theory saw self-organizing teams defining their own work as the core element of organizational design, humanizing work in the process, away from the mechanism of other approaches such as Taylorism and bureaucracy (Battilana et al., 2017; M.Y. Lee and Edmondson, 2017). The focus was on how people and technology could interact productively and in an empowering way. These concerns became widely espoused in Scandinavia, even becoming embedded as part of the founding principles of the tripartite union/business/government *Arbetslivscentrum*, Centre for Working Life, in Sweden, sponsoring policy innovations to improve the quality of working life.

North American management thinking, which, because of the power of its numbers, dominates global English-language discussions, has long spurned notions of industrial and organizational democracy. There are, however, longstanding European traditions of organizational democracy in Scandinavia and of works councils in the Netherlands, Germany and Austria, which, with their traditions of participatory codetermination, have only been lightly discussed, if at all, in the dominant English-speaking management literature of recent years (Balfour, 2018; Lecher et al., 2018; Sorge, 2018). If management's right to manage through the domination of their perspectives and the authority of their positions is assumed as a taken-for-granted feature of the English-speaking world, there is considerably more mutuality and joint decision-making between managers and employees in these European approaches. In addition, there are deep-rooted traditions of cooperative design and management evident in many sectors of the global economy, especially in producer cooperatives, discussion of which is largely neglected in the literature.

One provocative defence of democracy is provided by Tonkinwise (2018), who stresses that the definition of who is an organizational stakeholder needs expanding to include marginalized peoples, by race, class or ability, as well as a wide range of non-users, people from across the whole-of-life supply chain and delegates representing future generations and non-human actors. Together with this expanded notion of democracy, organizations should, it is suggested, be engaged in advocacy of visions for the future that the organization is working towards and prepared to evaluate its work against as well as advocating participation in the profits from design for all involved – from makers and maintainers to users and end-of-life disposers and recyclers. It is a profound and radical view of organizational democracy as a key component of a fully societal democracy, serving as a safeguard of the public good, a view that inspires us with hope.

CONCLUSION

We see hope in business organizations consciously embracing the goal of functioning as a force for social well-being. It would be impossible and undesirable for government to oversee the operations of all business organizations to the extent of forcing all businesses to embrace the mission of being a force for good. Democratic government does have a responsibility, however, to ensure that organizations do not cause harm. History has demonstrated the totalitarian oppression that ensues from governments that adopt ideologically authoritarian assumptions. There are many variants of these expressed in the philosophies discussed in our ethical narrative which, depending on their proclivities, will label specific forms and designs of business activity as, *a priori*, either negative or positive.

On the contrary, as is demonstrated in our empirical narrative, a more nuanced position is that the impact of business activities on society *may* be positive or harmful. It is a matter of strategic choice, as we emphasize in our prudential narrative. We find hope in evidence of an emerging countermovement seeking to rein in corporate capitalism and consciously consider the needs of a broader group of stakeholders. The explicit inclusion of hope in the vocabulary of positive organizational scholarship is another indication that it should be embraced by organizations as a collective project (Cunha et al., 2019), emphasizing attention not only to present goals but also to future aspirations and impacts. The more that organizational voices are democratically invited to contribute to designing and stewarding the processes of organizational governance at not just societal but also organizational levels, the more we hold hope in the possibility that business might be organizing for societal progress as well as profit.

NOTE

1. Part of this chapter is adapted from Chapter 11 of *Positive Organizational Behavior* (Cunha et al., 2019).

7. Post-Pandoran hope for moving wisely beyond the neo-Promethean Anthropocene

Wendelin Küpers

INTRODUCTION

"What hope can we have for Planet Earth for 2035 and beyond?"

This chapter proposes that we can hope, still, again and anew, by learning from the mythical stories of Prometheus and Pandora's box. In particular, there is hope when we learn to become wiser, and move wisely beyond the so-called Anthropocene. The Anthropocene marks a specific age (from Greek *anthropo-* meaning 'human' and *-cene* meaning 'new' or 'age'). Historically, this epoch, which is still under way, has been emerging over a long period of time. It started when some of Earth's creatures (humans) began taming nature, an activity that intensified from the Industrial Revolution up to our contemporary late modern and capitalist society. Human activities and impacts are now seen as permanent, even on a geological time-scale (Steffen et al., 2011a, 2011b).

The notion of the popularized term Anthropocene implies an 'AnthropoScene' that is the staging of a set of narratives with profound implications, including the performativity of depoliticizing stories that render an obscuring, silencing and off-staging 'Anthropo-obScene' (Swyngedouw and Ernstson, 2018). These scenes, like any representation of environmental or organizational histories, involve a storyline with a theatrical setting that features a cast of key actors, agents, properties, and relations, and inevitably exclude other potential performers and relations (Cronon, 1992). We are currently witnessing a new transformation and reconfiguration of figures, characters, and their roles in performing a drama that makes all the world a stage sharing one interwoven destiny in a geo-bio-social becoming (Ingold, 2013).

Is there hope that the historical trajectory of the materio-eco-socio-cultural nexus can be transformed? Such transformation is even more challenging, as this nexus is characterized at present by the fateful dominance of capitalist interests and rationales, and technocratic power.

If we consider that the Anthropocene is a narrative between dystopian and eco-eschatological horizons of despair and hope, critical questions and quests emerge, such as: What does it mean to hope for a life worth living, while knowing about extinctive striving towards dying? Is misleading hope part of the problem? Can we still connect hope to a modernist-progressivist view of a better future? What about nostalgic and retrogressive hope? Where is a place for hope in times of 'catastrophes-to-come' and an apocalypse without the promise of redemption? Is there 'hope in the dark' (Solnit, 2016) and a tragic 'post-human comedy' (McGurl, 2012) whose fate is sealed (Morton, 2013, p. 7; Scranton, 2015), deciding, like the ancient emperor Nero, to fiddle, while the Earth and its stakeholders burn (Fiala, 2010)?

In contrast to this decadent and defeatist scenario, hope might serve as a virtue in the age of climate change. As such, it can function as a positive orientation towards the future that energizes and motivates action (Williston, 2015, p. 49). Thereby, hope may mediate an anticipatory responsibility in the present (Sardo, 2019). In this way, hope can play a vital role in reaching out and enacting anthropo-decentric transformational futures, 'this-sidely' of apocalyptic dystopia (Slaughter, 2004).

Accordingly, hope – together with grief (Head, 2016) – can serve to shift our relationship with(in) the Anthropocene and generate practices that change courses. As an active disposition for elaboration and collaboration, hope is an affirmation about values that involves adopting a way of being-in-the-world creatively, but without fixation on any preconceived solution (Teanor, 2015).

Since hope is both a proactive orientation and a response to the angst of the Anthropocene, it wagers hermeneutically that reality and living in reality are worthwhile. Furthermore, as hoping connects us to practical wisdom, it gives us energy to organize ourselves in the Anthropocene (Heikkurinen et al., 2016).

To elaborate this vision of hope, the following first briefly presents some ideas about hope and its ambiguities. To illustrate the link between hope and the so-called Anthropocene and wisdom, the myths of Prometheus and Pandora's box are discussed. Finally, the role of hope for an anthro-decentric transformation and some perspectives pointing towards an enlivening eco- or *zoë*-cene are put forward. As the Greek word *zoë* refers to meanings of life in an ecological sense, this eco- or *zoë*-cene can be understood as a post-anthropocentric age.

HOPE

Hoping is an integral and profound experience and process of human and other lives, but is also a contested concept and disputed category. This complex phenomenon and socially mediated capacity has varying affective, cognitive, behavioral, and socio-cultural dimensions and modes that have been interpreted quite differently.

Despite its variations according to the ontological and epistemological concerns of the time at which it was addressed, Ludema et al. (1997, p. 1030) state enduring qualities. For these authors, hope is born in a relationship, inspired by the conviction that the future is open and can be influenced, sustained by dialogue about ideals, and generative of positive affects and actions. With these qualities, hope and a socially enabling 'vocabulary of hope' (Ludema et al., 1997) may transform the status quo towards renewing life.

Before exploring the ambivalences and roles of hope in the Anthropocene, and retelling the story of Prometheus and Pandora, the following working definition and vision of hope is proposed:

> Hope is an embodied, emotional, individual, and/or collective inter-relational experience and imagined and storied process. It is embodied in the sense that it is a bodily means to be 'inter-affected' (Küpers, 2014) and thus 'effectuated,' moved by and moving with others, both humans and more-than-humans alike. As such, it functions as a potential generative and subversive force, an energizing medium for 'possibilizing' and creative, transformative practices. In turn, when connected to and qualified by practical wisdom, these future-related dimensions of hope may serve to enhance vitalities for organizing human and 'more-than-human' stakeholders.

Based on this understanding, the starting point for the following is that individual and social hope for a qualitatively different way of living (that is worth striving for) will become increasingly important in the Anthropocene. Before discussing the relation of hope, the Anthropocene, and wisdom, the following addresses hope's polysemy and equivocacy.

AMBIVALENCES AND AMBIGUITIES OF HOPE

If hope is to be compelling in a secular world, it needs to be more than simple expectation, passive anticipation, naive or irrational optimism, delusional wish-fulfillment or the means of an escapist flight from reality, thus an evasion! Nor can it be a laconic resignation to fate, a passive waiting for deliverance, whether theological or technological.

Historically and religiously, hope once played a different role. In Christianity, hope was constructed as one of the central virtues of a believer. It functions as part of faith, to justify actions, not bound to knowledge or evidence. Together with faith and love, hope played a guiding role not only for a good Christian life, but also for the goodness that secures the future in the form of salvation and a heavenly life after death.

However, the Christian theological virtue of hope was also seen as a source of belief in progress, which, combined with the Industrial Revolution, gave modernity its characteristically future-oriented developmental pathway.

Following this religious interpretation, the more secular view, taken by Descartes or Hobbes for example, saw hope as a motivating factor in human thinking and agency, leading to both rational and irrational actions. According to empiricists, like Locke and Hume, hope is that pleasure that the mind takes in thinking of the probable future enjoyment of delightful projects. Interestingly, for Hume it is a mixture of pleasure and pain that arises from the imagination of some pleasant but only probable future events.

Likewise, for Spinoza, the passion of hope is a form of pleasure, as the mind is affected by the idea of a future event, yet this joy is mingled with sadness as outcomes of the event remain unknown.

In contrast to optimistic interpretations, for Kierkegaard and other critical voices, hope can be the expression of a misguided relationship with the world. As such, it is unable to face the demands of human existence, but traps hopers into an illusionary, deceptive orientation.

Nietzsche's (2006) Zarathustra is radically critical about a consoling transcendental sphere, and thus warns: "do not believe those who speak to you of extra-terrestrial hopes!" (p. 6). Moreover, by prolonging attachment to insatiable desires, hope generates frustration, resentment, and a proneness to disappointment that can easily result in reactionary violence.

Keeping all of these ambiguities of hope in mind, the following focuses on its relation to the Anthropocene and then to wisdom.

HOPE IN THE ANTHROPOCENE?

Considering the above-mentioned ambiguities, this section explores the status, role, and tasks of hope in the so-called Anthropocene, which is making a global human impact on Earth and its evolution.

In this so-called Anthropocene age, we are increasingly learning about the irreparable effects and dramatic impacts that humanity – or rather specific human activities – is having on the planet. Gloomy, dystopian, and apocalyptic stories of disaster, decline, demise, and extinction are increasingly being told as part of an eco-eschatological 'dark ecology' (Morton, 2016).

The ongoing use and misuse of nature as a resource for instrumentalist progress- and growth-oriented economic practices and capitalogenic mechanisms have reached such a level that the Anthropocene would more appropriately be called the 'Capitalocene' (Moore, 2016).

What does hope mean in a world of anthropocenic globalized practices that have led us to transgress planetary boundaries and generate abysmal moves?

Can, should, or need there be hope while we are living in an anthropocenic world that is nihilistically so productive and effective to progressively move towards an eco-cidal collapse, characterized by the loss of not only diversity, but also meaning and ways of living?

Does the end of the world as we know it (and us in it), and the leaving behind of traditional understandings of nature and its mastery, make it possible to move towards a hopeful pathway?

Importantly, the Anthropocene is a malleable concept that accommodates several co-existing, at times contesting, narratives.

While the meaning of the Anthropocene remains disputed, new interpretations and distinct stories are emerging that affect ongoing conversations and practices. Ontologically, epistemologically, and practically the Anthropocene challenges familiar separations between nature and humans, culture, and so on that structure our order and knowledge of the world. The realization of humanity's material dependence and fragility invites us to rethink long-held assumptions about the autonomous, self-contained rational human subject that begins and ends with itself (Malm and Hornborg, 2014). The Anthropocene appears to bring to a close an anthropocentric understanding of power and governmental agency (Chandler, 2018, p. 16).

Can we still understand the Anthropocene not as a problem to be 'solved' in the logic of a modernist 'dis-course' of solutionism, but as an opportunity to be grasped to take a different 'course'? Are anthro-decentric transformations still possible that turn towards an enlivening eco- or *zoë*-cene via a wisdom mediating 'Gaian Praxecology' (Küpers and Gunnlaugson, 2017)?

What role would hope play in this? To answer these questions, we present first the Promethean tale and then the myth of Pandora's box.

PROMETHEAN STORY

We can understand how we arrived at this crisis of the Anthropocene and its junctures in history as well as the role of hope by recalling and reinterpreting the ancient Greek myth of Prometheus, which lays the foundation of our mastery over nature. Prometheus was a classical mythological figure, whose ambiguous, fascinating qualities offer revealing interpretations of our human condition and earthly situatedness. Prometheus, whose name means 'forethought', was a Titan hero and trickster who not only created (god-like) men from clay but provided them with fire, thus enabling progress and civilization, though it was stolen from the gods.

For Promethean man, the Earth appears as a storehouse of resources to be subdued, exploited, and controlled. In the endless pursuit of mastery, he abandons his responsibility as an observant caretaker, assuming instead the mandate of a technician and laying the foundation of our techno-human condition. With him, the Earth and all its inhabitants are turned into what Heidegger calls 'standing reserve' under the holding-sway of an occluding or concealing enframing or 'Gestell' of technological thinking. As such all beings and bodies are effectively perceived as resources. This ordering of the disposition of resources makes them as raw materials to be put to use and thus the earth turns into something for us to manipulate and produce.

To Promethean man, there are no 'ethical-moral' grounds to distinguish between one form of technological behavior and another, whether it is preserving or extinguishing a species, poisoning or detoxifying an ecosystem, enhancing life or spreading death. The only quest in this regime is how to find the most efficient means to any given end. Thus, for the Promethean god-like orientation, there are no limits, boundaries, or even guideposts for action and technological applications. For example, all forms of trans- and post-human manipulation and genetic engineering of our own species are Promethean realizations.

The agenda of Prometheanism is to celebrate and recalibrate human beings so that they have the ability to refashion their world and themselves by means of technological ingenuity. Accordingly, the Anthropocene is not only anthropocentric and reeking with the techno-triumphalism of Promethean man, but identifies the entire human species as the culprit of current changes in the Earth's spheres, in all its bombastic pomposity and misplaced narcissism of the heroic Prometheus.

The myth relates that, to punish his hubristic acts of transgression and claims of omnipotence, Prometheus was eternally tormented by being bound to a rock. As well as being unable to move, each day an eagle was sent to feed on his liver – the organ of ambition and envy – which would then grow back to be eaten again and again.

As mentioned before, the state of Promethean affairs in the Anthropocene calls for decentering an anthropocentric positioning, while problematizing tendencies towards re-elevated humans as reborn Prometheus (Baskin, 2015). Today, neo-Promethean Earthmasters use 'fire' in neo-technocratic ways that have led to global warming. The titanic masters of the Earth are now 'playing God with the climate' (Hamilton, 2013), while rivaling the 'great forces of nature' (Steffen et al., 2011b) of a defiant Earth (Hamilton, 2017, p. 41) by pursuing an updated eco-modernist agenda.

Promethean aspiration manifests itself in human attempts to remake nature, including 'objectified' human nature, to serve purposes and satisfy desires (Sandel, 2004). With this agenda and without radically changing the capitalist development, the human-centric, techno-managerial program is predicted to continue. This program is characterized by a hyper-accelerationist vision, in which big science, big data and big capital can find ways to save both Earth and earthlings (Neyrat, 2018). This sphere is run by techno-scientific, socio-economic elites, who claim to have the necessary tool-kit for readjusting the machine, so that things can 'hopefully' stay as they are.

What is needed is to improve our critical understanding of these anthropogenic practices that operate in that dangerous Promethean spirit, as well as our ability to question the eco-authoritative claims (Howe, 2013) of eco-modernists. In the misleading neo-Promethean heroic narrative, promise and false hope see humans actively co-constructing the Earth's forces as an adaptive terraforming by managing the Earth system to sustain civilization as we know it. More specifically, this approach sustains civilization for some, but turns into necropolitics for others via an immuno-biopolitical phantasmagorical scripting of a fully socialized nature (Swyngedouw, 2013, 2014; Swyngedouw and Ernstson, 2018).

How, then, can we respond to the Pelagian claim that humanity can achieve its own salvation by technocratic mastery and eco-technological management? We may affirmatively embrace our technological role in this co-evolutionary drama, including events in all of the geo-spheres – litho-, hydro-, and atmo- and biospheres, as well as techno-sphere (Cera, 2017).

The latter sphere will play an important role, as technology no longer just impacts and embeds into ecology but increasingly is an intrinsic part of the future habitability of the Earth (Lemmens et al., 2017, p. 124). Accordingly, terrestrial-oriented technologies are becoming more Earth-adaptive, for example biomimicry and eco-mimesis (Lemmens et al., 2017, p. 124).

However, an inter-evolutionary engagement acknowledges the wild, subtractive capacity of 'nature' as an un- or non-constructable Earth (Neyrat, 2018), emerging as a non-substitutable whimsical becoming that escapes the Promethean hubris.

What is called for is the inter-evolution and conviviality of species as co-creative partners in the planetary odyssey towards sustainable flourishing. How hope and wisdom are required for such a process is illustrated by a related myth.

THE MYTH OF PANDORA'S BOX

Continuing the story of Prometheus' theft of fire in Greek mythology, Pandora (meaning 'all-giving') was the first woman on Earth and was created as a punishment to mankind. Her gifts were beautifully evil, according to Hesiod's somewhat misogynist tale. Hephaestus created her from clay, shaping her perfectly, Aphrodite gave her femininity, and Athena taught her crafts. Hermes was ordered by Zeus to teach her to be deceitful, stubborn, and curious; in other words, to become seduction incarnate.

Pandora was given a box or jar that contained special 'gifts', but she was never to open it. Despite trying to tame her curiosity, in the end she could no longer restrain herself. When she opened the cursed box, all kinds of evils, hardships, and plagues were released. Thus greed, envy, hatred, mistrust, sorrow, anger, revenge, despair, sickness, and death were scattered across the world to torment humans.

Realizing what she had done, Pandora quickly shut the lid, and only one thing was left inside: Elpis, the personification of hope. Trapping the spirit of hope inside made it impotent in alleviating the ills of the world. Pandora's closing of hope inside the box has been interpreted in various ways (Verdenius, 1985).

In terms of climate change, one evil that came out of Pandora's box was fire from the monster's mouth, produced by supposed infinite growth, endless production, and boundless consumption. Our blind pursuit of profit and exploitation has led us to a level of carbon dioxide emissions that jeopardizes all life. The ideologically dogmatic responses to these pressing releases from Pandora's box of carbon trading, geoengineering fixes, and other myopic, time-wasting 'market solutions' dreamt up since then to hold back the inexorable tide of rising temperatures seem to give hope, but are not sufficient or are even misleading.

Yet hope remains in the box! Hope both belongs to and is separated from the category of human suffering, included in the box of miseries but kept from being released. It is an open question whether it was kept from

humans, or is still available to them as a potentially mitigating but ambivalent force that "always desires to be realized but never is" (Verdenius, 1985,
p. 68).

According to Hesiod, hope indeed stayed inside the box, because that
was Zeus' will; he wanted to let people suffer in order to understand that
they should not disobey their gods.

However, is the hope imprisoned within the jar full of evils to be considered a further bane, or a potential benefit for humanity, a medium for idle
illusion or practical wisdom?

HOPE AND WISDOM

For Hesiod, whose account of the Prometheus myth we recall here, hope
rests on the notion that, by experiencing trouble, a fool may become wise.
Likewise, among many other voices, Erasmus later cast the figure of hope
as "he whom mistakes made wise" (Barker, 2001, p. 32). Before extending
the relationship between hope and wisdom, the following briefly discusses
some ideas about what wisdom, especially in its practical form, means and
implies.

Without presenting here the complex traditions, understandings, and
role of wisdom in different cultures, times, and applications (Küpers,
2013), we focus on some hope-relevant qualities, specifically its function as
a virtue for guiding decisions and actions that serve the common good or
enhance societal well-being.

A historically informed and critical contextualization and cross-
disciplinary exploration of the multidimensional phenomena of practical
wisdom reveal its contemporary importance. It is significant for the wider
ecological, social, societal, and political spheres in which contemporary
business and economics play powerful, far-reaching, and often problematic roles (Küpers, 2013). Wisdom is understood as practical knowledge
and virtuous habit in praxis, and refers to a form of enacted moral
excellence to create flourishing and happiness (eudaimonia), individually
and collectively. As a concern for what is practically good here and now,
phronesis focuses on making the 'right' use of knowledge and preferential
choices or judgments for the prudentially doable actions of humans as
rational, social, and political animals.

Importantly, it includes embodied, sensual, and tacit knowing, intuition, and emotions in relation to character operating in situated realities
and specific circumstances, to value, respond, and act appropriately.
Accordingly, practical wisdom can be understood as an embodied and
reflective, morally committed doing (Kemmis and Smith, 2008). This

doing is situationally carried out at the right time, for the right reasons, and by the right means, resulting in the right consequences. Not only can hope motivate to enact a wiser life, but it can in turn be informed and guided by wisdom, since there is also the hope that we will learn from being wiser. But can the anthropos, who pursues 'progressivist' projects, really learn from the Prometheus and Pandoran myths and become wise?

It seems that only by endangering and almost despoiling the planet do we realize just how much a part of it we are, and always have been.

Instead of Promethean mastery of nature (Gehmann, 2004), the challenge will be to develop and share hopeful images, stories, and practices that offer a wiser 'mastery' as the embodied art of a resonant inter-relationship with(in) nature (Baskin, 2015, p. 16). This stewarding 'master-ship' would integrate the multiple addressivities of hoping, sometimes in the same telling (Carlsen and Pitsis, 2009).

We can have hope when we learn to communicate wisely using non-totalizing and non-normative, or even non-moralizing, images and stories (Zylinska, 2014, p. 46) that guide practices. There is hope when these media leave aside imprudent ambitions of human(ist) ascension and exceptionalism as well as its masculinist rationality, binary systems, and hierarchizing dualisms. Moving wisely away from the hubristic idea of 'anthropos' as a world-maker or apocalyptic destroyer towards more inclusive inter-evolution with 'more-than-human' beings in a sustainable existence calls for and achieves hope.

CONCLUSION: TOWARDS A HOPEFUL, ENLIVENING ECO- OR *ZOË*-CENE

Based on an understanding hope and its ambivalent links to the Anthropocene, we retold the tales of Prometheus and Pandora to make some connection to practical wisdom.

To conclude, the following addresses the need for hope in anthro-decentric transformations that turn towards an enlivening eco- or *zoë*-cene.

Wisdom-oriented hope has the potential to usher in an onto-ethical transformation and catalyst for an imaginary and practical shift. This includes a radical change of affective dispositions, perception, ways of conceiving, and habitus. Referring back to the proposed interpretation of hope as a somatic, semantic, social event that serves as an energizing medium will enable forms of different organization of work (Mouton and Montijo, 2017), coping and stress resilience (Ong et al., 2017), or well-being (Lee and Gallagher, 2017). Particularly, it will help manage human and 'more-than-human' stakeholders in responsive, responsible, and sustainable ways.

Bringing hope and wisdom together contributes to the emergence of a sensibility for re-visioning and re-enacting new temporal, spatial, and social imaginaries and practices, individually and collectively.

Both vision and imagination are forms of creative and aesthetic processing that see phenomena and meanings differently. Once energized by hope, envisioning gives sense to emergent patterns that can inform present and future possibilities. Belief in the attainment of shared dreams lies in the inspirational qualities of the capacity of images to astonish and exhilarate, and thus expand the horizons of what is livable.

Related to organization, to be effective, a hopeful vision of the future needs to permeate orientations, decisions, and actions that energize and empower all members to take movable pathways forward within affective atmospheres of hope (Thedvall, 2017). This requires embodied transformative metaphors and narratives for communicating and shaping contextualities and practices more wisely (Küpers, 2012a, 2012b). Instead of the seeds of dystopian hopelessness in hostile deserts of organizations, we need seedlings of hope to be cultivated for flourishing gardens of organizational *life*-worlds as part of more comprehensive 'hope-scapes' (Mattox, 2012).

Perhaps hope in the Anthropocene in relation to organizations can only be bounded and 'moderate-ing', in the spirit of an engaged 'letting go' that is 'satisficing,' while being open for future subversions, revisions, and refinements co-created with multiple stakeholders.

A post-Promethean, hopeful cultivation of life and post-anthropocenic turns (Arias-Maldonado, 2016) involves enlivening, shared sessions and sustainable cyclic successions towards an eco- or *zoë*-cene. As indicated above, *zoë* is interpreted here as a holistic meaning of life in its experienced and ecological sense, including the whole animated/animating Earth (Weber, 2013). A move towards *zoë* integrates the proto-wisdom of plants and animals in the sense of an eco-sophy.

For an integral wisdom practice borne and enacted by hope, bodies and embodiments of all involved are entwined with the natural and cultural world. Hope and wisdom together embrace a "relationship of 'inter-corporeity' with the biosphere and all animality" (Merleau-Ponty, 2003, p. 334–335).

An embodied mindfulness in the adequate spirit of wise hope, and hopeful wisdom may offer chances to reconfigure and inter-relate anew with ourselves and others, including stones, plants, animals, and biomes, all be(com)ing part of an unfolding nexus within our congenital aborning cosmos.

Further critical research and discussion of the concept and narratives of the Anthropocene in relation to hope provide opportunities to develop and enact more prudent, non-hubristic organizational and leadership practices. Enacted in everyday life, this can then contribute to making practically wise decisions, judgments, and actions for a hopefully more sustainable cycle of evolutionary unfoldment. Enacting here is an analogy of what Paul Goodman (1911–1972) envisioned: "Suppose you had the revolution you are talking and dreaming about. Suppose your side had won, and you had the kind of society/organisation that you wanted. How would you live, you personally, in that society/organisation? Start living that way now!" (quoted in Shantz, 2013, p. 20).

Then we can have hope for a wiser Planet Earth before and by 2035 and beyond!

PART TWO

Empirical and imaginative inspirations

8. 'Hope-full purpose': Time, oblivion, and the strange attractors of Pandora's box

Richard Longman

Hope . . . which is whispered from Pandora's box after all the other plagues and sorrows had escaped, is the best and last of all things. Without it, there is only time. And time pushes at our backs like a centrifuge, forcing outward and away, until it nudges us into oblivion. (Caldwell and Thomason, 2004, p. 275)

PRELUDE

Hope animates prophets, visionaries, and radicals. So, when Pandora replaces the lid of the box that is entrusted to her, it is these prophets, visionaries, and radicals who are left to conjecture as to why hope remains. Does hope remain to soothe the torments of humankind? Or is the contrary true, and hope is denied to humankind as retribution for the release of plagues and sorrows? Perhaps neither of these is correct, and hope is simply another evil: a false hope that, even in its absence, plagues and sorrows, torments and deceives. This unresolved conjecture – and the strange attractors of Pandora's box which predispose chaotic conditions to a more likely set of outcomes – offers further caution to those animated by hope. Hope, after all, is experienced in conditions which delimit, subvert, distract, and resist. Yet, if we believe these conditions to be worthy of challenge, then perhaps there is some hope.

A PREMISE FOR 'HOPE-FULL PURPOSE'

Hope is shrouded in conceptual ambiguity and contradiction; it appears easy enough to identify until one tries to capture it, when it reveals itself as little more than a vague floating signifier. Indeed, hope has rarely been discussed outside situations of the extremes: acute hopelessness (Fukuyama, 1992) or fantastical hopefulness (Snyder, 2000). Thus, whilst

85

hope has strong heuristic power in narrative, its existence as a tangible part of everyday organizational life is not clearly defined. This chapter argues that hope is deserving of closer attention because of its potential 'to grow and overwhelm . . . nontransformative perspectives' (Butler, 2001, p. 277). The chapter draws on extant literature and original empirical work – the latter carried out in *Medium*,[1] an online site of social journalism – to deepen understanding through critical analysis of an alternative empirical reality. My hope, ultimately, is that a transformative vision of hope may be drawn closer to the work of organizational scholars.

Latour (1999, p. 300) considers how we might go about organizing hope. He writes:

> [W]e seem to have exhausted the evils that emerged from the open box of clumsy Pandora. Though it was her unrestrained curiosity that made the artificial maiden open the box, there is no reason to stop being curious about what was left inside. To retrieve the Hope that is lodged there, at the bottom, we need a new and rather convoluted contrivance.

My convoluted contrivance is to unite hope and purpose. Whilst hope may pose a set of conceptual problems, purpose establishes some lines of thought which may be helpful in achieving resolution. Common conceptualizations of purpose tend to capture how it is utilized to meet an organization's needs (Warriner, 1965; Bartlett and Ghoshal, 1994; Basu, 2017). But this perspective only emphasizes the place of purpose in the instrumental processes and outcomes of organizing, rather than revealing any radical qualities that purpose might possess in this context. Instead, I draw on empirical material from a study of alternative organizing, where notions of hope and purpose unite to pursue wholly different ideological ends to those framed by a neo-Weberian rationalism. I propose that retrieving the hope that is lodged at the bottom of Pandora's box must be a purposeful act and, thus, that uniting hope and purpose demands a prefigurative practice which reinvigorates attempts at organizing. Furthermore, to engage in prefigurative practice requires us to become agents of change, living out relationships and practices that remedy our present shortcomings and characterize a better future. We see an example of prefiguration in Ostrom's (1990) critique of 'The Tragedy of the Commons' (Hardin, 1968). Ostrom argues that organizing need not resort to top-down regulation; she prefers to reinstitute the human as capable of self-governing its common resources. This prefigurative, commons-inspired approach to organizing resonates with the socio-ecological ideas of prophets, visionaries, and radicals such as Bateson (1972), Schumacher (1973), Sennett (2006), and Bauman (2011), whose hope-full and purpose-full approaches to organizing inspire pockets of scholarship and practice today.

In this chapter, I argue against organizing as the short-term optimization of resources for the self on the grounds that it leads to longer-term, sub-optimal benefit for the other. This requires that I attempt two things: firstly, to demonstrate how organizing for the purpose of delivering short-term interest is bad for the collective; and, secondly, to explicate how the hope of our collective selves might save us from our individual impulses. In doing this, I advance a conceptualization of hope that goes beyond soothing the torments of humankind and reveals 'hope-full purpose' as an effective guide for a common journey towards a new set of social relations (De Angelis, 2017).

HOPE, PURPOSE, AND THE COMMONS

Hope has received limited attention in organizational scholarship, and that which it has received is characterized by a conceptual breadth which delivers a variety of responses. Emblematic of one core view are Snyder et al. (1991, p. 287): they define hope as 'a positive motivational state that is based on an interactively derived sense of successful (1) agency (goal-directed energy) and (2) pathways (planning to meet goals)'. This reading of hope finds resonance with the reformist ambitions of the contemporary corporation, in which hope-full individuals are guided by conscious efforts to pursue specific ideological ends and appraise life goals in more affirmative ways. Contrast this with Ludema et al. (1997, p. 1026), who highlight the relational nature of hope, which is 'always engendered in relationship to an "other", whether that other be collective or singular, imagined or real, human or divine', and 'almost always portrayed as having a moral, spiritual, or religious dimension'. This orientation towards hope, an affirmative form of social discourse within a constructionist epistemology, responds best to this chapter's ambition of retrieving the hope that is lodged at the bottom of Pandora's box. Hope takes its place amongst communities of people, generates new possibilities for social relations, and mobilizes the moral and affective resources necessary to translate image into action and belief into practice (Ludema et al., 1997). As a shared construct, with transformative vision of a better future, and by means of a prefigurative practice, hope is well deserving of attention from organizational scholars.

Seen through a utopian lens, hope draws attention to the need for change, suggests a direction in which change must be made, and offers a stimulus to act upon that change. For Levitas (2010), hope is the defining characteristic of utopian thought. She builds on Bloch's ([1959] 1986) work, which argues that hope enables the imagination of new social institutions and practices, embedding new ethics and values. M. Parker (2002b, p. 2) posits that 'utopias are statements of alternative organization, attempts to put forward plans which remedy the perceived shortcomings of a particular present age'. The utopian thinking which refuses to accept that there is no alternative is not without its limitations; and, ultimately, how we respond to its limitations will define what becomes of hope. The strange attractors of Pandora's box predispose our thinking as well as our doing; and Lorenz's (1963) foundational theoretical work prompts us to consider the starting conditions of our thinking and recognize how the tiniest adjustment may have huge ramifications on our doing. So, taking inspiration from Havel (1990, p. 182), I advance a conceptualization of hope which 'gives us the strength to live and continually to try new things, even in conditions that seem as hopeless as ours do, here and now'. But hope, alone, is not enough; enter purpose.

Purpose is often captured in terms of 'the noisy declamations of those who, having lost all sense of purpose long ago, adopt the lapel-badge approach to values by bedecking themselves with Mission Statements, Chartermarks, Investors in People awards and so on' (Hoggett, 2006, p. 190). Hoggett identifies that purpose is 'saturated with value' which invests it with a transformative power such as we might associate with hope (Butler, 2001). However, implicit in Hoggett's description is the possibility for any teleological project to emerge which co-opts purpose for its own ambitions and risks the legitimacy of any organizational praxis based in hope. Purpose, thus, should be conceptualized and theorized carefully. In relationships between individuals we see how purpose relies on ambiguity to reach consensus. The definitions of purpose created by this consensus are little more than temporary fictions which bind collectives together and contain their individual differences (Hoggett, 2006). And purpose is inherently temporary and contested, requiring ongoing clarification as to its true ambitions. To address this, G. Moore (2012, p. 384) proposes 'a conceptualization of purpose in relation to the common good which is more than the simple aggregation of the organization's internal goods'. He captures something of that exchange of fiction which exists in the pursuit of purpose, and which does more than meet an organization's internal needs; rather, it embeds itself as part of a larger and interconnected whole. In emphasizing this connection, and in a careful treatment of purpose, Moore enables that step towards commoning and the social practices used to organize shared resources (Linebaugh, 2008).

'Commoning' is more than a fashionable term for cooperating. We are born into a commons (P.M., 2014): a set of shared practices and a social metabolism based on the production, preservation, and use of communal goods and services (Linebaugh, 2008). Implicit in the commons is 'a plurality of people ... sharing resources and governing them and their own relations and (re)productive processes through horizontal doing in common' (De Angelis, 2017, p. 10). So, to accept prima facie the tragic argument made by Hardin (1968) – that the world is dependent on common resources, but that individuals using these common resources will not cooperate to achieve collective benefits – is to condemn hope to the bottom of Pandora's box: a hope denied to humankind or, worse still, a false hope. Instead, Ostrom (1990) demonstrates how individuals might become collective and organize with the purpose of the advancement of shared, long-term benefit by challenging those deeply embedded assumptions of neoliberalism which privilege the leveraging of common resources for short-term and highly individualized gain. Ostrom presents commoning as an antidote, which traverses the individual and the collective and inveigles new possibilities of social relationships (which support and sustain not just the collective but the relationships and responsibilities that emanate from the collective). De Angelis (2017) warns how commoning is constrained by the power of capital and the state, and ponders 'what if?' we might remove these strange attractors which delimit, subvert, distract, and resist its potentiality. In this 'what if?' question, he identifies the commons as a place of hope: a place where hope-full purpose can thrive.

What if hope is a *reason* for doing things? Might purpose be a *tool* for doing those things? Purpose might help negotiate the passage from ambiguity to agreement, to create those temporary fictions which allow us to share collectively in prefigurative acts, and to realize some common, saturated value. Or does conceptualizing purpose as a tool simply facilitate a careless slip back towards an understanding of the world founded on instrumental rationalism? Perhaps a conceptualization of 'hope-full purpose' will allow us to situate, motivate, and facilitate our engagement in shared prefigurative acts? In so doing, we might (re)produce more hope-full social relations and reinvigorate the hope and the purpose of organizing. In this orientation towards a horizontal doing, hope-full purpose finds its spiritual home in the prefiguration of the commons.

THE COMMONING OF HOPE AND PURPOSE

I turn now to a set of everyday interactions which rebuff those characterizations of extreme hopelessness or fantastical hopefulness. The longitudinal, qualitative empirical work on which this chapter now draws was situated in an online site of alternative organizing and interrogates hope and purpose; during this period, archival work, participant observation, and semi-structured interviews were carried out by the researcher. The nature of the research site meant that this work was predominantly carried out online and facilitated by communicative technology, and the archival data that informs this study is largely represented by articles published online and the comments attached to them by readers. These articles are identified here as sources of data which help construct an empirical reality. Qualitative content analysis (Altheide, 1996, p. 16) was developed to interrogate hope and purpose within the data set through 'recursive and reflexive movement between concept development-sampling-data, collection-data, coding-data, and analysis-interpretation'. Tacking between materials and meanings helped interrogate the evidenced empirical reality, revealing things about hope and purpose which are intertwined in those approaches to organizing which embrace the commons in their defiance of conditions of hopelessness.

Turning attention to those vestiges of alternative organizing practice that sit somewhere infrequently visited by critical scholars, it befits the analysis that will follow to first provide some contextual detail.

IN SEARCH OF HOPE AND PURPOSE

The commons inspires discourses and practices of alternative organizing. Scholarly attention has already been drawn towards those responses to modernity which reject ideological modes of rationality (Baunsgaard and Clegg, 2012) and reproduce organizing practices and structures, conditioning local action and conventional wisdom (Adler et al., 2007). An important body of scholarship extends consideration of alternative organizing onto more radical ground (Parker et al., 2007; Parker, 2011; Kostera, 2014; Reedy et al., 2016) and challenges the social perspectives and norms of organizing that envelop us in their discourses and practices. This includes attention to commons-oriented approaches, ranging from collectivist organizing (Edley et al., 2004) to open-source technology (Pearce, 2012); approaches which share in challenging current discourses and practices and nourishing alternatives. The empirical work which is now presented was undertaken in *Medium* – a website which takes a commoning approach to social journalism. It was selected as a research site in order to connect with discourses and practices of alternative organizing, in a space enlivened by such discourses and practices, and specifically pertaining to hope. *Medium* has a hybrid collection of amateur and professional writers and embraces Creative Commons licensing as it responds to a large community of contributors sidestepping mainstream channels (Sussman, 2014). The hope of the commons in this space is pervasive and persuasive, and *Medium* publishes articles encompassing a rich discussion of blockchain, open-source technology, panarchy, sociocracy, and other organizing methodologies which attend to the horizontal doing of the commons rather than top-down ordering of mainstream responses to organizing. *Medium* is, itself, an expression of the commons, a space for sharing new ideas and resources, developing communities of thought and practice.

'The Purpose of Life . . .' and 'Foster a Sense of Purpose . . .'

Two articles provide an entry point to the discourses pertaining to hope and purpose in this community. The first introduces the ideas of Darius Foroux (2016). He states: 'What really makes me happy is when I'm useful. When I create something that others can use. Or even when I create something I can use.' He quotes Ralph Waldo Emerson: 'The purpose of life is not to be happy. It is to be useful, to be honorable, to be compassionate, to have it make some difference that you have lived and lived well.' With a flourish of rhetoric, he concludes: 'What are you *doing* that's making a difference?'

Two responses to this article posted by readers pick up on his conceptualization of purpose and the corresponding links he makes to hope. Louisse, who describes herself as 'desperately trying to live and not just breathe', articulates a staggering sense of hopelessness:

> I'm only 23 and I don't want to live anymore because I find no purpose in life. I have a good paying job, I take holidays often, I travel a lot but I am simply not happy. . . . I think, what the hell am I doing here? I don't know what I want to do to be useful to others yet, what I lack most is conviction. This is really great, thank you for this.

For Louisse, purpose is not found in happiness constructed from good employment or frequent travel. Purpose, for her, is elusive. Indeed, the absence of purpose causes deep, desperate hopelessness in understanding her own, individual existence. Louisse wants to be 'useful to others', and recognizes some residual hope that she, as an individual, might become part of a larger, collective self; she yearns for a sense of connection with others, believing that this would bring purpose. However, unsure of how she could realize this herself, purpose and hope remain disunited.

Similar themes are expressed by Matthew, a Lutheran pastor, who perhaps brings a spiritual or religious dimension to his understanding of hope. His response reads:

> Thank you. I am truly sick of hearing that the purpose of life is happiness. That's BS. Happiness is a fleeting emotion that comes and goes. . . . What we

define as the purpose of life will determine how we approach life. Well done with this article. Thank you.

Matthew refuses to equate purpose with happiness. Moreover, he claims that happiness is a short-term state which, in any case, has limited value; the purpose of life holds a longer-term benefit which is, by implication, a more valuable and hope-full endeavour. He clearly establishes the link between how we understand the purpose of life and how we prefigure the purpose of life, reinforcing that relationship between thinking and doing found in theory and practice which is shared and expressed in multiple realizations of the commons.

Louisse and Matthew wrestle with purpose in a way which accentuates their sense of hope. They find their own purpose ill defined and absent, yet they hold out hope for it. They seek purpose with individual relevance and collective coherence, and Foroux's article provides some sort of temporary fiction which binds them to the hope of the 'other' without crushing the 'self'.

The second article, by Kimber Lockhart (2016), is entitled 'Don't create a sense of urgency, foster a sense of purpose'. She argues that purpose 'is a deep understanding of the reasons behind our efforts'; it 'resonates with the impact we'd like to make on the world'; it is 'immersion in our cause'; and it is 'about going faster and smarter toward a mission we all see clearly'. Her suggestions identify purpose as something which underlies practice, connects with outcomes, and is shared, articulated, and understood. Furthermore, she identifies the latency of purpose: it is something that is crafted, an ontological construction, a temporary fiction which must lay out common ground for any collective of individuals.

Her article attracts response from Ian, a professional working in 'growth' for an online legal marketplace in Seattle. He says:

> This is great. Urgency without purpose is poison. It will burn everyone out, ultimately bringing down the team and creating churn. I think in startups or in product, creating a sense of purpose and illustrating the vision is priority #1, however, some form of urgency can be positive. Urgency can create excitement and heighten focus around a purpose. . . . You'll need everyone to be on board, but a finite timeline to do something great, with purpose, can fuel the fire. It can push the team past any self-imposed limits and produce great results.

The workplace focus of this article prompts a wholly different response. Ian regards purpose as a counterbalance to urgency. Urgency, portrayed as the pursuit of short-term gain for individuals, represents a distortion of the commons, where sustainable, long-term benefit for the collective is promoted. Ian identifies that, in a time-pressured environment, shared purpose can contribute to collective achievements. The constructed nature of purpose, for individuals and collectives, emphasizes its temporary and contextual qualities; this renders it susceptible to manipulation in the workplace, where it may be hijacked for commercial benefit rather than for common benefit. Perhaps in response to the conceptual hijacking of purpose for a short-term, individualized gain, a commoning approach to purpose legitimates long-term, collective endeavour, and mobilizes the moral and affective resources necessary to retrieve hope from the bottom of Pandora's box.

Lockhart herself conceptualizes teams with a high sense of purpose as engaged and as having a high output. 'Fostering a sense of purpose is different [to urgency]', she claims. 'It's a collaborative endeavor, and it requires trust that your team members will translate their sense of purpose into increased effectiveness.' Still, the language of mainstream organizations (e.g. 'faster', 'smarter', 'effectiveness', 'efficiency', 'growth') all feels a little incongruous around these more holistic conceptualizations of purpose, maybe emphasizing the predominance of the logic of the corporation, even in this alternative space. Moreover, it serves as a reminder that, even when we might hope for better things and seek the purpose that might help deliver on our hopes, strange attractors continue to delimit, subvert, distract, and resist.

The Hope of Purpose-full Organizations

Medium traverses the individual and the collective. The writings of Foroux and Lockhart explicitly link individuals to wider collectives, many identifying with professional communities embracing the commons, experimenting with self-organization, and expressing hope in their experiences of work and life. These collectives are given good coverage by *Medium*. There is widespread discussion of alternative organizational ideas which propose more hope-full and purpose-full ways of working; together, I argue, they articulate a sense of hope-full purpose. Capturing the mood of many individuals, these collective movements respond to purpose in statements articulating their beliefs. Four such collective movements emphasize their different, negotiated fictions. *Holacracy* distributes power, giving individuals the freedom to organize in a way that is aligned to the organization's purpose. *Teal Organizations* encourage individuals to listen to the purpose the organization wants to serve. *B Corporations* proclaim their approach balances purpose and profit, whilst *Sociocracy* claims it is values that give our lives purpose, and we act because we value (Rego, 2016).

Across the *Medium* community, purpose is presented as a unifying device; it is held up as powerful and responsible. Individuals gather here because they hope for similar things. Consequently, they become subject to similar promises, made by individuals and collectives, which are themselves contested. Tom, another *Medium* writer, disputes the claims of Teal organizing. He argues that 'an organisation isn't a separate soul or entity with its own purpose, it's a story of an idea which is gradually becoming reality . . . ultimately held by one individual author' (Nixon, 2015). For him, purpose is not a neutral, common resource, and he cautions against any presentation of purpose which is set apart from its political intent. This reveals that purpose, alone, may be problematic, but that commoning can re-frame purpose in terms of hope. It may be possible to engage hope-full purpose to affect a more sustainable temporal outlook which resists the habitual attraction of short-term, individualized gain in favour of a longer-term prosperity for the collective selves.

In this view, individuals express hope, sometimes in unconventional ways, but to serve a collective ambition. Nadia and Paul comment:

> I feel like I want to give up hope but I'm not ready to do that yet because I think that I should persevere for the sake of my children. (Nadia, in *Medium*, 2016)

> This is not a good time, but we must still hope. Something deep inside me tells me that things will change for us all. (Paul, in *Medium*, 2016)

Drawing on data from the commons of *Medium* helps enlighten our own discourses and practices by attending to an empirical reality whose expressions of hope redefine organizational purpose away from the justifications of the prevalent socio-economic conditions which are characterized by short-term gain and individual egoism. Hope-full purpose, or the search for hope-full purpose, can be observed in these individuals, in the collectives with which they connect, and furthermore in the common purpose that characterizes their shared hope.

PURSUANT TO HOPE

Exploring *Medium* (as a community whose collective expression of the commons is characteristically hope-full) draws the hope of the commons closer to the work of organizational scholars and demonstrates how hope is deserving of critical attention. In uniting hope and purpose, I have presented a portmanteau construction – hope-full purpose – which describes how retrieving the hope that is lodged at the bottom of Pandora's box might only be achieved with the assistance of purpose. This illuminates how uniting hope and purpose embeds a prefigurative practice which finds repeated and often unstated expression in the commons. And, in refusing Hardin's (1968) narrative of those using common resources not cooperating to achieve collective benefits, hope-full purpose offers an organizational alterity to the short-term optimization of resources for the self. Hope may still reside in situations of acute hopelessness or fantastical hopefulness; and, in that context, it is likely to remain lodged at the bottom of Pandora's box. Yet identifying expressions of hope within this specific empirical setting has highlighted its potentially transformative qualities, and demonstrated the relevance of organizing hope in the context of a community hitherto lesser explored by empirical research. Ludema et al. (1997) find hope in communities of people, in the new images of possibility for social relationship they generate, and in the moral and affective resources of prefigurative practice. Empirical evidence which inspires this chapter finds great sympathy with this description. To activate its transformative qualities, hope must remain a shared construct and become a shared practice; and this is precisely the purposeful transition from individual to collective which renders it so potent in the context of organizations.

POSTLUDE

The story of Pandora's box has inspired many readings, which give rise to a multiplicity of interpretations. If hope is simply another evil, then our efforts in this volume may be in vain; if this is the case, then the thread spun by the editors should reveal how our good intentions have helped pave the road to organizational oblivion. If hope is to be denied to human-kind as retribution, then perhaps we are guilty of misidentifying hope in ourselves or in our objects of study; my convoluted contrivance – uniting hope and purpose – establishes a conceptual link to suggest we do correctly identify hope and that we may share a pursuit of its promises. And, if hope is to be the soother of the torments of humankind, then this volume may enliven scholarship and stimulate debate which informs discourses and practices within organizations, such that we better attend to our present shortcomings.

I hope so.

NOTE

1. See https://medium.com.

9. Against organization – farewell to hope?

George Cairns

INTRODUCTION

This volume's editors called for deliberation on the notion of 'hope' within the domain of organizing. My immediate reaction was to posit that – in terms of current structures of power and dominance at a global level – there is little evidence of concerted action to promote goodness towards humanity or hope for the future betterment of the planet. In developing the polemic below, I draw first on the etymology of 'hope', where the word is not subject to singular definition in linguistic terms. While popular usage may see hope as a desire for some positive future state, dictionary definitions are generally neutral – hope as expectation or desire, but with no value attribution. So, if hope is merely a desire for something to happen, we must consider the human capability to wish for harm or damage to others.

My approach to thinking on hope starts with recognition that it is subject to contextual interpretation and meaning, informed both by individual beliefs and values and by shared cultural norms and behaviours. I adopt a similar approach to consider the terms 'organizing' and 'organization', rejecting singular notions of what they mean, particularly where these are derived from dominant models of organization in Western society – political, religious, business and social. This may be read as implying that I adopt a stance of moral relativism, whereby all approaches are held to be of equal value. However, this is not the case, as I hope to explain.

I argue that the way to some better social order – one that responds to the editors' call for 'hope, ideas and inspirations' – requires initial engagement in a programme of destruction: destruction of the notion of hope in organization as being something that is subject to singular, shared conceptualization of what 'hope' actually constitutes and, thereby, what is 'good', and towards what ends ideas and inspirations are to be directed. Such a proposal is, of course, one that is characterized by extreme risk – risk that the destruction is too limited or fails to materialize . . . or is complete and irreversible.

WHAT DO WE – AND CAN WE – MEAN BY 'HOPE'?

Explorations of the etymology of 'hope' give little clue as to its origins, with indications of Old English, Germanic and Dutch usage, but with all of these defined circularly in English as meaning 'hope'. In theological terms, 'hope' is defined as a moral virtue and the desire to achieve everlasting life – as the opposite of the sin of despair. For those of a religious disposition, this is presumably a positive definition of hope. However, the origins of the word 'hope' again remain unclear in the theological texts, often being a translation of the Latin *spēs*, which is in turn defined as 'hope' or 'expectation', returning us to where we started. So, what is 'hope'?

Oxford Living Dictionaries (2018) provide several basic definitions for the word, both as noun and verb. While normal usage and terms such as 'We can only hope' imply that hope is a desire for a positive outcome to any given situation, such positivity is not explicit in the base definitions given by Oxford, namely:

NOUN
A feeling of expectation and desire for a particular thing to happen.
VERB
Want something to happen or be the case.

We might cynically posit that there are many on this planet for whom hopes are desires and expectations for actions and events that would certainly *not* be perceived as positive or beneficial by the majority. Perhaps the term 'hope for the best' gives us a pointer towards the neutrality of hope; otherwise we have a double statement of positive thinking.

Your response to my thinking here on hope may well be 'So what?' My reply is to reiterate that 'hope' cannot be read as a shared concept of benefit and improvement for the many. Rather, it is a term that implies individual expectation and desire, where these are defined in accordance with personal beliefs and values. As such, hope may be either benevolent or malevolent in intent, and may be directed at purely personal satisfaction rather than some 'greater good' for humanity at large. This then poses problems in relation to what is meant by organizing hope. If hope is multifaceted and individual, the organization of it may simply be a case of classifying and categorizing different types of hope, rather than understanding them, their origins and meanings, and responding to them with some form of action directed at improvement of the situation of those who hope.

HOPE AND THE INDIVIDUAL

Thinking of goodness and hope as specific to the individual and being imbued with personal beliefs, desires and expectations can be read as aligning with the political rhetoric of recent decades, grounded in the dogma of Thatcher and Reagan. Here, the notion of individual freedom and choice is central to the message, whatever the reality might be. However, contrary to the oft-quoted (and misquoted) Thatcher statement 'There is no such thing as society', the aims of businesses and politicians within the related free market economy are to bring cohesion and conformity – you should be an individual, but only within the constraints of whatever brand marketing campaign or policy statement is thrust in your face through the media or, nowadays, whatever fad dominates the social media scene.

In being promoted as individuals, humans are constantly bombarded with messages of hope, of achieving: fame through 'reality' television; fortune through investment in bricks and mortar or pieces of paper (or by betting on a lottery or some sporting event); or beauty through using the right cosmetics and wearing the most fashionable clothing. If we are not exposed to such messages, we exist in some part of the world which is deemed of no consequence to the powers that be and can be left in peace – although there are few if any places that cannot offer something to 'the market', whether as consumers of unnecessary products or suppliers of resources to produce more of these products. Yet, as more and more people are subsumed into the global market, so more and more become redundant within it. When I was a teenager in the 1960s, the promise was of a future of leisure and luxury as robots undertook work processes. But, for many, this 'leisure' turned out to be manifest as retrenchment, redundancy or precarious employment. As Gray (2002, p. 159) pointed out early in the new millennium, the reality of mechanization for many is that 'a new phase of the Industrial Revolution is underway that promises to make much of the population superfluous'. He went on to say that 'The function of the new economy, legal and illegal, is to entertain and distract a population which – though it is busier than ever before – secretly suspects that it is useless' (p. 160).

Over the past half-century, many – including myself – have considered how society was being defined in terms of either Orwell's *Nineteen Eighty-Four* or Huxley's *Brave New World*. Our contemporary situation indicates that this is not an either/or choice, but a both/and reality. We are subjected to constant surveillance in streets and buildings and to the voice of a 'Big Brother' that expresses views that will be fact today and 'fake news' or 'alternative fact' tomorrow. At the same time, we are entertained 24/7 by a myriad of channels of communication, subsumed by the *soma* of a never-ending stream of reality television, interspersed with a barrage of advertisements for a multitude of potions to relieve our pain of being. But, as Gray (2002, p. 41) points out, with reference to Schopenhauer and Indian philosophy, 'Individuality is an illusion. Like other animals, we are the embodiments of universal Will, the struggling suffering energy that animates everything in the world.'

In a world that faces catastrophic climate change, that is beset by physical and ideological conflict, and where socio-economic disparity and fragmentation continue to grow, I see dominant structures of power as urging individuals to define 'hope' in terms of their personal social status and acquisition of 'goods', rather than in broad social and environmental aspirations towards goodness to redress the excesses of older generations.

At this point, you may think that I see no positive side to the concept of hope. Bear with me.

WHAT HOPE IN ORGANIZATION? ON THE NATURE OF CRITICAL THINKING

If I am to see some trace of optimism for a positive hope for the future, I might look within my own area – to the academic world. Are we academics not free to engage in research and writing to explore the problems of society and the environment and to propose ideas for their resolution? I do not need to spend much time on going over what is already known, that contemporary academics are subject to managerialist performance measurement that relies on metrics of little relevance to society – 'top' journal articles, research funding (preferably industry funding), and 'top marks' for teaching from the customer base of paying students, who themselves have been subject to performance measurement in accordance with some national standards throughout their school lives.

More than 30 years ago, Paul Feyerabend (1987, p. 315) pondered presciently that university professors

> serve masters who pay them and tell them what to do: they are not free minds in search of harmony and happiness for all, they are civil servants. . . . and their mania for order is not the result of a balanced inquiry, or a closeness to humanity, it is a professional disease.

In recent years, particular criticism has been aimed at the business school as the source of the woes that have persisted in the wake of the 2008 Global Financial Crisis (GFC) and other corporate scandals, even from within its own ranks (e.g. Podolny et al., 2009). In the *Harvard Business Review*,

Petriglieri (2012) presented a view of the business school as a 'beacon of instrumentalism using its pulpit to proselytize an amoral view of the world, peddling theories that justify managers' selfish elitism', where the academics are 'clueless, a distracted caste moved by "physics envy" to churn out arcane research that bears little relevance to business in the real world'. If this research is of little relevance to business, what chance is there of it being meaningful to society at large and impactful for a better future environment?

While we might spend our time productively sitting in contemplative judgement of ourselves as poor academics, pondering the fate of the business school as a form of organization, do we then risk failure to address more pressing problems facing the fundamental lifeblood of all human organization – planet Earth? While French president Emmanuel Macron (BBC, 2018) has highlighted in the US Senate that 'there is no Planet B', scientist Dr Mayer Hillman (Barkham, 2018) asks if accepting that there is no reversal to our destruction of 'Planet A' will likely result in 'the end of most life on the planet'. Rather than leading to eventual hope for a positive trajectory, this line of thinking will most likely fall into the camp of Gray's (2002) *Straw Dogs* and the thesis that we humans are merely one form of animal life on this planet – one that is arrogant and erroneous in its beliefs of self-importance. That is not a very hopeful thought. . . . So, in the words of Lenin, 'What is to be done?'

If we are to find some common ground for humanity to have hope for a positive future and to find ways of becoming organized, it is my view that we must reconceptualize notions of hope and organization through initial rejection of what they *currently* mean to many.

WHY 'AGAINST ORGANIZATION' AND 'FAREWELL TO HOPE'? REVISITING THE WORKS OF PAUL FEYERABEND

The heading for this chapter was inspired by my memories of the titles of two books by Paul Feyerabend ([1975] 1993, 1987) that were fundamental to my early academic thinking, namely *Against Method* and *Farewell to Reason*. Having read both books several times in an attempt to understand the argumentation implied by the titles, I realized that (in terms of my own interpretation) both can be viewed as ironic. Full reading of the first book shows that Feyerabend did *not* argue for rejection of method. Some readers may have taken the title as a true indication of his thinking, since he ventured into discussion of the role of anarchism as an approach to investigation in scientific research, with an early presentation (Feyerabend

[1975] 1993, p. 14) of the view that the '*only principle that does not inhibit progress is*: anything goes' (italics in original). However, in the Preface to the second edition (referenced here to the third edition), Feyerabend ([1975] 1993, p. vii) acknowledged that he 'had no problem in putting on the anarchist's mask' as a joking response to his friend Imre Lakatos. Beyond this, again in the Preface to the second edition ([1975] 1993, p. vii), he stated that '"anything goes" is not a "principle" I hold . . . but the terrified exclamation of a rationalist who takes a closer look at history'.

To my mind, Feyerabend's text is a provocation to stimulate critical reflection on the limitations of method that is defined only in terms of the researcher and her/his intellectual context, with no regard to the culture and values of those who are subject to its application. Having considered the particular problem of dealing with conceptual and perceptual relations that cannot be discussed through the lens of rationality – being subject to 'covert relations' that are socially contextual – in the final chapter Feyerabend presented what I consider to be the key statement of the book. He wrote that 'It is conceited to assume that one has solutions for people whose lives one does not know. It is foolish to assume that such an exercise in distant humanitarianism will have effects pleasing to the people concerned' ([1975] 1993, p. 266).

Similarly, he argued against a blind acceptance of reason, where that reason might be seen as *unreasonable* by those subject to its line of argumentation. Feyerabend argued that much of what is termed 'reason' in thinking about the situation of the *Other* is based on dogmatic self-righteousness. He saw this as applying even to those who viewed themselves as critical thinkers, considering that '"critical" philosophers define human relations in their own intellectualized way. Congratulating themselves on their tolerance they are either ignorant, or dishonest, or (my own conjecture) both' (Feyerabend, 1987, p. 85). I wonder if he would have applied the same interpretation to the group of self-designated 'critical management' thinkers (here, I do not exclude myself from the reflection prompted by this question). It was from reading Feyerabend's work that I developed my own sense of the need to understand the *Other*, not as an object to be observed and interpreted by me, but as an active participant with me in mutual inquiry about *their* problems in *their* terms. Whether or not I have ever succeeded in this venture is a moot point.

Feyerabend (1987) placed blame for the lack of meaningful engagement with the excluded not only on those who sought to exploit them, but also on those who professed to be helping them. He argued that contextual knowledge in many parts of the world 'was severely damaged and partly destroyed, first by the gangsters of colonialism and then by the humanitarians of developmental aid. The resulting helplessness of large parts of the so-called Third World is *the result of, not a reason for*, outside interference' (1987, p. 298) (emphasis added). In critiquing those who express their intentions of goodness in dealing with others, he was particularly scathing about those of a religious persuasion. He expressed the view that 'All religions are good "in principle" – but unfortunately this abstract Good has only rarely prevented their practitioners from behaving like bastards' (1987, p. 299).

Feyerabend's works lead me to posit that speaking against hope and organization is not to reject them per se, but to challenge the reader to think deeply and critically about how she/he both perceives them in theoretical terms and then carries these perceptions into the field of practice in engaging with others, even with the best of intentions of addressing their hopes and helping them to organize to fulfil them.

TAKING ANARCHISM SERIOUSLY – REFLECTING ON THE WRITING OF PIERRE GUILLET DE MONTHOUX

Before I delve into the work of Guillet de Monthoux, let me draw again on Feyerabend (1987, p. 285), who outlined two alternative interpretations of anarchism as a mode of inquiry. While he may have expressed a view that he accepted the title of anarchist as a joke, he thought very seriously about what it means to be an anarchistic thinker. He posited that anarchism 'can be interpreted as a demand for an open exchange that seeks understanding without being tied to specific rules. But it can also be interpreted as a demand for acceptance without examination.' The first interpretation opens an unlimited field of possibilities for social inquiry and understanding that paves the way to invite the *Other* to come on board as an equal and valued partner. However, the second interpretation presents the challenge – or danger – that all views and opinions must then be treated equally, with a moral relativism that defies comparative judgement of what approach to problem resolution is 'more good' than any other.

In his excellent discourse on notions of 'art and anarchism for business administration', Pierre Guillet de Monthoux (1991) presented a range of options for how anarchistic ideas might be enacted in the domain of organization, offering illustrative examples of each. These include: the 'natural organization' which is subject to no external control, being freely regulated from within; the unselfish community of 'peaceful Communism'; the 'self-governed co-operative' in an autonomous society; and 'mathematical mutualism', whereby a just distribution of resources is achieved through mathematical modelling and bookkeeping. The key point of note in Guillet de Monthoux's explication is that the anarchistic model of community in all its forms *is* organized in some way; it is *not* anarchy. However, its form of organization does not conform with the norms of dominant political and business institutions, with their formality, bureaucracy and desire for order and unity. He points out that 'The notion that decision-making is often messy, insecure, incomplete, unavoidably arbitrary in some degree, existential, and intuitive, having its final grounds in a moment of spontaneity, is something the bureaucratic mind has great difficulty in accepting' (1991, pp. 250–251).

Guillet de Monthoux (2014) later broadened the scope of his views on anarchism as a lived concept. Here, he posited anarchism's appropriation by and incorporation into the agenda of neoliberalism in the USA – promoting the anarchistic notion of the self-motivated and self-interested capitalist individual. However, he also argued for anarchism's ongoing value as informant of action in the fields of art and aesthetics, as long as we have awareness of it being a concept that (like critical management?) can be absorbed, 're-branded', ignored or suppressed at will by powerful actors. Looking at the political landscape of 2018 – notably in the USA but also in countries as diverse as Turkey, Venezuela, Poland, Italy and Australia – it is possible to identify how notions of self-interest and self-motivation without regard for any external regulation or control appear to have become dominant. Here, we see political anarchism, bordering on anarchy in some cases, but where the benefits are confined to the few, with disregard for the many.

As the fundamental ideas of socialism, liberalism and communism have been appropriated by the powerful and corrupted to suit their own interests over those of others, so we see that anarchism is not exempted from such instrumental distortions. Thus we must seek to identify and elaborate its positive potential to provide a way of looking at and living in the world, a way in contrast to basic binary divisions of good/bad, us/them or right/wrong that embraces ambiguity, complexity and chaos, but a way that requires some form of organization to frame and enable its inclusiveness and benefits without becoming exclusive and stifling.

SOME THOUGHTS ON HOPEFUL ORGANIZATION, OR ORGANIZING HOPE

As Feyerabend (1987, p. 301) opined, '*What counts in a democracy is the experience of the citizens, i.e. their subjectivity and not what small gangs of autistic intellectuals declare to be real*' (italics in original).

In arguing against the concept of organization as it is currently understood in many contexts, I do not reject the need for forms of organization for humans to survive and prosper. However, I see that, as formal institutions argue for the need to be organized, they frequently acknowledge only their own preferred form of organization – be it political, economic or social. In the world at present, their arguments in favour of their own form of organizing tend to be set out in binary terms, whereby you are either 'with them' or 'against them'. If you don't agree with them, you are wrong! The proponents of such organizational forms give the air of being objective in their views, derived of logical and rational thinking. There is pressure on the listener and reader to accept the presented rationale without examination, in line with Guillet de Monthoux's (1983) second definition of anarchism. However, closer examination and analysis in accordance with a broader set of fact- and evidence-based criteria will often expose a limited and exclusive rationality presented as 'truth' and 'logic'.

To my mind, we are currently faced with a range of organizational forms that offer an air of diversity yet are mostly exclusive in nature, serving the self-interest of those who hold power within them, and based on a bounded rationality yet designed to present the appearance of being entirely rational, inclusive and mutually beneficial for all. I see a need for the deconstruction and elimination of these forms of organizing before there is any hope – as in desire or want – for an alternative form. As long as the populace at large, particularly in powerful nations, is 'satisficed' by the *soma* of adequate comfort, nourishment and entertainment, and can be persuaded to see the situation of the *Other* as being acceptable (migrants held in camps on Nauru?), unfortunate (residents in post-hurricane Haiti?) or necessary (workers in third world sweatshops?), there seems little chance of such deconstruction. It appears that action can only be elicited – perhaps too little, too late – after the event of direct impact on those with the power to bring about change. Even then, as where the Arab Spring turned into a dark winter, the powerful of some persuasion most likely will rise to the top and seize control.

However, if we look into history, we can find evidence of alternative forms of human organization (not to mention the myriad examples of self-organizing in the natural world). The anarchist communities of the Paris Commune and the Spanish Federation of Workers' Societies may have been short-lived, but we must hope that the lessons that they can offer contemporary society will at some stage be resurrected. It would be sad if the promise of the self-organizing society for mutual benefit was to be lost and the only legacy of thinking on anarchism became a corrupted reference to the anarchy that prevails in countries like Somalia and Yemen.

HOPEFUL ORGANIZATIONS

If we are to have hope of seeing the emergence of self-organizing communities working for some shared sense of common good, then we must find ways of allowing expression of individual desires and expectations, of giving them all consideration within a truly democratic conversation. However, we must also find ways of making often difficult choices between competing demands upon finite resources to meet these individual desires. It must be possible to elicit common hopes that, if fulfilled, will provide the greatest benefit to the community of individuals from which they are drawn. Such common and localized desires should outweigh individual wants, particularly where these are based on narrow self-interest. They should also take precedence over desires that might be imposed by others from outside the community for their own benefit, even when there is the promise of some great 'good' to be offered in return – in the form of 'development aid' or some other charitable donation.

As we watch a world that appears to be collapsing into chaos and anarchy (October 2018: synagogue massacre in Pennsylvania; right-wing, anti-environmental president elected in Brazil; Brexit shambles; migrant caravan heading north to face the US military being drawn up along the Mexican border . . .), we *can* find hope for a more positive future in small initiatives at the community level. I offer three examples to, hopefully, inspire your thinking:

- *The Hedgehog Self-Build Housing Co-op, Brighton, UK.*[1] Established in 1996 to address the lack of access to affordable housing by groups in society, this project has thrived over the following decades. It demonstrates how individuals can come together, with support from formal institutions, to create homes, a community, and new opportunities for personal development. This community featured in the very first series of the television series *Grand Designs* (1999, Series 1, no. 3) and again over a decade later (2012, Series 12, no. 12). At the second visit, host Dr Kevin McCloud elicited accounts of how the community membership had remained stable and mutually supportive and, also, how members had fulfilled their individual hopes and dreams of betterment.
- *Yackandandah Community Development Co., Yackandandah, Australia.*[2] This small town in north-east Victoria has a long-established culture of self-determination and resilience. Yackandandah featured in the ABC Australia television series *Back Roads* (2016, Series 1, episode 3), where presenter Heather Ewart met with community members who told their stories of how, having

seen the closure of local banks in the 1990s and facing closure of the town's filling station in 2002, the Yackandandah Community Development Co. was formed to maintain essential services in the face of withdrawal by national businesses. Currently, the town aims to become 100 per cent based on renewable energy sources by 2022.

- *The Totnes Pound, Totnes, UK.*[3] The Totnes Pound is a 'parallel currency' established in this English town to respond to what the community termed the 'leaky bucket' of the mainstream economy, where money spent in local branches of national businesses 'leaks' out. Again, the town faced closure of local branches of national businesses yet saw the need to maintain services to the community. Here, the local currency is interchangeable with the pound sterling, but funds can only be spent within the town limits in local businesses, building a circulating flow of economic activity within Totnes. Starting from the use of paper banknotes, the Totnes Pound is now an electronic currency.

I will not attach a label to any of these examples – whether anarchistic, communist, socialist or otherwise. That is for the communities to decide if they wish. However, I would posit that they each demonstrate examples of self-organization and self-determination, born from within the community, that might be equated with the earlier examples of the Paris Commune and the Spanish Federation. What is different is that each of these has gained wider support from formal institutions and is seemingly thriving on its own terms. I encourage *you* to seek out similar examples in your own country or region, and to consider how you might support them, spread the word about them, and encourage others to emulate their thinking.

SO WHAT? SEEKING DIRECTION FOR THE FUTURE. NO CONCLUSIONS, MERELY POINTERS TO A WAY OF BEING AND THINKING

At the start of this chapter, I encouraged deconstruction of the terms 'hope' and 'organization', and rejection of their use as constituted by powerful actors. However, this destruction must not be read as encouraging full-frontal attack on current actors and institutions of dominant power, to be replaced by yet another set. Nor does rejection of one order of hope and organization open the door for an approach of moral relativism, where all approaches are considered equal. Rather, I consider that we must adopt the intellectual approach of Feyerabend – dissecting and disrupting extant understandings of organization and hope, to prompt new critical reflections on our own positions within these, and the positions of others outside them. The key aim must be to find a minimum common ground within different world-views that will provide hope for a better shared future while enabling true diversity and individuality at the local level. We must consider how an anarchistic approach to reconstituting organization in search of hope for humanity can – and should – draw inspirations and ideas from all sources, even those that seem to be intellectually opposed to it.

NOTES

1. See https://unofficialculture.wordpress.com/2015/06/15/self-build-iii-self-build-for-social-rent-hedgehog-co-op-and-the-segal-method/.
2. See https://www.smh.com.au/lifestyle/is-this-australias-most-perfect-country-town-2016 0602-gp9pjw.html.
3. See https://www.totnespound.org/what.

10. Idealists and dreamers: Struggling for more resilient communities via alternative organisations

Anna Góral

INTRODUCTION

According to Zygmunt Bauman (2012), what has been known to us – the structure of power and its institutions, organisation of the space that surrounds us, and patterns of behaviour that have so far been perceived as guarantors of the stability of local community development – has been shaken. At the same time, David Korten emphasises that the past conviction that the key to success, as well as the source of happiness and hope for a better tomorrow, is money, markets and business care is illusory. Recent history has shown us that those are the main factors causing inequality and the growing social stratification of our communities, which have to deal with a growing number of crises surrounding them (Korten, 2015). In the face of ongoing changes, formerly stable organisations are questioned, especially traditional public institutions, as they do not always seem to satisfy the needs of society, as evidenced, inter alia, by a deepening decline in confidence in the public sector (OECD, 2018). Thus, it is interesting to observe the constantly growing number of people engaging in alternative (often called non-governmental) organisations in the public and private sectors – foundations, associations or informal groups – which can be seen as people's attempt to build a better future (Dany, 2013).

In recent years, these phenomena have been of interest to researchers of organisations and management who are increasingly looking at the emerging alternatives to organisations in the public and private sectors that are based on the idea of creating a better reality that focuses on the human being and his or her needs (see Parker et al., 2007; Wright, 2010; Bogacz-Wojtanowska, 2013; Reedy et al., 2016; Kostera, 2018).

Therefore, it seemed important to look more closely at the problem of non-governmental organisations (NGOs) in the context of organisational resilience. As a research area, I chose NGOs: foundations and associations.

It was particularly interesting to me to understand why people establish NGOs and decide, often despite adversity, to act within their structures, hoping to create more sustainable and crisis-resistant communities. In this sense, NGOs are often perceived as more effective, open to the needs of the environment, flexible and humanitarian.

As a result, the aim of this study was to look in depth at the activity of three NGOs I selected and to reflect on what drives their members to work. Based on interviews with the activists of the three selected NGOs, I had a chance to understand how they and their stakeholders define their place and role in co-creating sustainable and resilient local communities.

THE CONCEPT OF ORGANISATIONAL RESILIENCE

As was outlined in the above introduction, reflection on the contemporary organisational reality, which is subject to constant transformations of a more or less complex nature, shows it is constantly under the influence of sudden and unexpected changes.

In the literature on management and organisational science, there are two different ways of defining *organisational resilience*. On the one hand, it is seen as the ability to regenerate and return to the state that pertained before the unexpected, difficult, often traumatic situation that affected the organisation (cf. Weick, 1993; Balu, 2001; Gittell et al., 2006; Lengnick-Hall et al., 2011). On the other hand, some researchers, when analysing organisational resilience, assume a broader perspective that reaches beyond the organisation's ability to rebuild, expanding its conceptual scope with the organisation's ability to develop and creating new, not necessarily positive, changes that affect it (cf. Weick, 1988; S.F. Freeman et al., 2004; Jamrog et al., 2006). In this second approach, the organisation's ability to learn and actively seek new paths that will enable it to develop is highlighted.

The scientific discussion in the literature is mainly dedicated to the analysis of individual case studies of organisations – of the public sector or more often business organisations. Researchers in their studies pay attention to such features of resilient organisations as flexibility, agility and adaptability or look for model, more universal practices that can be used by organisations to build or strengthen their own more resilient environment (cf. McCann, 2004; Lengnick-Hall et al., 2011). However, David Korten (2015) and Wolfgang Streeck (2016) turn our attention to the fact that today we may observe a growing number of individuals and organisations that believe that there might be a different development path for their communities – one that will bring them hope and happiness and help organise local communities in a more sustainable and resilient way towards the changes happening around them.

Lengnick-Hall et al. (2011), analysing the literature dedicated to organisational resilience, point out that researchers distinguish three groups of organisational features that have an impact on the formation of organisational resilience broadly understood. The first group consists of the so-called cognitive features, which include a strong orientation towards a sense of purpose and sense of action (Weick, [1995] 2016), sharing values and building a shared vision (Coutu, 2002). The second group consists of behavioural traits, which Lengnick-Hall and Beck (2003), comparing the employees of resilient organisations to the popular TV series character MacGyver, understand as the ability to fully, and sometimes unobviously, use their, usually limited, resources to solve emerging problems. On the other hand, the last group consists of the so-called contextual features, i.e. the organisation's ability to build a sense of security, develop social capital, divide power and develop a wide network of contacts (Lengnick-Hall and Beck, 2005). According to researchers, organisations with these characteristics are able to create a resilient reality for themselves. Interestingly, the three groups discussed above are commonly affiliated with the non-governmental sector, which is characterised by a strong sense of mission and a sense of action (Bogacz-Wojtanowska, 2016), the ability to cope with difficult situations with limited resources (Korten, 1987; Salomon and Anheier, 1992), and the ability to operate in wide cooperation networks (Adamiak et al., 2016).

According to *Global Journal* (2018), there are an estimated 10 million NGOs worldwide, which their creators, and increasingly also the recipients, perceive, on the one hand, as a place of realising their own passions, dreams and interests, but, on the other hand and often above all, as a space for creating a better reality for local communities. In this context, it is worth looking at the alternative organisations – their roots, organising methods, motives for action and plans for the future, as well as the challenges they face every day – in order to reflect on what drives their members to work: a sense of mission, faith in the rightness of their actions, or madness.

MATERIALS AND METHODS

In my research, I decided to focus my attention not on the already existing forms of organisation rooted in our society and the strategies for survival and development they adopt in the face of change, but on the phenomenon of the development of alternative organisational forms that evolve in society under the influence of changes taking place in their environment.

The research area for my search was three Krakow-based NGOs: Klika, Nowe Centrum and MiLA. The organisations that were the subject of my research met the following criteria: 1) they were oriented towards achieving social goals; 2) they had been actively and continuously acting for local communities since their establishment, which was understood as continuing involvement in projects dedicated to their community; and 3) they were interested in development and thus in sharing their history and their reflections about their 'here and now' and their future. Cooperation with each of the surveyed organisations lasted approximately two months. The research that constitutes the basis of this text was carried out in 2017.

Conviction about the need to stop for a moment and reflect in depth on the organisation was the basis for designing the research forming the basis of this text. I decided to think about what makes people establish NGOs and choose, often despite adversity, to act within their framework

Table 10.1 Characteristics of the surveyed organisations

Organisation name	Fundacja Nowe Centrum	Fundacja MiLA	Stowarzyszenia Klika
Goal	Support for people threatened with social exclusion as well as promotion of the idea of volunteering.	Support for rural development through activities for local entrepreneurship and the development of cultural heritage.	Helping people with disabilities, aiming at their integration in society.
Target group	Children, youth and elderly people living in Nowa Huta (a Krakow district).	Local communities in rural areas.	The disabled.
Main activities	– Street working. – Street rocket. – Running a community centre.	– Support for the development of local products. – Development of eco-museums. – Training in the field of social economy, incubation of entrepreneurship in rural areas.	– Conducting occupational therapy workshops. – Supporting cultural and artistic activity for people with disabilities. – Organisation of free time for disabled people. – Professional activation of disabled people.

Source: Own work.

in favour of more sustainable and resilient communities. Taking up the task of understanding this phenomenon, I decided to conduct ethnographic research, which allowed me to better understand the point of view of people and organisations directly involved in working in NGOs, focusing on organisations working for members of local communities at risk of social exclusion. As emphasised by Paweł Krzyworzeka (2015, p. 34), 'Ethnography not only allows discovery but also provides a detailed empirical material that, if properly used, can be used to create a convincing and inspiring academic narrative.'

The research was based primarily on in-depth interviews:

- Individual interviews with members of the organisations and stakeholders (two interviews in each organisation). In the text, extracts from interviews were marked with the first letters of the organisation's name and the number of the subsequent interview (e.g. NC-1).
- Group interviews with members and employees of the organisation during the project (one interview in each organisation). In the text, extracts from interviews were marked with the first letters of the organisation's name, the letter 'G' referring to the group interview, and the number of the subsequent interview (e.g. NCG-1).
- Group interviews with the organisation's stakeholders during the project (one interview in each organisation). In the text, extracts from interviews were marked with the first letters of the organisation's name, the letters 'GI' referring to the group interview with the stakeholders, and the number of the subsequent interview (e.g. NCGI-1).

In addition, the organisations' statutory documents, their websites, and profiles in social media, as well as other materials documenting their activities (including films, publications and photo materials), were subjects of the research. Also, in order to inspire the members and employees of the organisation to reflect, I conducted creative workshops, and several times I accompanied the organisation's members in their daily work.

Constructed in this way, the process allowed exploration of the following issues in relation to the surveyed organisations: their roots, how they are organised, their motives, and dreams and plans for the future. Also, an important element of the study was a reflection on what kind of impact the organisations actually have and can have in the future on their members and the environment they work in and whether those ideas are considered by their beneficiaries to be utopias or real alternatives for building a meaningful future for their communities.

THE PATH TOWARDS RESILIENT COMMUNITIES: A CASE STUDY

The organisations I study have different longevities. The oldest, Klika, has been operating continuously since 1971, MiLA started in 2010, and the youngest, Fundacja Nowe Centrum, was established in 2012. All three were grassroots initiatives and, as their leaders and members emphasised, born of the need to do something positive for their surroundings, initially implemented in the form of informal activities, which were at some point transformed into third-sector organisations.

Klika's roots are found in a group of friends who in their college days decided to help people with disabilities – initially helping them, among other things, with everyday shopping, and over time getting more and more involved in the social activation of the group. For the founding members of the MiLA Foundation, inspiration for action was the desire to put their competences and expertise in the field of cultural heritage management to better use by encouraging the business activity óf rural residents, as well as a sense of insufficiency in public sector jobs at that time – everyone had previously worked in higher education institutions. Nowe Centrum was established, according to its members, 'on the initiative of a group of people wanting to create new quality in working with other human beings' (NCG-1). The members focused on support for seniors and children – residents of Nowa Huta at risk of social exclusion – after noting deficits in this area of activities undertaken by public institutions responsible for supporting these groups.

The Nowe Centrum Foundation is a totally secondary activity for its members. When asked about the reasons for establishing the Foundation, my interlocutors gave various answers. One of the animators of Nowe Centrum, speaking about her motivation, tells the story of one of the Foundation's pupil:

> Wojtek comes to our classes. . . . He lives with his grandmother . . . but she is quite ill and not strong. The only thing she cares about is food and sweets, so Wojtek has plenty of them, and that's why he is like that, and besides he just hangs around the area. He recently came to us, but he comes every day immediately after school and stays until closing time, even on Saturdays. This is probably the only place where he wants to be, because here someone talks to him, helps, cares, and he has friends here. Neither the school nor the local social welfare centre [MOPS] is interested in him, because he has a grandmother. . . . Here at Nowe Centrum we are focused on people just like Wojtek. We want to give them a chance for the future, help them, because we see that no one else will. . . . The Foundation gives me freedom and capacity to act. I can be true here by helping others. Besides, I see that what I do makes sense and brings joy to my kids. Do you understand? (NC-2)

The core of Klika is a team of several people who decided to devote their efforts to the disabled, as in their opinion the existing system of social institutions does not care about them to a sufficient degree. Marcin, who works in Klika as a manager, draws attention to a sense of meaning and opportunity:

> You know, we have this boy among our charges who has muscular dystrophy. Practically all the time since childhood he has been in a wheelchair. A really nice guy. . . . His greatest dream was a trip to the mountains. But how to do it? And then I thought that I would help him no matter what and that we would fulfil his dream. I gathered a group of 16 boys and 13 girls. That was crazy! [Laughter.] We carried him one after another on this frame on our backs. It took us all day, three times longer than normal, but it worked! You should have seen that joy! . . . Yes, then I really felt that what I do makes sense. (K-2)

The idea of getting involved for the benefit of local communities was based on the conviction of my interlocutors that the public institutions with which they were often professionally involved, despite the objectives of these institutions, did not completely fulfil their functions. Thus, one may say that the organisations I studied deliberately seek 'otherness' – the implementation of their functions and tasks differently from the way the public or private sector implements them. The existing, 'traditional' system of social support, although well developed, seems to focus on satisfying the basic needs of its charges related to, inter alia, medical care or housing. Klika's charges define this help as 'ensuring survival', and they think that there is a lack of 'something more' in the system that would allow for getting outside the four walls of the house and personal growth (KGI-1).

In the statements of my interlocutors, although not explicitly expressed by them, there was the motif of a sense of mission, or willingness to fulfil their and their charges' dreams and implement the impossible. Members of the organisation that had decided to operate in the non-governmental sector had dreamed of being able to pursue their passions, help others and make the world a better place. They had a high sense of mission in their activities, and wanted to have a greater opportunity for efficient impact on the environment to which they devoted a lot of time and energy, not only during working hours but also in their free time. This is also how they are perceived by the recipients of activities undertaken by the foundations and associations which are the subject of the studies: 'They are always available, and not only during office hours' (NCGI-2).

At the same time, importantly, the organisations sow in their communities a kind of seed of development that they hope to cultivate together with their charges. The manifestation of this is the moment when my interlocutors notice that their charges, under the influence of the activities undertaken in the researched foundations and associations, begin to dream – about more than just surviving. They begin to discover their potential and look for opportunities for its development. Over time, their dreams, when the activity within the studied organisations increases, are more and more bold, but in the opinion of the respondents also more and more real. The enthusiasm and almost tangible willingness of the members and employees of the non-governmental sector often constitute an inspiration to take action for their charges, which is what gives them hope for a better future.

Something extremely important for my interlocutors was a sense of responsibility for their actions, which is their important driving force. As members of the MiLA Foundation emphasise, 'the organisation and everything that is related to it – space, structure, activities – is ours, from beginning to end' (MG-1). Activity in an NGO is for them a source of emancipation, which they lacked in other workplaces. Clearly perceptible in the statements of my interlocutors was the desire to feel agency in the environment in which they operate and which gives them work within the framework of NGOs, and the adversities that my interlocutors encounter on the way often have a strengthening rather than a weakening effect.

However, the path chosen by the surveyed organisations, as Marcin from Klika emphasises, does not always 'come up roses'. My interlocutors constantly have to deal with problems and obstacles. On the one hand, these result from a turbulent environment that does not provide them with 'safe' operating conditions. Among the main problems, they point to difficult financial realities, mainly referring to the lack of a stable source of funding.

However, my interlocutors, despite the difficulties they face, try to explain the need to face the problems, the sense of mission and the importance of their activities. Clearly visible in their statements are attempts to idealise their activity and to reaffirm themselves in their sense of performing it, even if sometimes it collides with brutal reality, not only organisational but also on the part of recipients who do not always seem to appreciate the NGO's activity.

Each of the organisations at some point came up against the proverbial wall and had to deal with a crisis. Their sources were different, including the sense that, in developing, the organisation became increasingly bureau-cratic and gradually formalised, like traditional public sector institutions (Klika's case), which is perceived as a sign of failure: 'We wanted to be different, but at some point we were unable to avoid it, or maybe we had no idea how to do it differently . . . and we still do not know. And that's probably the biggest problem that is blocking us now' (KG-1).

For others, this is a recurring question about their actual impact on the

environment, whether their work and involvement really are important for
the recipients, whether the presence of the organisation produces positive
effects in the environment that are perceived by the recipients, or whether
they are simply treated as another social welfare centre.

> Sometimes I ask myself, what would happen if we were not there? Would the
> residents notice it? And I do not think I know the answer. And this is, unfortu-
> nately, the worst position, because I do not know if what we do here, on which I
> spend every moment of my free time, makes any sense at all. (NCG-1)

A recurring cause of frustration is also the feeling that some of the
completed projects have failed and so the dreams of my interlocutors
have not been fulfilled. For some of the members and employees of the
organisations surveyed, the accumulation of such factors at some point
becomes an insurmountable barrier leading to a kind of burning out, loss
of enthusiasm and, as a consequence, resignation from the activities of
the organisation. However, many people remain and, despite obstacles,
continue to pursue their mission.

A sense of the importance of persisting in my interlocutors and the
necessity of their actions is stronger than the difficulties encountered.
This is apparent because, during the interviews, apart from reflection
on the problems, statements about positive aspects of work in the non-
governmental sector appeared at the same time. The significant positive
aspects of everyday life are associated primarily with people: everyday
relationships with colleagues with whom they form a community of
friends, family, and those for whom the everyday efforts are undertaken.
The humane dimension of the activities of the NGOs surveyed seems to
be the key one, for which it is worth, in the opinion of my interlocutors,
undertaking the effort to change the surrounding reality. This seems to be
most fully underlined by the idea, mentioned earlier, which is at the heart
the Nowe Centrum Foundation, which was established to 'create new
quality in working with other human beings' (NCG-1).

Through their attitude, the interlocutors show that despite the hardships
and failures they can continue, learn from the failures and draw conclusions
from them for the future. 'Now we know why they rejected this project. We
will write a better one next time . . . and I have a better idea now' (KG-1).

DISCUSSION: NGOs AS THE AXIS MUNDI OF THEIR LOCAL COMMUNITIES

The members of Nowe Centrum, when asked during the workshop about
how they imagine themselves in a few years' time, drew a tree with large

branches which was firmly rooted in the space they co-created. Their story of the drawing they had created was a specific reference to the idea of the axis mundi, which according to ancient beliefs is a stable element of the universe. This picture was the externalisation of the dreams of my interlocutors, who believe that their work and involvement will become the axis around which a stable local community will be built and that the Foundation will be a refuge for its charges, a place where they will always be able to come and around which the local community's life will revolve. This explains the interlocutors' strong sense of mission and sense of action (Bogacz-Wojtanowska, 2016). They clearly strive to encourage the seed of hope, which they planted at the very beginning of the Foundation's activity, to grow and take root, becoming ingrained in the local community, and to spread, reaching an increasing number of people in need. In this way, they are trying to build a stable environment that satisfies the needs of their community (Korten, 2015). The members of MiLA and Klika dream in a similar way, and in their thoughts of the future go even further by building an ideal picture of the world in which organisations similar to theirs will not be needed at all. These dreams, however, seem to my interlocutors still distant ideas about the future, and the scale of their achievements so far is underestimated and constantly perceived as insufficient. However, they are not giving up, as they see the need to constantly strive towards more resilient organisations, and to have the strength to learn and to seek new paths (Weick, 1988; S.F. Freeman et al., 2004) despite difficulties (Salomon and Anheier, 1992).

Interestingly, observing the surroundings of the surveyed organisations, these dreams do not seem so distant or *unrealistic*. In many cases, they can even be considered to be already implemented. This is evidenced by statements from the charges of the foundation or association. In their statements, they talk not only about what has already happened but also about the future, about further undertakings in which they will participate thanks to the NGOs. This suggests that these organisations will last. When they think about it, they find it hard to imagine a future without the people who form Nowe Centrum, MiLA and Klika. They greatly appreciate their daily work, treating them as extraordinary and unique people. Sometimes it is difficult for them to understand how it is possible that these 'crazy, wonderful people' devote so much time to them and want to work and spend time with them, even their own time, which 'is due' to the family. They talk about them warmly and with respect, and even as family members, which is clearly underlined by the charges of Nowe Centrum and Klika, although, as they admit, they may seldom talk about it. The bond with the environment created by the organisations studied here seems almost palpable. It also shows a new, people-centred paradigm (Korten, 1987) as a driving force for the action of these NGOs.

In their dreams, first of all, my interlocutors do not think about themselves and their own direct benefit, but first and foremost about the local community that they operate in and its wide network of stakeholders (Adamiak et al., 2016). Klika imagines a new business idea that will ensure stable employment in workshops for disabled people, who thus will not have to stay at home. For Nowe Centrum, the vision of the future is new headquarters – a local social innovation incubator which will be the centre of activity of the 'old' Nowa Huta. MiLA envisages the possibility of providing constant support for young rural residents interested in economic activity in the area of local heritage.

SUMMARY

Idealists and dreamers, but also activists, social activists and altruists – this picture of alternative organisations emerges from the research I carried out. Such organisations are created by extraordinary people who have found the meaning of their actions in work for sustainable local communities, often undertaking, like Don Quixote, the proverbial tilting at windmills, deciding on uncertain, unknown and difficult tasks, believing that their engagement will have real impact on the people for whom it is undertaken. The organisations examined decided to implement difficult tasks. In the face of crises, progressive social stratification, and the growing threat of exclusion of such social groups as children, young people, disabled people or residents of rural areas, they decided to devote their time and energy to these groups, recognising in their commitment an opportunity to implement the idea of inclusive, sustainable local communities.

The main objective of my study was to examine the problem of alternative organisations in the context of organisational resilience. It was also important for me to learn why people establish non-governmental organisations (NGOs) and decide, often despite adversities, to act in favour of creating more sustainable and resilient communities.

I attempted to show in the text that the very idea of alternative organisations seems to be a sign of a new way of thinking about a community-building process and organisations where people, the artefacts they create and the values they hold constitute a basis for the creation of a given space. In this, I am trying to show, as David Korten (2015) underlined, that there is a future built on values other than money, market and career. The organisation of NGOs often takes the form of a group of people who want to achieve the set objectives together, on the basis of the values and beliefs they share. People, not procedures, are the priority in the organisations I examined, and all activities are devoted to them. Thus, a resilient organisation is one that draws attention to the human being who in fact forms the basis of the local community.

My research leads to the conclusion that the surveyed NGOs are structured, focused, shaped and managed by, and in response to, the requirements of the present time, in which contemporary societies function. They are an attempt to build a stable community undertaken as a result of the conviction that the existing forms of organisation and management seem to fail to fulfil their functions, especially in relation to the human beings they serve. They strongly represented the people-centred idea of development (Korten, 1987). However, as I tried to show in the chapter, their work, and the impact they create, is not something that happens only here and now. In the case of the organisations I studied, it is a process that took a long time, starting from the college days of my interlocutors. They needed time to get rooted in the communities they work with and to become their active co-creators. Thanks to their hard work, strong belief in its meaning and hope for a better future they managed to become recognised as the axis mundi of those communities they co-create.

The conclusions I present may be treated as an inspiration for more interest in alternative organisations' management, in particular in the area of building organisational resilience based on the people-centred paradigm. Such an approach may be an interesting alternative, stimulating a greater involvement of the community in its life, and as a result in its sustainable development, and an important step towards more human organisations and society.

11. Cadriste (R)Evolution

Markus Kallifatides

INTRODUCTION: FROM DESPAIR TO HOPE

The three cardinal virtues of Christianity, faith, hope and love, perennially served, much as in all monotheistic religions, as an opium for the masses. Faith, hope and love as moralizing imperatives are, to my mind, the discursive expression of the material dominance of the few. Faith, hope and love all stimulate serenity and contentment among the many. The opposite virtues, of disbelief, despair and hate, may however well serve as an antithesis in the necessary transmutation from moralizing imperative to rational reality in which there would be good reasons to believe, foresee a brighter future, and love one's fellow animals. Disbelief, despair and hate all stimulate uproar and energizing discontent.

In my estimation of how things are, there is plenty of disbelief, despair and hate to go round, which is, then, good grounds for hope for change to come in the form of political decision resulting from social movement. Another good ground for hope is that social science has given us knowledge of what the underlying problem is: the irrational, contradictory social formation referred to as capitalism that constitutes our life form, that is, a social formation in which private ownership of the means of production, be it parts of nature or human constructions, is the dominant principle of organizing social life. This formation may be analyzed according to the simple formula of "money, commodity, more money," which in turn is but a special case of the more general formula to which human history subscribes: "power, weapons, more power," as shown for instance in magisterial texts by the great Canadian political scientist and Brennerian Marxist Ellen Meiksins Wood (1942–2016) (e.g. Meiksins Wood, 2002), to whom I believe I owe much of my understanding.

This chapter assumes – against all the "contemporary nonsense" (Meiksins Wood, 2002) – the Marxist position that patriarchy, explicit racism and formal colonialism were indeed successfully challenged in the post-World War II era, of course without obliterating these pre-capitalist phenomena, because these were barriers to capitalist expansion.

As we speak, capitalism is doing away with its own and more recent (19th- and 20th-century) constructions, the centralized nation-state and democracy. This is why victimized people are both angry and disoriented. Furthermore, the chapter speaks to a class alliance in which an avant-garde and the proletariat are conjoined in the "social-democratic" construction of (more) socialist societies.

In this chapter, as any Marxist must, I emphasize that this simple formula of "money, commodity, more money" must be superseded in order for there to be good grounds for faith, hope and love in a world of grotesque inequality, violence and environmental destruction. The optimistic prediction formulated by Karl Marx more than 150 years ago was that human beings, when reduced to commodities themselves and experiencing this denigration together, would eventually rebel against those other human beings who, through the mystification of property rights and the magic of money, have aggrandized themselves into gods. He was obviously correct. From 1850, when Marx was pretty clear about how things work, a string of social movements established both democracies and dictatorships, vastly improving the lots of national majorities in particular in what became the affluent nation-states of the West. None of these uprisings, however, put an end to capitalism, which is why it was there all along to make its formidable comeback in neoliberalism, the crisis of which we are now experiencing.

In the transformation to post-capitalism, money must be invested in something other than commodities, and the "return on investment" must be something other than more money. And weapons must be used to create something other than more power. Both would have to be an expression of self-limitation on the part of the strong. In this chapter, I propose that one seed for this (r)evolution is in decent supply in many high-income nations' middle classes; with substantial collective holdings of financial capital (money), democratic states and non-governmental organizations (NGOs) already in place to manage it, and better-than-ever knowledge of conditions of the social and natural world, as well as a prolonged experience of meaninglessness and its corollary cynicism, the urban middle classes may well, once again, come to serve as the avant-garde of the global proletariat and the global peasantry. Previously, the avant-garde edge was concerned with ending patriarchy, explicit racism and formal colonialism. This time, it is about ending capitalist imperialism altogether, thereby putting capital back where it belongs: in a prison run by a democratically elected government and administered by a cadre of managers.

Sweden, once a shining star of reformist social democracy, has in recent decades been neoliberalized and financialized into a run-of-the-mill Western nation-state – and this within the frame of the USA's informal empire, with its military doctrine of "war without end" and attempt at comprehensive global control (Meiksins Wood, 2005). However, this tiny nation – Sweden – has retained some particularities, including the espoused values of many of its citizens. In this text I suggest and dream of an awakening through an urban and "cadriste" (r)evolution within the discourse and practice of Swedish institutional investment.

GROWING AWARENESS OF THE REAL PROBLEM: CAPITALISM

In one of his many interventions in Swedish public debate, professor of human ecology, and one of the few Swedes alive with the potential for world-historical significance, Alf Hornborg (see for example Hornborg et al., 2007) suggests that capitalism is the problem. He underscores the importance of "general-purpose money" enabling the exchange of anything for everything else.

> Since the 18th century, such money has put beyond reproach the increasingly fast exchange of consumer goods for the natural resources and ecological context used to produce them. They now allow us to exchange rainforests, coral reefs and oil reserves for Coca-Cola and video games. The same idea makes us see it as natural that food for ill-nourished children in Zambia is valued in the same currency as the one played with on Wall Street. We have thus learned that ecosystems, human lives and trivial pass-times are exchangeable on the same market. (Hornborg, 2017)

For decades now, individual active capitalists (Marx's term for all sorts of business leaders involved in the direct exploitation of surplus value) have enjoyed the support of rather passively organized collectivities of middle- and working-class citizens in high-income nations. Through pensions and insurance savings, primarily reappearing as interest-bearing capital or portfolio investment, majorities of citizens have come to share in the pecuniary benefits for capitalists of an international order of liberalized trade and capital flows within what is effectively political anarchy in the world system and increasingly authoritarian market dominance in defined geographical spaces. On the other side of that pecuniary coin are of course the costs of these things, for instance the morally reprehensible conditions of millions of laborers in globalized production networks (Milberg, 2008) and the continual degradation of the biosphere (H. Rogers, 2013).

The specificities of our current situation are that the USA has come to be controlled by the land-owning elite of the South, losers in the American Civil War but not quitters. In unbending manner, this elite has fought against democracy, including Roosevelt's New Deal (Selznick, 1949). In neoliberalism, it has successfully re-established its proprietary structure of labor-intensive mass commodity production in trans-national and trans-continental production networks while supporting and celebrating the hard work of right-wing populist movements under the Stars and Bars of the confederate flag (Fletcher, 2016).

The European Union once threatened to become a social-democratic challenger worthy of picking up the glove in the absence of the Soviet Union and its fallen empire. Through a formidable build-up of economic power backed by even more formidable military power, the USA has contained this threat for quite some time (Meiksins Wood, 2005), with capital mobility across national borders and especially across the Atlantic being central to this strategy, and with institutional investment one of the prime ideological and practical vehicles for it (Harmes, 1998).

Awareness of the downsides to liberalized trade and capital flows is surely growing, not only within academic enclosures. Within the policy discourse surrounding and featuring so-called institutional investors, matters such as abhorrent labor conditions, gender inequality, corruption, pollution and so on have all come to the forefront in policy initiatives from the United Nations, the OECD, the European Commission, the International Labour Organization and the WWF. "Corporate social responsibility" (CSR) and "responsible investment" (RI) have become large institutions in themselves, an industry featuring hordes of advisors and service providers enabling money managers to enact CSR and the Principles for Responsible Investment (PRI) (Nyqvist, 2015). The trouble is that CSR and PRI as enacted are largely unrelated to the material realities of producing better labor conditions, less gender inequality, less corruption or less pollution. The bulk of any such improvements in increasingly global supply chains or networks (and there are improvements!) come from a convergence of material interests among corporations, governments and international NGOs, such as in matters regarding "food safety," that is, food that is safe to consume, not safe provision of food to those who are hungry (Davis et al., 2018). The ideational dimension of this lack of correspondence between corporate/government/NGO talk and action resides in the ideological idea that money-making can be combined with the making of whatever other good one wishes to accomplish: a Nirvana notion that all good things can be accomplished simultaneously. The thinness of this basic idea provides a good explanation of the thickness of the practices surrounding CSR and PRI. Confusion, or, as Bourdieu would have had it, misrecognition, forever remains easier to breed in a fog of disinformation. This disorienting fog has been in ample supply from the community of institutional investors, to which I now turn my attention.

THE REAL OF INSTITUTIONAL INVESTMENT

The subterrain of modernity includes a passion for the Real, Žižek (2002) teaches. On the topic of "responsibilization" of institutional investment, a seasoned senior manager of a large Swedish institutional investment company alludes to the Real of the practice and discourse that has preoccupied him for quite some time:

> Well, nobody stays away from buying American government bonds. Yet, these are the ones that finance the acquisition of weapons. And if the weapons are used, they do the warfare. So, if you oppose weapon manufacturing, you shouldn't really buy US bonds either. As long as they use the weapons. So there are some simplifications, shortcomings to all that thinking, very difficult to reconcile if you're really serious. But it's developing gradually and that's very good. (Senior manager, Swedish institutional investment company)[1]

The thickness of these increasingly "globalized" practices of institutional investment, ostensibly in accordance with principles, may obscure the vision even of critical observers. Swedish social anthropologist Anette Nyqvist ends her substantial and illuminating field work on the everyday activities of people working as institutional investor representatives based in Sweden by remarking and asking:

> Most of us are today not only co-owners in thousands of corporations around the world but also – indirectly – financial market actors, investors and speculators. We buy the service and hand over responsibility, let the fiduciary capitalists do the job. Stick our heads in the sand, hope for return on investment and keep quiet. Are we happy then? (Nyqvist, 2015, p. 231)

Some probably are happy. Some probably are not. Indeed, some research indicates rather common outright phobic emotions vis-à-vis financial markets (Holgersson, 2018).[2] Those are empirical questions to be asked and answered by research. A troubling point about the quote above is that a scholar with so much time invested in the topic is guilty of a conceptual slip of the tongue when explicitly debating what she has studied so extensively. In most cases, Swedish middle- and working-class individuals do not, at least not only, "buy" the service. On the contrary, institutional investment in Sweden, as elsewhere, is to a significant extent organized in civil society's not-for-profit organizations and by government. Unless one defines paying membership fees to one's union or taxes to one's state as "buying," these "services" are organized within democratic rather than dictatorial organizations such as corporations. The overarching decision-making rule in Swedish institutional investment is "one person, one vote," to be compared to the corporate rule of "one share, one vote." By the end of 2017, the Swedish National Pension Funds held financial assets valued at 1436 billion Swedish kronor, approximately 30 percent of Swedish gross domestic profit (GDP). An equivalent amount of financial assets was held by the three major corporatist and non-profit pension and insurance companies, jointly owned by the Confederation of Swedish Enterprise and the national union federations. To this, one might add the labor movement-affiliated insurance companies, with assets worth another 10 percent of GDP. I would like to put forward the notion that this is good grounds for some hope of transformation to come, unless we agree with Alf Hornborg (2017) also on the point that "the poor masses of the South have no benefit of democracy in Europe" and consider this to be an eternal fact.

The suspicion that the poor masses in the global South gain very little from Northern democracy is reinforced by a critical re-reading of the reality of democratically organized institutional investment. As Anette Nyqvist (2015) makes clear, the objective of investment is maximum returns. That is the implication of Swedish legislation regarding national pension funds and insurance companies, as well as bank-run and other investment funds. It also happens, and Nyquist fails to address these matters, to be the implication of legislation regarding Swedish foundations, including the Wallenberg and Handelsbanken foundations, in effective control of corporate empires spanning some two-thirds of Swedish industry. If any uncertainty was still lingering out there, Swedish corporate law is unambiguous on the matter of the purpose of the corporation: the purpose of the corporation is to produce profits for its shareowners (unless otherwise stated in the corporate constitution).

There is (as yet?) no legal obligation on the part of individuals to maximize return on investment. It is still legal to remain an alienated shareholder and let oneself be a relative loser on financial markets. Ample research on the economistic colonization of Swedish everyday life (e.g. Lindqvist, 2001; Forslund, 2008) suggests that government and financial market intermediaries have interacted in strongly promoting a sense of there also being such an obligation among larger strata of the population. For individual active capitalists, generating profits is primarily a means to build greater corporate empires, something that these individuals appear to believe is tantamount to doing something good. Here the ideological notion of active capitalists "creating jobs" rests on forgetting that competition among capitalists suggests that new jobs imply old jobs lost elsewhere, along with the perennial shift of all sorts of social and environmental costs to others while benefits are retained as profits (Korten, 1995).

All this has not hindered a lively discourse in recent decades on "environmental, social and governance" (ESG) issues among institutional investors, but always within the overarching frame of maximum return

Organizing hope

on investment as the ultimate objective of corporate activity. (For the comparative and critically important case of the United Kingdom and the City of London, see Kallifatides and Larsson, 2017; cf. Talani, 2011.) It is a case of real business as usual, talked about in sometimes fanciful hyperbolic terms, especially at all those special events at which institutional investor representatives meet to portray themselves, to themselves and to others, as not only "active" but also "responsible" owners.

Nyqvist's (2015) anthropological study allows us to take part in these recurring events at which "everybody," i.e. asset owners, investment managers, and professional services providers involved in "responsible investment," meets. They meet at nice venues anywhere in the world. There are exalted speakers and fine cocktails, and there is intense networking. Representatives of Swedish institutional investors partake in these proceedings in order to develop skills in the core competence of responsible investment: dialogue with corporations. This dialogue in turn also takes place anywhere in the world, at nice venues, and entails fine cocktails and intense networking. Quite a few of the informants whom Nyqvist met with during her field study describe the entire thing as something of a religion, or at least a social movement. Conversion to the creed is quite often mentioned as that which is involved in transforming financial market actors into "responsible" actors. As far as religious conversion goes, this particular instantiation appears to be a rather modest variation, to say the least.

> We as investors do want the companies to focus on their business idea and produce more profit. We don't want the board and management to be preoccupied with lots of other matters because they have "stepped in it" and done something. That is what we always explain to them. We are just monitors. (Institutional investor representative, in Nyqvist, 2015, p. 222, my translation)

Or:

> We are supposed to generate profit, and then we are supposed to take ethics and the environment into consideration. You invest in companies because you think that you will make money. Else you could buy a sweater. And then you would have a new sweater to wear. You invest in stocks because you want return on your investment, or else you do something else with the capital. This is always to be remembered. It is no charity. (Representative of the Swedish Ethics Council, in Nyqvist, 2015, p. 223, my translation)

Quod erat demonstrandum. Business as usual.

The anthropologist concludes her discussion (Nyqvist, 2015, p. 231) by suggesting that the only category of people who have remained silent in the wide public discussion on responsible institutional investment are the customers of institutional investment organizations, i.e. the large crowd of ordinary citizens, most of whom work outside finance. As the reader of this chapter must by now be able to anticipate, I come to a somewhat different conclusion. The discourse and practice of "responsible" institutional investment are what has both stimulated and silenced the multi-headed crowd of ordinary people. This is the most important effect of that discourse. It is a formidable power-effect. That kind of power-effect is what this as well as many other forms of ideology in the Marxist sense accomplishes; it stimulates the accumulation of private wealth and silences the alternatives of investing in collective well-being. It is to such alternatives that the chapter now turns, in order to give these alternatives voice.

AMPLE EXPERIENCE OF THE SOLUTION: DEMOCRATIC ORGANIZATION

One author who does not quite share Alf Hornborg's, or possibly my own, dystopianism regarding our future is Dutch political scientist and representative of the Amsterdam school of international relations Kees van der Pijl (2005). In line with a tradition of predominantly French elaborations of Karl Marx's unfinished theory of the transition from capitalism to socialism, van der Pijl pinpoints the class representing a society without class within a class society. This class has been given many names; the one preferred by van der Pijl is the French "cadre." The American sociologist Erik Olin Wright (1997) refers to it as the class of people in "contradictory class locations," both subordinate to capital and superordinate to labor, tasked with the overall job of maintaining social order, thus securing capital accumulation within capitalist (class) society by elaborating notions as well as practices of planning and solidarity.

Van der Pijl is hardly alone in his overall description of the political landscape of the interregnum and the line taken by the cadre within it. His empirical investigation of the particularities of our immediate (Western) history in these terms is hard to match. What he shows is that the political orientation of the cadre depends on whether it opts to look up, protecting the privileges of the ruling class that employs it, or down, to the protesting and suffering majority of the population. If the cadre directs its gaze downward, the cadre will feel and think it necessary to challenge capitalist strictures, individual property, market competition and all that, and suggest more organization. Evidently an exponent of a Brennerian, political Marxism, van der Pijl concludes: "Only through the cumulative momentum of a series of particular, largely contingent episodes can we hope that the forces capable of imposing limits on the capitalist exploitation of people and nature can prevail, and the suicidal drive of neo-liberalism reversed" (van der Pijl, 2005, p. 166). So how do we stimulate this cumulative momentum? Insistence on foundational notions is one possible path of action, emphasizing that the very point of democratic organization is debate about objectives, while the point of dictatorial organization is efficient accomplishment of a given objective. Money must be invested with some other purpose than to make more money in order for there to be any such thing as "responsible investment."

Swedish political economist Magnus Ryner (2007) has highlighted the historically highly significant notion of a Swedish model, and its role as proverbial Sorelian myth in the politico-economic imaginary, not only in Sweden but elsewhere too.[3] The democratic socialist and finance minister Ernst Wigforss (1881–1977) coined the concept of provisional utopia. It is to formulating and dreaming of such a provisional utopia that I now turn, in the spirit of maintaining, or perhaps creating, some hope. In this particular "futurible," as French authors may dub it, a new Swedish model is born.

PROVISIONAL UTOPIA: INSTITUTIONAL INVESTMENT BEYOND CAPITALISM

In the Swedish model developed out of the ashes of the Great Depression of the 1930s, investment in social services, health care, housing, infrastructure, knowledge and skills was conducive to strong economic growth, with globally exporting industrial corporations based in Sweden beneficiaries of social peace and labor productivity. This old Swedish model was attacked by domestic and global capital in the 1970s, was kept on financialized life support in the 1980s and was effectively killed by a right-wing government in 1991–1994. The model was kept in its coffin by the Social Democrats when they returned to office in 1994, while being used as a phantasmatic projection of national glory. Since then, Sweden has experienced mass unemployment and growing discrepancies in conditions of life, including income and wealth inequality. Financialization has served to postpone renewed crisis up to the present day. Sweden appeared to have weathered the Financial Crisis fairly well, but it was only by a surge in privatized Keynesianism in which increasing indebtedness among Swedish households kept the domestic economy going while protecting the exporting sector from loss of competitiveness (Belfrage and Kallifatides, 2018a, 2018b).

In this, my day-dream, things have changed. In this, my imagined future, formulated as if it had already happened, written in the past tense, it was at this particular historical juncture, described above, that new alliances were formed. A class alliance of the cadre, the (liberally minded) urban middle classes and un- and underorganized wage laborers (the "reserve army" in Marx's terminology) was formed around the traditional policy objectives of the Swedish model of the 1930s: work, housing, education, health care and child care. For everybody. Not for profit. This class alliance, clandestinely supported by a few among Sweden's (many) super-rich, engaged in fierce confrontation with the increasingly xenophobic strata of organized labor drawn to the successor to Swedish fascism and Nazism, and the intellectually and morally corrupt suburban middle classes (the petty bourgeoisie) drawn to the overtly hypocritical project of the Conservative/ Neoliberal Party portraying itself as the new labor party, in reality concerned only with further reductions in taxes (Kuisma and Ryner, 2012).

The radical step taken was a massive investment program geared to addressing the most pressing of social problems for large strata of the Swedish population and electorate. The housing shortage caused by one of the high-income world's most liberal housing policy frameworks from the late 1980s to the present day (Christophers, 2013) was diminished through the provision of "green" housing, with investments in public infrastructure securing the use and exchange value of that housing, including special purpose housing, such as accommodation for the elderly with a need for care in the home, in new and renewed residential areas around the larger urban centers, along with selected re-settlements in the wastelands left behind by urbanization, de-industrialization and de-agriculturalization – and all financed by the collective savings of the Swedish citizenry in public and corporatist pension funds and insurance companies (amounting to approximately one Swedish GDP). The first order of the day was a sell-off of (in prioritized order) assets in off-shore tax havens, US interest-bearing assets, real estate outside Sweden, funds of funds, and funds exchanging these foreign financial for domestic real (estate) assets.

This, together with outright bribery of the Swedish police force and health care nurses, occurred in the form of pay increases and increases in the number of work colleagues, fully financed within the removal of what was the world's most neoliberal and thus austere fiscal policy framework (Erixon, 2015). Medical doctors and lawyers, the strongest of the professions, were lured to come on board too, almost for free, by allowing them more autonomy in the running of the health care and judicial systems, in exchange for a limitation on their entrepreneurial (for-profit) inclinations.

This short-term resurgence of a class alliance in favor of democratic socialism prepared the ground for a number of long-term policy development processes with the two overall ambitions of shifting the balance of power back from capital to labor and from those now alive to those not yet born. Five broad and old-school public inquiries were immediately launched and tasked with mandates to come up with radical policy proposals on the following topics:

- Is economic growth a policy objective to be abandoned by the kingdom of Sweden? (With the explicit possibility of the inquiry answering "yes.")
- How should government promote free and fair trade? (With the possibility of the inquiry proposing selective customs barriers, subsidies, bans, and all sorts of infringements of so-called "property rights.")
- Should Sweden remain in the European Union? (With the possibility of the inquiry coming to the conclusion that Sweden should leave it, or radically modify its stances on many issues within the Union.)
- Should government pursue public interest banking? (With the possibility that one or several Swedish banks should be nationalized in one form or another.)
- Should Sweden de-neoliberalize financial markets? (With the possibility that Sweden should reinstitute capital controls at its borders.)

CONCLUDING REMARKS

Struggle is what is Real, Karl Marx underscored. Ellen Meiksins Wood insisted that ours is a struggle of democracy against capitalism. Reforms, the former finance minister of Sweden Ernst Wigforss propagated, are the way forward. What was suggested in this chapter is a re-invigoration of Swedish democracy, with the explicit aim of putting capital back where it belongs, in a prison run by government and monitored by those strata of well-educated managers that a particular French tradition refers to as "cadre." In the "cadriste" and urban (r)evolution hinted at in this chapter, the capitalist imperialism expressed in the notion and the practice of general money is overturned. This practice of general money to be invested/divested anywhere at any time with any purpose is finally reined in, for instance by institutional investors representing popular majorities rallied into a decisive counterattack on the capitalist imperialism up till now pursued in their name. Indeed, such a (r)evolution would be very much in accordance with the Swedish model yet to be realized.

NOTES

1. This quote comes from an interview conducted by and reported in the book by Einarsson and Kallifatides (2017), which unfortunately is available only in Swedish.
2. The dissertation of Martin Holgersson (2018) contains a valuable survey of much literature regarding the relation between ordinary citizens in contemporary high-income societies and financial markets, including the reference to Burchell's (2003) intriguing work.
3. The French union supporter and philosopher Georges Sorel (1847–1922), an individual who was a political infidel, elaborated this insight that social myths (such as the one of a "Swedish model") may be of pivotal importance to the mobilization of collective action. The myth is not reality, nor is it deceit. It is a possible future grounded in the present.

12. The hope of discomfort: Using democratic citizenship education for transformative learning

Tali Padan

INTRODUCTION

The 21st century is increasingly being portrayed as a period of inter-regnum, a time when the old system no longer works, but there is no new one in sight (Bauman, 2012). Symptoms of the interregnum, which include continuing inequality and injustice, the process of globalization and migration, anti-democratic movements and concerns about civic and political engagement, have brought great uncertainty but have also been some of the major drivers for the renewed interest in democratic citizenship education around the world (Osler and Starkey, 2006). Democratic citizenship education (DCE) is defined as 'the preparation of young people to become knowledgeable, active and engaged citizens within their democracy' (Naval et al., 2002, p. 109). Such thoughtful and responsible democratic citizens, according to Crick (2000), have the critical capacities to weigh evidence before acting and thereafter exert influence in the public sphere.

DCE is not a simple knowledge acquisition process. Reviews and inquir-ies into DCE indicate a broad conceptualization of the learning process, involving not only political literacy but social and moral responsibility as well as community involvement (Veldhuis, 1997; Council of Europe, 1998; Crick, 1998; European Commission, 1998). Individual responsibility and community involvement require a participatory experience, i.e. engaging students in elections and class parliaments (Naval et al., 2002), but they also present a potential tension between an individual's need and what each sees as the collective good. A key theme emerging out of DCE research has been the need to address the tension between supporting diversity and unity (Figueroa, 2000; McLaughlin, 2000; Banks, 2004; Hahn, 2005), in essence the tension between the unique individual and the common collective. I suggest that addressing this tension requires first exploring the discomfort behind it and using it to its fullest potential. For this, transformative learning theory offers a useful framework.

Developed by Mezirow (1975), transformative learning is a process triggered by an experience of discomfort, or what Mezirow calls the 'disorienting dilemma', which motivates individuals to critically reflect on their own assumptions (Mezirow, 1997) and therefore become more reflective, open and emotionally able to change (Mezirow, 2009). While some streams within DCE do emphasize these aspects (Apple and Beane, 1999; Pearl and Knight, 1999; Veugelers, 2007), they do not purposefully work with the discomfort that arises naturally from group dynamics in democratic processes.

This chapter proposes a DCE method in which a reflective inquiry into these group interactions, guided by a facilitator, motivates individuals to question and challenge their own assumptions, often an uncomfortable process of destabilizing the known. By doing so, individuals have the chance to become detached from their existing ideas, beliefs and judgements. Discomfort is therefore used as a way to encourage the transformative learning experience.

As in the classroom, society's current uncertainties in these times of interregnum present a hopeful opportunity. I argue that the opportunity is not to fix and replace the current system with another but to use this discomfort as our societal growing pain, perhaps towards a collective transformative learning experience.

DCE: A CALL FOR DISCOMFORT

It is generally not controversial to recommend that DCE be implemented in schools in places like the USA, Canada, Australia and Europe. The controversy, however, lies in *how* this type of education is implemented (Davies and Issitt, 2005). This is because there are varying types of perspectives leading to educational objectives that generally range from adaptation to personal emancipation to collective emancipation (Veugelers, 2007). This is somewhat aligned with the UK's Crick Report, from an advisory group that set out goals and ambitions for DCE in the UK, where these three dimensions are described as political literacy, social and moral responsibility and community involvement (Crick, 1998; QCA, 1998).

The first objective, adaptation or political literacy, requires the teaching of values and norms. In this type of cognitive engagement, the learner gains an interest in politics and a clear understanding of the principles of democracy (Whiteley, 2005). However, a variety of research studies have already demonstrated that DCE requires a process broader than just knowledge acquisition in order to make an impact on one's attitudes and actions (Council of Europe, 1998; Crick, 1998; European Commission, 1998). Personal emancipation, therefore, goes a step further than this type of cognitive learning and focuses on choice and individual responsibility, requiring a development of critical thinking skills and handling criticism (Veugelers, 2007) as well as a focus on moral and ethical behaviour (Osler and Starkey, 2006). The third dimension, collective emancipation, includes social awareness, cooperative learning and reflection (Veugelers and Zijlstra, 2004) through an engagement with the community.

These last two dimensions – personal and collective emancipation – are in fact the foundations for, as well as the causes of, the tensions in our democratic systems. Making a choice between these two aspects for the direction of DCE would in fact be missing the opportunity to highlight and work with this tension. It is precisely the conflict between the individual and the collective that brings up much division, often leading to an ideological battleground. Teachers are often not used to or trained to use this battleground as a source of learning. Research into a group of secondary school teachers in the UK found that teachers saw some of their students as having 'undesirable' attitudes but were not confident in their own abilities to positively address socially sensitive issues (Wilkins, 2003). This is common beyond the secondary school as well. DCE methods in all types of educational settings encourage challenging the learners and incorporating the affective dimension, including caring (Noddings, 2010), but they rarely directly address the affective dimension which includes discomfort, i.e. conflict, rejection, guilt, anger and shame. These are mostly regarded as emotions to avoid, reject or resolve.

This same attitude is mirrored in our societal discussion of the state of our democracies. Those ideologically different are the 'others', whom we avoid, reject, or attempt to fix. The discomfort that we feel in this ideological difference, however, could be the key ingredient to guide us towards a reflective and transformative inquiry into ourselves.

TRANSFORMATIVE LEARNING THEORY: BETZAVTA

As long ago as the early 20th century, Dewey ([1916] 1980) made the link between democracy and education through his emphasis on the lived experience. Education scholar Freire (1970) also believed that learning should be linked to the learners' experience. He saw transmission of knowledge as a 'banking' concept of education – depositing, receiving, filing and storing knowledge, as in a bank transaction. Freire's ideal educational process involved an emancipatory element, as learners would be liberated through the learning experience. Kolb (1984) also supported these ideas in distinguishing a learning not rooted in the cognitive acquisition of knowledge. His aim was not to replace cognitive and behavioural learning theories but to add experience as part of the holistic and integrative perspective on learning. The focus of his theory was on the process, rather than the outcome, of learning.

Building on this foundation, Mezirow (1975, 1991, 2003, 2009) developed a theory of transformative learning, in which Freire's (1970) idea of emancipatory education is carried out through a critical assessment of one's assumptions. Mezirow distinguishes 'emancipatory knowledge' as 'knowledge gained through critical self-reflection, as distinct from the knowledge gained from our technical interest in the objective world' (Mezirow, 1991, p. 87). Mezirow's transformative learning theory is defined by this critical self-reflection that transforms problematic frames of reference in order to make them more open and inclusive (Mezirow, 2003). What is unique about Mezirow's transformative learning theory is that its first step is a disorienting dilemma. It takes a disorienting dilemma to trigger a process of transformation that allows a person to make his or her own interpretation, rather than follow an authority (Mezirow, 1997), and to become aware of fixed assumptions so as to be more open and reflective (Mezirow, 2003). Mezirow describes the transformational process as one triggered by a difficult life event that launches one into a process of critical self-examination and self-reflection. Initially, Mezirow and other scholars wrote about unintended disorienting dilemmas, for example a loved one's suicide (Sands and Tennant, 2010) or the diagnosis of a chronic illness (Barclay-Goddard et al., 2012). But, as the theory developed, it also became a tool for educators to use in their classrooms. This meant that a disorienting dilemma could be a deliberate part of the learning experience, used to launch the process of critically examining one's assumptions and beliefs.

One such experiential learning method, developed in Israel in the late 1980s, is called Betzavta (Hebrew for 'togetherness'). Betzavta was developed by a group of educators, who started the Adam Institute, an organization founded against the background of increasing ethnocentrism and hostility towards democratic principles in Israeli society (Wolff-Jontofsohn, 2002). The 1985 murder of peace activist Emil Greenzweig, as well as several school reports which highlighted serious failures in the teaching of political education, especially in the areas of peace and democracy, prompted a few educators to start the Adam Institute, among them its director Uki Maroshek-Klarman. From its release in 1988, Betzavta emerged as a new concept for the Israeli political education system because of its experiential learning method as well as its focus on the subjects, rather than democracy as a system (Wolff-Jontofsohn, 2002).

Betzavta contains a series of activities that practise dealing with conflict by transforming it into a recognition of a dilemma, rather than an ideological battle, and from there finding new ways to move through the conflict together. Through different activities and games, the process in Betzavta highlights the competing tendencies at work in each of us, both for and against democratic principles, so that an external conflict can be understood as an internal dilemma. Participants are guided to see their own dilemma so that they can no longer externalize the wrong as an attribute of the 'other'. Through this, they are able to come out of the conflict in a way that acknowledges the equal right to freedom for all individuals and to solve the conflict in a way that works for as many people as possible.

USING DISCOMFORT IN BETZAVTA

The facilitator of the Betzavta method sees the group as a micro-society. Rather than bringing up examples or case studies from other contexts, the natural dynamics of the group present their own case study and allow the participants to be confronted by their own behaviours and beliefs. Anyone who has been through Betzavta training knows how intensive this approach can be. In fact, the facilitator often starts with a 'warning' about the upcoming process's inclusion of uncomfortable moments, which can bring up emotional states such as anger, boredom, frustration and even shame, guilt or fear. Resisting the onslaught of these emotions is also a part of the process, and this resistance can be expressed as judgement, division or conflict. However, warning participants at the beginning of the process only serves to sensitize them to the type of environment that they will be a part of. As Betzavta is an experiential method, the facilitator gently points out these forms of resistance throughout the process, so as to turn the reflection inwards and guide participants either to transform their rigid standpoint into a dilemma or to become aware of an emotion that they are resisting. For the past five years, I have been delivering Betzavta training and workshops to a variety of groups, diverse in age and culture. The process is best unfolded by giving a few examples from previous training courses.

Are You Free?

The activities in Betzavta often start with a blank page. A very simple introductory activity, for example, asks small groups to come up with a definition for freedom. They are given some time and then present their results in the larger group. Following this, there is a larger discussion about freedom, what it means for different people and what are its limitations. 'My freedom ends where another one's freedom begins' is a common expression heard during this round. The facilitator challenges participants to look more critically at this statement. Where does one's freedom end? If this is a subjective perspective, who decides this? Participants see the difficulty in organizing society using a term that has such different meanings for different people. Many experiential learning methods would stop here, as the participants have been sufficiently challenged and have come out of the conversation with more questions than answers. However, no disorientation or discomfort really occurred, as the participants could still hold the conversation at a distance from themselves. The facilitator therefore asks the following question: Are you free?

The Betzavta method includes a reflection process that uses three cards – red, yellow and green – on which participants put down their answers of 'no', 'maybe' or 'yes' to the facilitator's question. After hearing this question, there is often a pause. This is already an interesting learning moment, as the group has just spent an hour intricately exploring what freedom means. But when they are asked to reflect on their own freedom, some more time is needed to account for the shift between thinking and self-reflecting. Self-reflection requires an intimate look into one's own experience. This is already the functioning of Betzavta, to differentiate a theoretical reflection from one based on experience. The participants start to put down their cards, usually a mix of red, yellow and green, with some putting all three cards down. There is then another round of discussion, which noticeably has a more intimate feeling to it. Participants are now sharing from a place of experience.

The Betzavta method practices this shift into self-reflection with each activity, and it allows for a reflection on what comes up as this shift occurs. This addresses DCE's acknowledgement of the need for a more participatory and experiential process, rather than a purely cognitive one. This means that participants do not merely analyse concepts within democracy, such as freedom or equality, but they check whether in the present moment they are free or equal within the group. As a result, they connect with their own experiences and sharpen their self-reflective capacity.

Who Can Live on Our Island?

After working through a few activities on the fundamental principles of democracy, including freedom and equality, participants are given a chance to design a country of their own. Their task is to invent a country and come up with criteria of who has the right to vote and who has the right to be elected in their new country. Initially, it seems like an easy task – most of the participants wish to be open so they start off by allowing everyone to vote. However, without the interference of the facilitator, the group starts to find flaws with having no limitations, as they examine the ways it leaves room for corruption, misuse, and failure to protect equal rights. They therefore start to put restrictions, often including age but also extending to many different components, including experience, political knowledge, criminal background, residence status and so on. They then have to figure out how these criteria will be measured. For example, those who suggest political knowledge as a limitation need to figure out how to test this knowledge and who carries out this test.

The groups come back to the circle, and, as each group presents its result, other groups ask questions and bring up dilemmas. These can sometimes be emotional, if the participant is defending a certain group that is excluded. Recognizing the dilemma moves the conversation from a debate style of winning an argument to a place where both sides are recognized. It also allows a seeing of what lies behind certain perspectives. For example, someone could be offended about the choice to exclude the mentally disabled from voting, while another could see it as a way to protect people from being taken advantage of. Understanding these perspectives shifts the conflict into a dilemma and allows people to empathize with, rather than judge and critique, the other.

In another example from this same activity, I once had a group who created a country called Harmonia with values of peace, love and generosity. When the time came to reflect on the process, most of the participants put down a red card to mark they were not satisfied with the process. When asked about the red cards, it turned out that the process of coming up with Harmonia was not harmonious at all. In fact, it was mostly dictated by one member of the group who wished the country to look this way. Upon examination and reflection, the group realized that this country would never survive with these values, because individual behaviours would not align with the country's collective values. Thus the values would only be superficial labels, rather than lived experience. The discomfort in this activity took place on two levels: first, the experience of being in a group where one person is dominating the conversation (jokingly known in Betzavta as 'the good dictator'); and, second, the reactions that come as a result of this experience, namely judgement, frustration and conflict. What happens in the Betzavta process is that one becomes aware of these experiences and reactions. By not pointing out specific formulas or moral lessons, Betzavta allows each person to reach deeply into his or her own experience and simply observe what comes up. To present a 'right' way of being would not only be arbitrary based on each facilitator's moral reasoning but in fact block the participants from a deep examination into themselves. Often frustrating to the participants, Betzavta does not give easy answers but rather guides a process of self-reflection that puts each person in charge of his or her own learning process.

This addresses DCE's objective of social and moral responsibility but does not do so through the transfer of idealized democratic norms. It allows individuals to reflect on their own set of moral values and to see that even the most idealized moral disposition can create conflict. The learners experience that the block towards a functioning and peaceful society is not necessarily an effect of someone's wrong opinion or belief, but conflict can occur when someone is strongly attached to or identified with his or her beliefs. Rather than trying to convince or argue with the other, the person rather sees this conflict in him- or herself, and in the process the other is more likely to turn inwards as well. The individuals are then better equipped to deal with diversity and difference, targeting also DCE's third objective of community involvement.

If I Am Judging the Group, Then I'm Not Part of the Group

A central component of the Betzavta process deals with the group making a decision together. If there is a class decision that would traditionally be made by the teacher, this can be given as a Betzavta activity for the group. For example, in one nine-session elective course for bachelor students, I planned eight of the sessions and let the class decide what they would like to do in their last class. As it turns out, this was the most memorable yet frustrating activity that many students reflected on in their final assignment. Because the activity was given towards the end of the course, students already had been challenged about the existing dynamics, and many of them wanted to try out new and more inclusive ways of working together. In the effort to include the voices of the 25 students sitting in a circle, they found the decision-making process to be lengthy and awkward. Not everyone wanted to speak, and yet a few students wanted to make sure everyone was included, without forcing anyone to speak. A lot of assumptions were made, but not many of them were voiced. The process felt as though it dragged on until a decision was reached, which included all raised suggestions but with no plan about how these tasks would be carried out.

The students did not quite realize that this was an activity until I gave them the red, yellow and green reflection cards and asked them to reflect on the process. The more vocal students expressed their frustration that there was 'indifference' in the group. Others less vocal called it 'flexibility'.

Highlighting this difference enabled the different perspectives to be seen but also showed how judgement can cause division and conflict. This was further highlighted when one of the less vocal students expressed that she was frustrated by how long it took the group to make a decision. I asked her if she was part of the group, and she paused and said that she was. With that simple question, she realized and then later expressed that, by judging the group, she was putting herself outside of the group, and that relieved her of any responsibility to participate. This, in turn, was causing the judgement of 'indifference' by others, creating a rift built on assumptions and judgements.

Studies into DCE often call for active and engaged citizens (Crick, 1998; Naval et al., 2002; Banks, 2004), suggesting a one-way journey towards making the inactive active. The Betzavta method addresses this call, but without placing a higher value on the active. The facilitator equally challenges both the active and the passive participants, allowing them to see how they affect each other. This enabled the student in the example above to notice an unconscious habit of making a division between herself and the group. That realization in itself was already a turn towards a more responsible disposition, because she then saw herself as part of the group, therefore equally able to have a voice and an influence.

BETZAVTA'S LIMITATIONS

The job of a Betzavta facilitator is not to try to fix anything for the participants, convince or even present a different belief system, but merely to ask questions that guide participants into their own introspection. This, of course, does not always happen. For one reason or another, some people are not able or willing to reflect deeply upon themselves and might in fact put up even more resistance. The facilitator's job is to present the opportunity, when it is possible, and it is up to the participant to use it or not.

Additionally, it takes some practice and experience to facilitate using Betzavta. The facilitator must first have been a participant in Betzavta training, as well as have received further training to become a trainer. True to Betzavta's intensive focus on experience, a training manual is not sufficient to guarantee an effective facilitation. Betzavta requires being present and listening. Therefore, there is very little preparation that a facilitator can do, and it is often better not to come in with too many pre-existing ideas. Being 'fresh' to the process is helpful, and this is difficult for many traditional teachers.

As the group experiences moments of tension and discomfort, so does the facilitator. In fact, in some cases, the participants turn against the facilitator as the cause of their discomfort. The facilitator must, in a sense, be comfortable with the uncomfortable and allow for these projections to take place, while still guiding the participants towards dilemmas. The facilitator must be able to witness this projection and discomfort, without identifying with it, a process that takes time and practice.

CONCLUSION

The process of Betzavta as described above lends itself to many uncomfortable moments. This is because the facilitator is guiding the group through an untraditional learning process, different from cognitive learning, and into a reflection into each learner's own experience. Such a process of shifting the reflection inwards brings discomfort in the form of undesired emotions, especially when triggered by interactions with others. Fortunately, we know from Mezirow that transformative learning is initiated by a disorienting dilemma, which is usually unintentional. While the Betzavta process does not artificially produce a disorienting dilemma, the mere process of working with a group and reflecting on the process of working together inevitably brings up some friction. Betzavta does not shy away from this, and in fact the facilitator uses these tense moments to guide participants to dig deeper into what lies behind their discomfort.

Our societal interregnum contains much of the same discomfort on a macro-level. We tend to externalize what is going wrong with the state of the world by blaming it on someone or something. We then suggest ways of fixing what is wrong, and in doing so we generate hope for a better future. But we may be limiting our own experience if we avoid the discomfort too quickly and only focus on the journey back into the comfort zone.

In our rapidly changing and evolving world, the skill needed will not necessarily be a good strategy or more cognitive knowledge, but rather the skill of being able to deal with life as it comes – the good, the bad, the ugly, the uncertain – and being able to do this individually and collectively. In fact, the ones who can transform challenging experiences into learning experiences, as in the process of Betzavta, are the ones who will benefit the most. They will be able to define themselves less by their own beliefs and be more able to work constructively with others who are different. The upcoming turmoil, instead of being our greatest anxiety, can transform into our greatest learning experience. This is the hope of discomfort.

13. Technologies of the commune: A bridge over troubled water?

Daniel Ericsson

According to Michel Foucault (1988), 'Know thyself' is the fundamental knowledge principle in the modern world. Throughout history, human beings have tried to understand themselves by playing out different types of hermeneutical 'truth games' and adopting processes that are supposed to lead them to some sort of self-enlightenment and self-control. Confession, meditation and dream interpretation are examples of such 'truth games' or, as Foucault also calls them, 'technologies of the self': epistemological processes that 'permit individuals to effect by their own means or with the help of others a certain number of operations on their own bodies and souls, thoughts, conduct, and way of being, so as to transform themselves in order to attain a certain state of happiness, purity, wisdom, perfection, or immortality' (1988, p. 18).

Technologies of the self are intrinsically interwoven with a given society's basic conditions and dominant truth regime, and as such they vary by time and place. Over the centuries and over the continents, they have thus faded in and out, and blended into more or less coherent wholes with profound consequences for people's everyday lives – for better or worse. The technologies of the self that form – and are formed by – late global capitalism are in this regard no exception, and it could be argued that this regime thrives upon a very specific amalgam of Christian and Stoic technologies of the self, and that it is organized accordingly. On the one hand, it rests upon Christian obedience, the sacrifice of oneself by complete subordination; on the other hand, it presupposes Stoic *logoi*, the teaching of oneself by passively listening to the voice of the master, memorizing what is said, and 'converting the statements one hears into rules of conduct' (Foucault, 1988, p. 35); in addition, it stipulates Stoic *gymnasia*, the training of oneself by physical abstinence and privation in order to test the independency of the individual.

Without these technologies of the self, capitalism would be more or less devoid of its meaning. Without obedience and logoi, the top-down, mediated division between capitalists and workers as well as consumers

– between the ones controlling the means of production and appropriating surplus value, and the proletarians creating the surplus value, first in production and then in consumption – would (probably and hopefully) be wildly contested; without gymnasia, the capitalist universe of ever-increasing return on investments, interest rates, risks and calculus of net present values would (probably and hopefully) collapse. Training oneself to be able to postpone utility serves as the backbone of capitalism.

Rethinking capitalism thus equals rethinking capitalism's technologies of the self – a proposition that speaks in favour of exploring alternative epistemological truth games. If one is interested in moving beyond the present-day interregnum depicted by Bauman (2012) and believes that capitalism is part of the problem, then such alternative epistemological truth games might bring goodness and hope to an otherwise despairing stalemate. The purpose of this chapter, therefore, is to narrate an emancipatory epistemology that is neither self-centred nor directed towards self-discipline. Tentatively, I name this narrative 'technology of the commune'.

A PROTAGONIST WITH A UTOPIAN CAUSE?

My narrative starts with a protagonist with utopian connotations: the prosumer. Once upon a time Alvin Toffler (1980) coined the term in relation to what he believed to be the future of capitalist markets. On the one hand, he argued, demand for standardized products for the masses will decline; on the other hand, demand for mass customization will increase. To satisfy this latter new demand, the consumers will have to partake in the production processes, especially in regard to design of products and services, Toffler argued. Producers and consumers will have to be brought together into a new actor category, the prosumer; and production and consumption processes will consequently have to fuse into one, prosumption.

Two decades later, Richard Normann (2001) would elaborate upon similar ideas in his book *Reframing Business: When the Map Changes the Landscape*, as he addressed the new strategic business paradigm that he suggested is in the offing. According to Normann, industrialist production and mass consumption are successively being replaced by a new way of doing business in which prior systems of value creation are reconfigured. The actors leading this transformation of business landscapes are 'prime movers', actors characterized by a specific perspective on both customers and skills. Unlike manufacturing industrialists who seek to bring their goods cost-efficiently to markets made up of passive customers, and unlike service-oriented entrepreneurs who seek to establish, manage and nurture relationships with their customer base, prime movers act on the basis that their crucial skill is to create value together with the customer. For these actors value is neither something intrinsic to products nor a matter of customer need satisfaction; value is instead a joint co-creation, and can as such take many forms of (inter)subjective expression.

To establish opportunities for joint co-creation of value, Normann (2001) envisions that prime movers will reinterpret existing value creation systems and revaluate existing divisions of labour and coordination mechanisms. Existing bundles of activities are to be dissolved, or unbundled, and re-composed, or rebundled – and previously unseen organizational roles and rules will follow. In these processes, the prime mover mainly acts as systems integrator, while the customer takes the position of prosumer, that is, at the same time acts as both producer and consumer of value. Not for nothing, Normann's prime example is IKEA, which proffers the customer the opportunity to perform value-laden activities s/he otherwise would not have been able to do (i.e. warehousing, transportation and assembling of furniture).

As Normann (2001) depicts it, the unbundleability and rebundleability of activities are driven by three interrelated forces: 1) on the one hand, the actor's creative imagination and, on the other hand, technological innovations that make it possible to 2) separate information from physical artefacts, a force Normann identifies as dematerialization, and 3) spread information easily across space and time, a force Normann acknowledges as liquification. Taken together, these forces interact with each other to open up a range of organizational opportunities with regard to time (when things can be done), place (where things can be done), actor (who can do what) and context (with whom things can be done). Opportunities like these, Normann then argues, can result in an increased density of time, place, actors and contexts.

Since Normann wrote his book, ideas like his on prosumption and prosumers have mushroomed among scholars. The double issue of the *American Behavioral Scientist* (cf. Ritzer et al., 2012) on the subject is a clear expression of this interest, but it might just be the tip of the iceberg, since much of the research effort on prosumption/prosumers is implied in adjacent areas such as value co-creation (Prahalad and Ramaswamy, 2004), 'Wikinomics' (Tapscott and Williams, 2006) and productive consumption (Laughey, 2010).

For some researchers prosumption/prosumers are a reflection of profound changes in society such as the invention of digital technology and the increased importance of the so-called creative industries (Ritzer et al., 2012). The world as we know it has for these researchers simply entered 'the age of the prosumer' (cf. Ritzer et al., 2012; but also McLuhan and Nevitt, 1972; Toffler, 1980; Kotler, 1986). Yet for other commentators the prosumption/prosumer phenomenon is intrinsically intertwined with the capitalist regime, and as such even implied in the works of Karl Marx (cf. Ritzer et al., 2012). According to this latter perspective prosumers and prosumption are not particularly new social phenomena; rather, they are 'primordial' (Ritzer et al., 2012, p. 379), and as such they raise important questions as to how prosumption relates to democracy and capitalism. For instance, is prosumption to be understood as part of a capitalistic co-optation strategy to subsume consumers (Comor, 2010), or does it represent a new form of capitalism (Ritzer and Jurgenson, 2010)? At the heart of these debates are issues of relations between labour and capital as well as different views on copyright and ownership.

But what if 'the age of the prosumer' represents something completely different (cf. Ericsson, 2010b) – something that might already be sowing the seeds of capitalism's own destruction?

COMPOSING UTOPIA

Plot twist. If one were interested in investigating the future, where would one direct one's attention? To history, some would say. To imagination, others might proclaim. Study the music industry, the French economist Jacques Attali ([1977] 1985) argued, as he provided ample evidence that changes in the political economy of music portend greater changes in society and have done so throughout history in the sense that there is homology between different historical modes of music production and the way societies have been organized.

Chronologically, Attali ([1977] 1985) identifies three different prophetic homologies: *sacrificing*, as a mode of sacral music economy, foreboded pre-industrialism with increasing division of labour and specialization, market and hierarchy controls, and transitions from user value to exchange value; *representing*, as a mode of music production based upon symbolic representations by means of sheet music, preceded industrial capitalism with proprietary rights, markets and exchange values turning into stock values; and *repeating*, as a mode of mass production of music detaching it in time and space by means of records and broadcasting, anticipated global capitalism with its unwarranted claims on increasing return on investments, alienated workers and consumers.

Attali ([1977] 1985), however, also envisions a new political economy of music that he believes to be a precursor to an entirely new social order that negates previously dominating modes of production – and consumption. This new political economy he conceptualizes as *composing*, a musical landscape in which actors create their own instruments and create music together in ways that transcend well-established dichotomies between musicians and audiences, that is, between producers and consumers. And this is where my protagonist re-enters the narrative: If one were to have faith in Attali's historical exposé and vision, what current reconfigurations towards composing and prosumerism are taking place in the field of music? And to what extent are these reconfigurations paving the way for alternatives to capitalism's technologies of the self?

The field of music has since the 1980s and 1990s undergone substantial changes owing to digitalization and inventions such as the MP3 format, file sharing and other types of streaming technologies. On the one hand, the power of the former oligopolistic music production and distribution machinery (cf. Björkegren, 1996) has been offset by the new technologies. On the other hand, artists and audiences have been empowered to produce and consume music outside the prior given confines of the music industry. The changes have, however, not taken place without deep controversies; the debate on copyright infringements has at times been very harsh, with differing claims on immaterial copyrights and conflicting ideas on legitimate distribution of income flows (cf. Alderman, 2001; Lessig, 2004; Duchêne and Waelbroeck, 2006; Flint, 2009).

Many of the activities in the field are indeed still based on traditional notions of producers and consumers. The music industry is still alive and kicking, although the introduction of streaming services has turned previously dominating industry logics somewhat upside down. In the good old days the industry made its money on record sales; nowadays so-called 360 deals are more and more broadening the revenue basis, making the artists into touring merchandise machines (cf. Marshall, 2013). Some of the strategies employed in the field could, however, very well be understood as fruitful attempts to bridge the traditional producer–consumer chasm and thereby to ease the alienating troubles associated with the repeating mode of production (cf. Chaney, 2012; Choi and Burnes, 2013).

One such example is the American independent multi-media company Aquarian Nation, which, by the means of (among other things) new technology, has created a prosumer community in which music is produced, distributed and consumed in novel ways (cf. Ericsson, 2007, 2010a, 2010b). Much of the prosumption activity of Aquarian Nation revolves around the company's founder, singer–songwriter Francis Dunnery, and the 'house concerts' that he performs all over the world. By playing at home, in the living rooms of his fans, Dunnery blurs the binary distinction between producer–musician and consumer–audience. However, by also inscribing into the concept a non-binary division of labour and coordination, the house concerts seem to challenge the very basis of the binary distinction of capitalism. The host of a house concert finds him/herself drawn into the production process, on the one hand acting as (among many other things) concert organizer, marketer and arena provider and, on the other hand, acting according to designated responsibilities to create a special atmosphere on the evening of the event, whereas Francis Dunnery's (dis)-position as a consecrated musician/producer is considerably downplayed. Dunnery and the host, instead of upholding contradictory (dis) positions between them, are both part of the production process and, in a sense, also both part of the consumption process.

The involvement of the host does not, however, end at the threshold of the host's living room. The prosumer (dis)position of the host is even more accentuated after the concert, as the host is encouraged to write about his/ her experience of hosting a house concert. These texts are later published as testimonials on Dunnery's website. At times Dunnery here also presents short documentaries in which the hosts get to play the leading role (cf. Ericsson, 2010b).

This collaborative aspect is also highlighted every year in October, when all of the hosts are invited to Dunnery's home town of Egremont, Cumbria, to take part in a charity event. The event is staged by the non-profit organization the Charlie and Kathleen Dunnery Children's Fund, founded by Francis Dunnery, and involves social dinners, concerts, happenings, special guest performances and auctions of memorabilia. The event ends with a joint Sunday walk around one of the many lakes in the Lake District.

Initiatives such as these clearly give the hosts the opportunity to become something other than mere consumers of music. If one were to translate the way Aquarian Nation works with the hosts into traditional music industry logic, the hosts, for example, act as financiers, promoters, arena providers, ticket vendors, caterers and event makers. Of course, they might not actually be part of the artistic production, but their contributions in terms of joint composing of the house concerts may very well induce a similar experience and feeling. This is not the least made apparent in the testimonials the hosts are encouraged to post on Dunnery's webpage[1], and to which I now turn in order to chisel out an alternative epistemological truth game.

TESTIMONIALS ON PROSUMPTION

Some of the testimonials focus upon the musical abilities of Francis Dunnery in a humble and fan-like manner, and some of the voices raised seem to identify themselves with the 'traditional' (dis)position of a receiving consumer, a listener. In many of the testimonials, though, the experiences point in directions that imply that the value created is not solely a matter for the musician and artist, but a collective matter – and effort.

One such direction highlights the equal footing of the hosts and the artists. Dunnery is frequently referred to as a 'friend': someone who used to be an abstract artist has now turned into a concrete fellow being. 'He is so much like a part of the family that my youngest son assumed I had known him since my schooldays', and 'Francis reminds you of a friend you've known forever' are representative accounts of this (dis)position, as are these words from one of the hosts, who states that 'They say that you should never meet your idols because they never live up to your expectations, but this was certainly not the case on this occasion as Francis is a thoroughly nice guy and a great pleasure to be with.'

On the theme of equal footing are also those who take the artistic message into deeper consideration and experience some sort of unity of the artistic product and the process that they as hosts are part of: 'Through humour, story, and song, Francis shows us what we all already know deep down inside: we are all the same, we are one.' This experience of oneness echoes in several of the testimonials, specifically expressed in terms of 'together' and 'conversation'. Here are some of the voices:

I wanted to bring people together to share that experience – and for 90 minutes for all of us to be part of something more than our collective solitude.

As soon as he started playing the opening chords to 'Chocolate Heart' it was obvious we were all in the Jacuzzi together.

I'm honoured to play a part in this unique and awesome journey. We're all in this together.

I was not let down, the whole night was a perfect mix of strangers coming together with their own stories of the past and present; together with the excitement of an artist appearing right in front of our eyes and the most bizarre thing . . . in my conservatory!

The guitar playing was incredible, and we so enjoyed his 'conversation' with all of us. The music and camaraderie was really special – thanks soooo much for inviting him again and making all the arrangements for a superb evening!!

Another direction of experiences highlights the transformative character of the house concerts, on the one hand stressing Francis Dunnery's lyrics and the messages of a 'changing life' and, on the other hand, identifying the uniqueness of the house concerts. It seems not only as if several of the hosts have experienced the unity of the product and process, but also that the product and process bring profound changes to how music actually can be experienced. One of the hosts makes reference to Dunnery's 'American Life in the Summertime', a song which opens his *Fearless* album, in which Dunnery criticizes the record industry: 'The words that keep coming back to me through this whole process, the invitation, the evening, everything, are these, "A record company clone, NOT ME."' Another host writes that he suspects that '[O]ne reason Francis enjoys these house concerts so much is that in performing them he transcends the Musician label that he has identified with for his entire life. These are not concerts at all in the traditional sense. They are uniquely engaging lectures on the mechanics of life.' And yet a third host appreciates the house concerts as 'game changers':

> From someone who has hosted and/or attended more than one show, it's next to impossible to sum up the experience in one paragraph. As live music events go, these house concerts are a game changer. . . . [H]e levels us with a stark honesty that surreptitiously leads everyone in the room from a place of worldly distraction to a place of humility and warmth.

For some hosts the transformative character has a more physical dimension in which the house is refurnished into – and reconsidered as – a concert hall, while for others the very same transformation is experienced as having almost a metaphysical dimension. 'The lounge became a "shuttle" taking the occupants on a journey to "inner space",' writes a guest at one of the house concerts, whereas a soon-to-be host wants to be part of something that he experiences to be almost 'larger than life':

> I thought about it. Then I went to a house concert, and it was amazing. I sat in a room of (almost) complete strangers and felt more at ease – at home – inside myself and my own skin than I had in months. Okay, so you may be thinking Big deal. It's a concert – you don't KNOW other people at a concert. Pffft. But, you see, I was in someone's house! Imagine going to the home of someone you don't know, paying them $30 (roughly) for the privilege and then sitting on their furniture to hear a concert. Dude. Seriously. It's transformative. By the end of the night I knew I wanted to host a house concert myself. I wanted that . . . energy in my house. I wanted to bring people together to share that experience – and for 90 minutes for all of us to be part of something more than our collective solitude.

A third direction of hosts' experiences is directed towards the collaborative aspect of the event. The testimonials are full of hosts' descriptions of themselves as 'event planner', 'ticket vendor' and 'food provider', as well as concert hall owner, but there are also descriptions of face-to-face interactions out of the ordinary in which hosts, guests and artist work together in producing and consuming music. Here is an excerpt from one of the hosts who had 'a certain mission':

Francis chilled and chatted with all the house guests, but I had a certain mission which I needed to complete. My best friend, his name is Peter Jones, is blind. He lost both eyes following a very aggressive cancer attack at only 13 months old and is now a professional musician, he has been since just 14 years of age. Unscripted and unplanned, Pete played Francis a few bars from one of his own songs, I know how unusual this is for Francis to do but, again, what a fantastic man to encourage this . . . and encourage it he did!! They both then went on to duet to about 25 minutes of impromptu Genesis!! I can only glean from this that Francis was relaxed and felt happy enough amongst us to let this happen. We all felt like we'd known him for years, he shared his time, his life, his lows, and his friendship with us, and my house guests were totally blown away by these 'added bonus tracks'!!!

PROSUMERS AS SOMETHING ELSE?

The hosts' experiences of being on an equal footing, transformation and collaboration bring somewhat different imageries to the fore, if one, for instance, were to compare them to the traditional 'faces' of consumers that Gabriel and Lang (1995) drew attention to in their deconstruction of different discourses on (capitalistic) consumerism. Arguably, the hosts could be grasped as 'choosers', 'communicators' and 'identity-seekers', and perhaps also as 'rebels' and 'explorers', but it seems as if the hosts 'escape' being (entirely) subjected to the capitalist discourses on consumerism. They are simply experiencing and enacting themselves differently; they seem to position themselves in opposition to the dominant logic of the record industry (or in a wider perspective to the capitalist regime), and they seem to bridge the industry's chasm between producers and consumers from what could very well be conceptualized as a prosumer (dis)position. The prosuming hosts are clearly something other than the alienated consumer of music once envisioned by Theodor Adorno ([1936] 1989; see also Adorno and Horkheimer, [1944] 1997).

In the perspective of Normann's (2001) ideas on how a new strategic thinking breaks with traditional industry logics, the staging of the house concert seems to correspond rather well to the unbundling and rebundling of activities that enables new (dis)positions. And thus the hosts' (dis)position surely is contrary to the former taken-for-granted (dis)position of the record industry, where consumers were expected to stand passively at the end of the record plants' conveyor belts, receiving ready-made products – or to stand star-struck in a crowd listening to an artist perform on a distant stage.

Normann's (2001) idea of consumers as co-producers is, however, slightly at odds with the hosts' experiences of being on an equal footing with Francis Dunnery. On the one hand, the prefix 'co-' in Normann's concept gives the consumer an inferior (dis)position with respect to the producer, as if the consumer (still) is seen as some sort of appendix to the producer; on the other hand, the notion of the consumer as an appendix to the producer is not counterbalanced with a notion of the producers as co-consumers. The co-producer concept in Normann's framework thus seems to be biased towards a footing that is less equal than that experienced in the realm of Francis Dunnery's house concerts.

In other words, the house concerts seem to foster a different type of pro-sumer from that outlined by Normann (2001) – and by his many scholarly colleagues who have immersed themselves in the prosumer phenomenon. But is it really something else that is going on in the field of music, other than capitalist business as usual?

TOWARDS AN EMANCIPATORY TECHNOLOGY?

Let's take a look at the knowledge mediated by the prosumer type at the house concert, and the technologies used to foster that specific knowledge. How do they materialize in relation to the capitalist technologies of the self?

First of all, it seems as if there is little focus upon the self at the house concerts. Instead of getting to know yourself better, it seems as if you get to know 'the other' better – and at the same time get to be reminded of what you already know, that is, that 'we are all the same, we are one', as it was expressed in one of the testimonials. The truth game played out at the house concerts thus is not an individual one: in terms of both content and process, it seems to be a communal one. Instead of sacrificing oneself, the road to a higher state of mind is paved by the hosts' affirmation of social assent.

Second, the communal truth of oneness seems to thrive upon con-versations with strangers. That is, instead of looking inwards for self-enlightenment in accordance with many of capitalism's technologies of the self, the house concerts seem to encourage people to embrace each 'other' with open arms – and together investigate their common ground. This has, of course, epistemological bearings: instead of striving to fixate their understanding of themselves and locate it in an essential self by means of monologues, the hosts are engaged in trying to understand their collective existence and its many transformations by means of dialogues. In this regard, the house concerts allow room for neither Stoics striving for independency nor Stoics passively taking in their master's voice as the truth, the whole truth and nothing but the truth.

Third, being open to others and the transformative character of life, the communal truth game has little to do with self-control and self-discipline. Rather than taking control of oneself, it seems to be about giving up control in relation to the world, and seizing life's 'unscripted and unplanned' moments, as one of the hosts phrased it. The fundamental principle at work at the house concerts seems to be a kind of disciplined disobedience in comparison with the Christian self-subordination.

In conclusion, the sense moral of my narrative is this: the field of music is currently being reconfigured (cf. Chaney, 2012; Choi and Burnes, 2013). The alienating dichotomy between producers and consumers is being rescinded, and new prosumer (dis)positions are being installed. These (dis)-positions rest upon knowledge principles that either nullify capitalism's truth regime or turn it upside down. Technologies of the self are being replaced by technologies of the commune, technologies that free the prosumers from (at least some of) the yokes of capitalism.

If Jacques Attali ([1977] 1985) is right when he says that changes in the political economy of music forebode greater social changes, then technologies of the commune could very well be the future. I hope he is right.

CODA

Ironical twist. As I was preparing this chapter, it came to my attention that Francis Dunnery was updating his webpage. The first thing you now see when you visit it is the heading: 'Know thyself.' But that is another story . . .

NOTE

1.   The testimonials were posted on francisdunnery.com between 2007 and 2013.

14. "Dad, Do Not Cry": Imagination and creativity on their own terms in inclusive cities and communities

Agata Morgan

Creativity is a very interesting research topic across various disciplines, including organization and management studies. Comprehensive theories of organizational creativity were proposed by Amabile (1988, 1996), C.M. Ford (1996) and Woodman et al. (1993), discussing the creative process from the psychological point of view and observing it within social systems. As they all point out, creativity and innovation are interdependent and strongly affected by the social environment, and they are perceived as very important factors in the knowledge-based economy. Great effort is devoted to fostering them both, as in the "creative class" concept developed by Richard Florida (2002), where the creative class is seen as the new main force providing socioeconomic development of cities. This chapter also focuses on creativity but, in particular, on the creativity which increases social cohesion in cities and communities and generates new and useful social ideas. After the initial fascination with the "creative class," urban researchers (including Florida himself) and local policy makers tried to address (yet again) the more complex and seemingly more difficult problem of *social inclusion*. Why is there a gap between creativity (or the "creative class" as defined by Florida) and social inclusion? Is it possible for the creativity to foster social inclusion in an organizational context? Starting with a closer critical look at Florida's concept, its effects in real cities, and criticism of it, I would like to discuss examples where imagination and creativity have contributed to developing more inclusive cities and communities, giving a voice to those who had been silent and excluded.

CRITIQUE OF FLORIDA'S CONCEPTS OF CREATIVITY AND THE "CREATIVE CLASS"

In 2002, Richard Florida claimed in his popular and best-selling book *The Rise of the Creative Class and How It's Transforming Work, Leisure, Community and Everyday Life* that creativity is the main factor fostering development of contemporary cities and communities. He stated that traditional economic factors such as access to natural resources or transportation routes, or even tax breaks, have ceased to be important factors for locating business; instead, companies have started to follow the people they need, people from the "creative class: people in design, education, arts, music and entertainment, whose economic function is to create new ideas, new technology and/or creative content" (Florida, 2002, p. 8). In his opinion creative people are attracted to places offering a bohemian life style, with chic coffee shops and a vibrant music scene, and they want to live in proximity to similar types, severing their ties with more traditional communities. Therefore he has advised local authorities to stop worrying about tax breaks for companies or building stadiums for the masses; instead, he has urged them to compete in providing the best living conditions for the "creative class" in their cities in order to attract the best companies and highly paid jobs. Florida's concept of 3T – namely technology, talent and tolerance (Florida, 2003, p. 10) – that he describes as playing a major role in the economic development of the city was very alluring for many researchers and city governors for almost two decades, and authorities in many cities such as Austin, Barcelona and Brisbane paid for his expertise and followed his advice. In the case of some cities ("superstar cities" according to Florida, 2017) such as New York, London, Hong Kong, Los Angeles, Paris and a few others, this strategy aiming at attracting a creative class proved to be to a certain extent successful, but the majority of people in these cities, as well as in other, more provincial towns and regions, were left excluded from the prosperity zone (Houston et al., 2008; Florida, 2017). Criticism of Florida's concept has been much wider, and includes questioning his definition of the creative class as different from human capital (Glaeser, 2004), and calling it too broad in its scope (Markusen, 2006); also criticized has been Florida's blindness to race issues (although this is combined with the promotion of tolerance for gays and other minorities (Reddick et al., 2014)), his promotion of place marketing and consumption (Peck, 2005), which are causes of gentrification, and probably the most troubling implication of Florida's concept, which is the exclusion from prosperity of the majority of people. Florida has estimated that the "creative class," as he defines it, makes up about 30 percent of the US workforce (2002), which leaves out 70 percent of the working population. In addition, members of the "creative class" often are already the most advantaged group of people, having the highest level of education and the highest income, while the remaining 70 percent includes people working in the service sector (although many artists and actors work as waiters or have other low-paid jobs) and a shrinking group of blue-collar workers. His definition of creativity and the creative class was misleading, and his approach led to unwelcome results. In 2017 Florida published a new book on urban crisis, where he identified "five key dimensions of the New Urban Crisis." All five of them addressed problems with the gentrification of "superstar cities" populated by the "creative class" and with growing inequalities between these cities and regions populated by the majority of ordinary people. Florida recalls his childhood in a working-class family, while expressing his concern with the growing social and economic disparities between various groups of city inhabitants (Florida, 2017, p. xviii), but it was exactly the neoliberal urban policy previously advocated by him that has contributed to the gentrification processes in "superstar cities," driven out of town many average people working in the service sector, and in the end harmed those cities and their inhabitants. As Florida observed in 2017, "It's hard to sustain a functional urban economy when teachers, nurses, hospital workers, police officers, firefighters, and restaurant and service workers can no longer afford to live within reasonable commuting distance to their workplaces" (p. 6).

Some researchers tried earlier on to turn our attention to the logic of neoliberalism, including urban neoliberalism, which has inevitably led to a lack of social fairness and a narrowing of social opportunities. (For example, Law and Mooney (2009, p. 290), when discussing neoliberal urbanism in the deindustrialized city of Glasgow, refer to more general publications on liberalism by Harvey, Klein and Bourdieu.) Law and Mooney state that neoliberal urbanism as "a mystical entrepreneurial conception of the market threatens to turn local planning into a facilitator of inward capital investment rather than moderator for the public good" (2009, p. 289). When we have in mind the public good we are able to look beyond the constraints of present arrangements and think about different possibilities in the ongoing process of creating social contracts. Some solutions may be difficult to accept at first sight, but there is still some room for changes, negotiations and adjustments. As Martin Parker has noted, "ideas about 'markets', 'efficiency', 'productivity', 'profits' and so on must always be understood as contingent social agreements, not naturally occurring phenomena which are subject to timeless laws. Including the environment, equality and ethics into such forms of calculation does not pervert them, rather it clarifies their purpose" (2018, p. xi).

The attempt to perceive neoliberal ideas about the market and efficiency merely as "contingent social agreements" was observable in post-socialist countries in the 1990s in the behavior of workers and middle management. Elizabeth Dunn ([2004] 2017) conducted an in-depth study while working for 16 months for a privatized baby-food factory in Rzeszów, Poland in 1995–1997. She was investigating how neoliberal management practices sought to remake workers as individuals of varying qualities – and how workers resisted it. She reported various interesting strategies of resistance used during the process of privatization. Although they were not successful at the time, nevertheless they show other possibilities for organizing more ethical work relations. One of the adopted strategies is particularly striking – middle managers refused to consider the work efficiency of a particular person as the only factor in the evaluation process during redundancies. Instead, they tried to assess the family situation of each employee, taking into consideration sources of income of the other members of the worker's family and the worker's ability to face unemployment. They were not promoting a lack of work ethic but simply trying to perceive their workmates as part of a wider community, not only as a replaceable labor force, and took into consideration workers' responsibilities toward dependents. This may be described as an attempt to include ethical choices in the job evaluation process, while making sure that all members of the community are provided with some support. It may go against common convictions about job assessment, but, when we realize that we all want to live in prosperous communities without deep social disparities, our point of view may alter. Maybe we should start thinking differently about job efficiency and profit as the main factors in work organization. Drawing from this example it is possible to imagine more solidarity-based and worker-led social economies as well as more inclusive communities and cities, but there is a need to develop a new narrative, which isn't just about creative and innovative growth but about inclusion being a part of prosperity. This new narrative should address the majority of those who are less successful and who remain silent about the most pressing social issues, which are contested, suppressed or overwritten by other associations, especially when political actors seek quick legitimacy.

ARTS-BASED RESEARCH METHOD

There is a question about choosing the appropriate methods for identifying these important social issues in local communities, especially from the perspective of decision makers with well-paid jobs. A very interesting method is arts-based research, since "artists often see themselves explicitly as a public conscience and as responsible for using their talent in ways that critique power and inequality and advance community" (Markusen, 2006, p. 1937). Although those artists who address important social issues usually do not belong to the Floridian "creative class," especially in terms of income level and social acceptance, as Ann Markusen has observed they "remain a powerful source of articulated opposition to societal status quo and a major force for innovation" (2006, p. 1922).

In this chapter I present the work of the visual artist Łukasz Surowiec, mainly his street art, for two reasons. Firstly, I believe that art possesses a unique capacity to get to the core of our humanity, and visual art gets there more easily, flying above words and language and stimulating our interest in learning more about its message and its context. Secondly, it is interesting to observe how street art provokes very intense and direct contact with the local community, particularly when it addresses important local problems.

The arts-based research method is based on the conviction that our understanding of social reality is more complex than that provided by a scientific discourse. Furthermore:

> If understanding depends upon the forms that promote it and if these forms are diverse in character – that is, if they come in varieties – then it is reasonable to assume that there are different forms of representation. These forms of representation need not be discursive, although in our culture they probably would have a discursive character to them. Discursiveness, however, is not a required feature of the form. The presence of nondiscursive experience provides for an awareness that when artistically crafted enables us to grasp some aspects of the meaning of things. Nondiscursive theory is not an oxymoron as long as our conception of theory is expanded beyond the narrower confines of traditional scientific discourse. (Barone and Eisner, 2012, p. 156)

Perhaps the most important value of art is its ability to capture and exploit our attention, so I shall start with a picture (Photo 14.1), and its context in a discursive form will follow.

MURAL AS A COMMUNICATION TOOL

In 2015, during a wave of strikes of miners in Silesia, a coal-mining region in Poland, young artist Łukasz Surowiec painted in the regional capital city of Katowice a very interesting mural, entitled "Dad, Do Not Cry." It is actually an original child's drawing enlarged to the size of the back wall of a three-story communal building, located in the working-class neighborhood of Załęże, where many families of coal-miners used to live and are still living now. There is something very moving about this picture of crying miners and about the comforting words "Dad, do not cry" coming from a

Photo 14.1   Łukasz Surowiec, "Tato, nie płacz" [Dad, Do Not Cry]

small child, six-year-old Zosia. This picture is rebellious because it displays
something we like to hide within the walls of our homes – it is our despair
and fear about losing our job and not being able to provide for our family.
During our meeting Surowiec shared with me the story that inspired him
to make this picture. In 2015 he was invited to participate in the Street Art
Festival in Katowice. At the same time there was a wave of strikes in local
coal-mines, because on the basis of a decision by the national government
four coal-mines were to be closed within a year and 5000 miners were to be
made redundant (MIW, 2015). Surowiec thought that in the circumstances
it was important to make a visible sign in the public space which would
address the local problem of workers facing unemployment. A political activist named Marcelina Zawisza from the radical left-wing Partia
Razem paid him a visit and showed him photos from the ongoing miners'
strikes and some pictures made by children from a local kindergarten.
The children had been asked to express on paper their emotions related
to the strikes and their family situation. Surowiec perceived this idea of
their school teacher as "quite brave and radical." One of these drawings,
made by Zosia Tabiś-Hubka, immediately got his attention, and Surowiec
contacted her parents (her father worked for the Makoszowy coal-mine,

one of the four to be closed) to ask if he could use Zosia's picture. With their permission and Zosia's involvement, Surowiec enlarged the painting and put it on the wall of the red-brick communal house at 14 Kupca Street in Katowice. It shows three persons dressed in miners' uniforms with their typical hats (festive outfits) standing in front of a mine shaft and crying. As Zosia has explained in an interview, the person in the middle is her father, a miner, on the left is her grandfather, who also worked in a coal-mine, and the smallest person by the mine shaft is herself. She drew herself dressed in a miner's hat and in tears, like the other two, because she also did not want the mine to be closed (Sobczyk, 2015). In her naïve, childish way she reminds us that she is also part of the mining community, she identifies with the mining culture which is important for her family, and she wants us to take into consideration her feelings and her situation. Surowiec believes that Zosia's drawing draws our attention to the fact that she and her family are not only losing jobs but also losing their identity, that we failed as a society in organizing the process of social transition from mining identity to some other job identity. As he puts it, "the financial situation of a given mining company is more important than the social situation of the whole community" (Surowiec, 2018). When I asked Surowiec if he had had any hope of the picture changing anything in the miners' position, his answer was that all he wanted was to make the problem visible. In this particular artistic project he wanted to make an individual problem, the problem of an individual family, visible in the public space, by working with the scale, by enlarging a small paper drawing and putting it on the wall, on the street. He believes that art changes our awareness (Surowiec, 2018). And in fact he did make miners' unemployment visible; his mural was easily seen from all the trains passing between Katowice and Gliwice or Wrocław. He received very intense media coverage, both from the local and national papers and from television stations (bed, 2015; Sobczyk, 2015; *TVN24*, 2015). The mural drew many strong reactions, both enthusiastic and critical, across the country, as well as in Silesia itself. In August 2018 we could still read comments made by the online readers below the articles. As Łukasz Surowiec has noted himself, "I think this mural is simply genuine and powerful because it was not artificially made. It comes from people and it is for people. Actually, I was playing the role of an animator or a curator rather than an artist imposing his artistic view."

I went to see this mural right after my interview with Surowiec and found out that it was half-overpainted with a tag (Photo 14.2), making it impossible to decode the original message. As Jessica Allen explains, a tag is "a stylized name or signature done with various materials, such as a marker or an aerosol spray can, often freehand. . . . A person who tags is known as a writer or bomber" (Allen, 2013). I wanted to talk to people living in the

Source: Photo A. Morgan.

Photo 14.2   Tagged mural (August 3, 2018)

neighborhood about this painting and its tagging, since it was obviously a
time-consuming tagging, which couldn't have been done without attracting attention, but their reaction to inquiry was hostile. On the way to see
Surowiec's mural I saw many others painting on various Katowice streets,
also on the commission of the Street Art Festival, but the paintings had
been left in their original form (as I knew from electronic media). They
were not tagged. When I was trying to discover why this particular mural
had been tagged, I found online other tags made by the same graffiti artist

(or group?) using the nickname BIK CRU. As I observed, they did not usually tag other pictures on legal walls (a legal wall is a wall where one can paint with the permission of the owner). BIK CRU paints mostly on trains and illegal walls.[1] I came to the conclusion that BIK CRU did not like Surowiec's mural and that there was something upsetting for them in its message, since they had decided to cover it with such a large tag. As I learned from another street art artist, Iwona Zając, an artist who makes murals must be ready for discussion about her/his artistic vision, and must be ready for tagging if someone does not like it.

I have asked myself what might have been so upsetting in Surowiec's mural. Maybe in a masculine culture, based on the hard work of blue-collar workers, men who are traditionally the only breadwinners in the family, it is not acceptable to show weeping men, as Zosia and Łukasz did. However, this was not the case with Zosia's father, who proudly stood for a photo in front of his daughter's drawing (Photo 14.3).

It is difficult to say whether Surowiec's mural made any impact on decision makers, but I like to think it did, since the story has a happy ending (happy considering its circumstances). The four coal-mines were not closed immediately as planned; the process was extended for several years (with

Source: Photo: Dawid Chalimoniuk/Agencja Gazeta. Photo courtesy of Agencja Gazeta (retrieved from https://katowice.wyborcza.pl/katowice/51,35063,18180057.html?i=0).

Photo 14.3   Zosia and her father

the consent of the European Commission), and the miners were offered jobs in other coal-mines or provided with compensation in the event that they wanted to leave (JD, 2018). This story is very special, since through its lens we can observe social change in a local community that restores our hope in better, more inclusive cities and communities. In my opinion it serves as an example in which creativity is used for a greater good, for helping others and for giving a voice to those whose voices have been ignored. What makes Zosia's story so powerful is the fact that those voices were heard and heeded. I am not totally sure if it was due to Surowiec's artistic project, but I strongly believe that we (ordinary members of local communities as well as decision makers) should look more carefully at contemporary artistic projects showing in public spaces, especially at projects which are referred to as very controversial or even repulsive. We might find something that will shake our opinions and make us think more profoundly about seemingly familiar issues. Later in the chapter I present some more controversial artistic projects by Łukasz Surowiec, sharing my dilemmas and ambiguity during my first confrontation with them.

ART AS SOCIAL INTERVENTION

"Dad, Do Not Cry" was Surowiec's first mural but not his first artistic project to address pressing social problems. His other projects have dealt with the problems of homelessness and unemployment. All of them were radical and brave, but some of them, in my opinion, were difficult to accept, like his idea of paying with alcohol (Alccoin) for work performed by homeless people (in the project Black Diamonds, after he realized that many of these people had an alcohol addiction problem). During our interview I had to struggle to remain open-minded about his ideas, to try to refrain from making quick, self-righteous judgments, but I am not totally convinced. But who knows? As Surowiec said, describing another of his projects, "We were trying to focus our ideas around that which was possible, and everything is possible in art. Right? Art allows us to work on the margins, it allows us to transcend all obvious and certain things, including customs, status quo" (Surowiec, 2016).

Maybe we should try to follow his advice and have more faith in art. I found his other projects very interesting and some of them seemingly less controversial. In my opinion his idea of a "warm monument" called the "Statue of Social Relations' Victims" [*Pomnik Ofiar Relacji Społecznych*] (Photo 14.4), dedicated to homeless people, is particularly interesting and really important. He envisages an empty roller or several rollers, about two meters wide, connected to a municipal heating system. The statue would

Source: Visualization courtesy of the artist (retrieved from https://sztukapubliczna.pl/pl/
od-dziecka-chcialem-robic-rzeczy-wazne-lukasz-surowiec/czytaj/6).

Photo 14.4   Łukasz Surowiec, "Statue of Social Relations' Victims"

be "turned on" in cold weather, letting everybody in need warm themselves
up. The heating costs would be distributed among city inhabitants so "they
could share the warmth with those who are deprived of it." People who
were not able to find a warm place for the winter could meet there. This
monument is meant to be a form of representation for the homeless who
freeze to death during each winter as well as a lifesaving aid for those who
are alive (Surowiec, 2018).

When we look at this idea it seems to make perfect sense, and it seems
easy to implement, but in fact it is not, as Surowiec has found. He tried to
interest the city of Wrocław in this idea during their preparation to become
the European Capital of Culture 2016. To his surprise he learned that they
had already tried to implement a similar idea with the Tauron energy supply
company, but it had not worked out. They had placed "warm benches" in
the city, but "homeless people had slept there, so the city authorities had to
give up the idea." At this point Surowiec realized that his point of view was
so different from the point of view presented by the local administration
that it was impossible to find any common ground (Surowiec, 2018). When
we look from the organizational point of view at this opinion of the city

administration we quickly notice that we desperately need new narratives and that we have been brainwashed and stripped of compassion for other people. It is hard to accept the position that warm benches should be provided only as a pleasure for those who do not need them. Why don't we make a decision within our competencies with a view to "sensemaking," as Karl Weick describes it, with a view to making connections and of creating our surroundings ([1995] 2016, p. 46) for inclusive cities and communities? Some artists cannot understand this, nor can they accept it, so they try to redefine our reality with new ideas, as Surowiec describes:

> Public authorities have their ready-made prescriptions for the world around them but when I look at the world around me I see many homeless people in the winter, and a great number of unemployed protesting on the streets, so it is clear that these prescriptions are no good, that their solutions are not working out. Many times I have tried to confront public authorities, presenting them with my prototype solutions, and although I knew they were quite radical there is still room for discussion. In the case of homeless people, we (myself and the homeless) have written several letters suggesting they build an estate of cheap houses for them in the center of the city (not somewhere far away, behind the forest or beside the train tracks) to make this problem visible, to include in the community those who are excluded. The administration thanked us for our interest but they said they have their own solutions, which are more efficient as they believe. In my opinion it is hypocrisy in the structures we are part of, structures where there is no place for the weak. We pretend there is such a place but if there really is such a place for them, it is somewhere far away, outside of the society. Homeless people know it well, so they act in unacceptable ways in order to force us to put them there, into a "better place." They break windows in shops in order to go to prison for the winter. It is the only place we offer them. (Surowiec, 2018)

For me this is a very disturbing diagnosis of our society. Surowiec makes the radical statement that we (people in institutions and organizations) cannot hide behind laws and regulations, because they are merely social constructs, such as the regulation that an intoxicated person cannot stay in a shelter for the homeless, even during the coldest nights. Artists are aware of many hidden problems, and they are often brave enough to see the truth and to tell us what they see. It is possible to pass different laws and regulations, but the first step is to start thinking about the others, about the weak and silent members of our society. The next step is listening to them, without presumptions and judgments. We can imagine a better world, a world with compassion and hope. We can start talking and writing about it or even visualizing it, with a view that, "When we say that meanings materialize, we mean that sensemaking is, importantly, an issue of language, talk and communication. Situations, organizations and environments are talked into existence" (Weick et al., 2005, p. 409).

What kind of situations, organizations and environments shall we talk/write/draw into existence in order to have a more inclusive, more compassionate society? I do not know, but I am ready to learn along with many other people and from many other people, including artists, who see more. At the beginning of this chapter I mentioned a need for developing a new narrative, which isn't just about creativity and innovative growth, but about inclusion, being a part of prosperity in cities and communities. I believe there is no contradiction between creativity, innovation and social inclusion, but we should try to find an updated answer to the question: what is a good community? The fiasco of Florida's concept shows that the creation of a good community or good city requires more than providing the best living conditions for the "creative class" in order to attract the best companies and highly paid jobs. Such a policy leads strictly to gentrification. In order to live a good life we need a lot of different people, with various jobs and experiences. We need teachers and nurses and other caregivers living nearby. We need their ideas, compassion and involvement; we even need people facing serious problems such as unemployment and illness, because by helping them we – as a community – can maintain our humanity.

NOTE

1. See https://www.wykop.pl/wpis/27830213/o-co-chodzi-z-tym-bik-cru-w-katowice-to-jak as-orga/.

15. Street performances in hope for the future of the urban sphere: Human interaction, self-realization and emotive enactment

Marta Połeć

INTRODUCTION

Street performances may be perceived in many ways. Metaphorically, with regard to social roles in a specific context (Goffman, 2000), any social situation taking place in an urban public setting is a performance. More essentially, we can distinguish any human activity displaying an artistic intention as an unusual and exceptional act, which occurs in the public sphere for a shorter or longer time (Ratajczakowa, 2015). Here we should include such forms as street demonstrations (Tyszka, 1998), city festivals (Połeć, 2016) and varied occasional artistic events (Niżyńska, 2011). I believe that there might be a kind of activity that is even more basic, although still not apparent in common knowledge, which concerns street performance (Połeć, 2018a) perceived as cultural entrepreneurship (Ellmeier, 2003). This kind of activity is usually planned in advance and is carried out on a regular basis, although independently and unofficially rather than in an official, legalized way.

Street shows include various kinds of performance art, such as theatre, music, dance, new circus and plastic arts (Połeć, 2018a). Together they create a universal, rich phenomenon with established roots, although they are live and immediate. In particular, street performance has been subject to dynamic changes over the last few years (Połeć, 2017), especially when we consider the attempts by the stakeholders to benefit from the urban sphere (Klein, 2004). Currently, street performance as a human activity is commonly perceived in an ambiguous way. On one hand, it might be a form of self-development and presentation of outstanding talent to a larger audience (Połeć, 2018a). On the other hand, people may at the same time think of a performer as someone leading the life of a vagabond or even a beggar (Grygier, 2012). Thus, it poses a much more complex problem.

Among the interdisciplinary scientific publications, street performance is usually presented as a positive example in many aspects. According to Zuidervaart (2011), all art in public helps with the formation and renewal of a vital public sphere. What is more, in attracting spectators in the urban sphere (Doumpa and Broad, 2014), street shows make interacting with other people easier (Montgomery, 2015). More specifically, street performers carry out an untypical form of human activity with social meaning (Tupieka, cited in Libudzka, 2014), which especially deserves respect (Twomey, 2012). Not only does it demonstrate a unique lifestyle with social value, but it also shows the act of inspiring others by one's own decisions, hardiness and creativity. Although street shows stand out positively against the background of other urban issues such as gentrification, pollution, violence and anonymity (Klein, 2004), they are still unacknowledged, seen as marginal phenomena of low quality, disturbing the public sphere. In practice, these views are reflected in the regulations implemented locally.

People cherish hope because they believe that there is an external power that allows things to happen and, even if things go wrong, there is still goodwill at the core of the situation, even if it is not realized at the time (Meirav, 2009). During the time of my research I felt as though I gained a really positive attitude to life thanks to street performers and their work. I am convinced that my topic of research was worth devoting myself to, just because of its great human value. I am sure that the power of this activity reached not only myself, as a researcher, but other spectators and urban sphere attendees. Although the fortunes of the performers were variable and included difficulties and misadventures, I strongly admired their self-assertion and obstinacy.

I believe that the hope of street performers and the hope they awaken in other people can also be spread by considering and learning from their cases, analyzed through the perspective of human interaction, self-realization and emotional enactment. If you want to know what to do when you feel helpless, when there are new restrictions and when your circumstances are changing constantly and unpredictably, the careers of street performers may be something to consider.

METHODOLOGY

From 2014, during the four years of my project, I met hundreds of buskers putting on shows of various forms of art in the urban sphere of many Polish cities, mainly in Gdansk, Krakow, Lublin, Warsaw and Wroclaw.

I managed to form closer, more long-term relations with dozens of performers and to follow their fortunes attentively. The main ethnographic methods (Angrosino, 2015) I used during the fieldwork were participant observation, anthropological interview and field notes. I also strongly appreciated the significance of documenting the visual aspect of street performances by photographs and videos, and also the need to refer to other materials widely available in media discourse.

As an ethnographer, I feel as though I changed and developed during my research on street performances. Through experiencing and learning from my fieldwork, I distinguished four stages in my mental attitude to my work. At the beginning, I was strongly motivated, inspired and almost fascinated by this new area that I felt wanted to reveal itself to me. Then, after a few months, I unexpectedly felt some disappointment, which gradually grew. However, I became even more involved in my role of researcher, which was the next stage, as I was trying to do my best to separate my emotional condition from the duties which I was still carrying out. In the last stage, I finally found a mental state of reconcilement. At that stage I realized the wide range of impressions, imaginings and feelings present in my research. They appeared mainly in my thinking about the society I was investigating, but also in the constant contact with its participants.

These affects, to which as a researcher I also became subject, let me gain a sense of the emotional meaning of the performers' work. Furthermore, that was partly a cause of this progressive inconstancy, I believe. At first, I got to know the street performers mainly as the characters they themselves created. Next, I perceived them as real people. Finally, I managed to bring these two sides of their life together, although not always smoothly.

HUMAN INTERACTION

I believe street shows are strongly dedicated to human interaction, since this activity could not exist without the audience. For that reason we can look for hope in the coexistence of people in the urban sphere in many aspects. Because street shows are open to everyone, it enables the creation of an equal audience, diversified by age, gender, nationality and wealth. As it turns out, people have a tendency to interact with street performers more informally, as they do with someone already familiar, using an informal name or a nickname. Probably this kind of interaction, which still adheres to the unwritten rules of respect and politeness, may become a safe way of teaching soft skills and making contact in the public sphere. The street performers were keen to share their time with those who were especially interested in the performers' life and shows, mainly other buskers, journalists, social activists and so on. As a researcher, I mostly felt warmly invited to participate in their life too. Nevertheless, I often felt simply amazed to see what a personal and caring attitude was being presented by performers to people they had just met. Usually they were willing to devote more time not only to disabled and solitary people but especially to children, who could not afford any financial contribution and were not usually self-assured enough, as they tended to hesitate for a time instead of coming closer immediately.

While watching street shows, I could see many different interactions between performers and their spectators. I could observe their behavior and reactions, which were happening individually and spontaneously. Above all, during the show street performers share their own presence, talents, emotions and personality with their audience. However, I noticed a more complex role for their attendance in a public space, as people asked them for recommendations or to provide information concerning the urban sphere. Moreover, some of the audience were especially interested in the performers' activity, wishing to take pictures together, being curious about the details of this occupation and even willing to follow the performers on social networks.

An informal way of acting may also suggest a lack of social responsibility. Because of the character of certain shows and the possible unreasonable behavior of a single person, some performances may be risky both for the buskers and for the audience. That is why performers take care they have insurance in case of any accident. Although adults usually realize that some tricks may be dangerous, children have to be told during the show not to try them at home (Cassel, 2012). The majority of performances require the participation of a volunteer who will do some simple tasks in front of the audience, not really knowing what to expect. Then a sense of trust is essential if buskers are to be able to encourage volunteers to join them for a while. It is also the responsibility of a performer to take care of the space after the spectacle of a fire show or a bubble-blowing performance, till it is as clean and safe as it was before the show.

There are three important motivations in doing street shows: to benefit from them, to entertain people and to be admired. Any performer may easily lose it all by endangering people because of bad show organization. Obviously, no busker wants to risk anyone's health, to get into trouble or to spoil his or her image. Thus I believe that street shows provide a good example of interacting with usually unknown people, getting together in a way that is full of respect and sympathy. It definitely inspires one with hope to think of a specific informal activity in the public sphere where people themselves care about the unwritten rules. What is more, they appreciate these rules as ones which help to create a space for common friendliness and trust. Although I was on occasion witness to aggressive, rude behavior during the street show, mostly the person creating the disturbance was not a performer. Additionally, the audience reacted immediately to demonstrate their support for the artist.

In my fieldwork I observed that street performers were focused on interacting not only with the spectators but also with one another. Usually they were interested in performative street art events happening in their area. They were trying to familiarize themselves with other performers. They also had their favorites and watched their shows from time to time. What is more, they appreciated the sense of togetherness, understood as a specific kind of informal community linking them. They could form closer relations to provide constant mental support in their artistic development. This sense, above all, enabled them to share thoughts and ideas for the improvement of their everyday reality. Since formally street performance is not perceived as a business activity (Judgment, 1994), it is not obligatory for buskers to set up their own private business undertaking. Therefore, for example, they cannot count the activity towards social benefit in the event of illness. However, quite frequently in such cases they would receive help from performers they were friends with. As can be seen, buskers perceive themselves in a way as a self-regulating community rather than a competitive environment.

The mentioned examples of human interactions during street shows bring hope to believe in informal, independent initiatives in the urban sphere. The shows are created to bring together and entertain people, while at the same time they provide conditions of safety and support in friendly interactions with others.

SELF-REALIZATION

Street performance perceived as artistic self-realization brings many points of hoping. First of all, buskers often put on street shows to improve their economic situation. According to the story of street violinist Władysław Tomczyk, he decided to start a private undertaking based on making music on the street. Thanks to the performances, and helped by his unprecedented possession of a cash register in order to give receipts for donations, he was able to go into retirement (Połeć, 2018a). He decided to continue his cultural activity in the urban sphere, which became an important part of his life and a way of inspiring other people.

However, there are also performers who do not want to live long-term like street performers, but prefer doing the shows mainly seasonally or just for a shorter time. After losing one's job and while searching for another one, street shows allow the possibility of gaining different experience and providing some financial support. Many well-known musicians have experience of street performance in their careers (Łobodziński, 2011). Moreover, buskers giving various kinds of performance became appreciated after participation in talent shows. Others, thanks to their success on the street, decided to develop their activity and even start private undertakings. As a consequence, these actions allowed them to gain recognition and easier access to formal cultural and artistic events (Połeć, 2018b).

Secondly, the decision to organize a street show may lead to a breakthrough in which the performers learn new things about themselves and about who they were before. While comparing the experience with earlier experiences, people may learn something new about themselves. Some performers first watched other shows and took part in them as volunteers, just to find out if it was exactly what they wanted to try on their own. For others, a street show creates an opportunity to work out a new role. While trying it, they practice with an audience and more easily develop emergent technical skills in performing. Buskers rarely have an education in a specific field of art; however, they appreciate and enjoy the opportunity of developing their hobbies in the urban sphere.

Thirdly, street performance brings hope for personal development. One of the buskers I met described himself as a person who used to be shy and diffident. However, he was a fan of street shows and consequently followed some advanced performers. He managed to get to know them and to learn from them. After a few years he was an outgoing person, a successful street performer, a guest on many television programs and even the organizer of several significant events. Thanks to this, he not only achieved his personal aim of being a part of street performance reality, but also managed to popularize and change this reality appreciably.

What is more, I recognized certain managerial skills as essential in this kind of occupation. Informal street performers have to make most decisions on their own. These decisions might concern actions such as planning, organizing, communicating, advertising and achieving specified aims. They have to take responsibility for their actions, and also take responsibility for the audience, especially in the case of more dangerous forms of performance. To develop, they have to search for support, including in the formalities and legalities of their activity. Most of all they have to work on successful, informal cooperation with other people participating in the shared urban sphere.

In recent years several Polish cities have seen dynamic changes in matters of street performance regulations (Połeć, 2018b). The limitations put on the performative arts were diversified locally and as a result brought many problems. As it turned out, the cases concerned not only performances of low quality that were neither very interesting nor well prepared, but those that were outstanding. Among them were performances referring to intangible cultural heritage, for example those concerning the characters of mimes presenting figures of the devil and death, which not only are typical of Slavic culture in general but especially concern an aspect that is important in regional custom – the Nativity scene. Moreover, buskers performing redundant professions, such as organ-grinder, have met barriers to appreciating the value and validity of their artistic work (Połeć, 2018b). Owing to the strict regulations, even recognizable performers could not afford to perform on the street spontaneously, while satisfying the formalities turned out to be obligatory and carefully controlled (Połeć, 2017). In one city, at first the local limitations offended street performers, as they implied the street performers were beggars. Nonetheless, later street performing and begging were formally separated. The cases mentioned above relate to more controversial situations of what happened to buskers as a result of performances becoming subject to regulations. What is important is that these limitations could arise as a result of various minor conflicts in the urban sphere based on public order offences.

Finally, some kinds of performance may be closely related to the specifics of a region and its folklore, as in the case of a pirate character in Gdansk (Połeć, 2018b). In the beginning, the character was performed by Andrzej Sulewski informally, but later he became an official city representative. After his death, the local government organized a competition, won by Krzysztof Kucharski, a person strongly devoted to various historical initiatives in Gdansk. However, there also appeared an informal successor to Andrzej Sulewski – Leszek Włodarczyk, who was his friend. Although at first Włodarczyk continued Sulewski's idea, while performing on the street on his own, he presented new thoughts, which later enabled him to attain his own unique character. Moreover, the aim of organizing a competition by the local government was not only to remind people of Sulewski's character, but also to cope with the appearance of an aggressive pirate called Czerwony Korsarz who was spoiling the image of this character.

The sense of hope in the examples mentioned above shows that people and authorities are aware of the impact of outstanding street performers on the urban sphere. The act of appreciating artistic grassroots initiatives may lead to enhancement of cultural identity and the image of place. Because street shows refer to social and cultural aspects, performers can additionally provide information for tourists about history and local interesting facts. Moreover, the possibility of economic status improvement and development of artistic, technical and organizational skills while performing on the street helps newcomers in planning their careers. Although the idea of implementing regulations for street performers seems to be reasonable, the previous effects of regulation implementation raise questions about their effectiveness and final purpose. Going back to hope, the conviction of performers, that their misunderstandings should and can be clarified informally, shows that people who are strangers can manage their theoretically conflictual plans while still getting on well together.

EMOTIVE ENACTMENT

Although the participation of a spectator in a street show usually happens accidentally and briefly, it may be a huge emotive experience. Indeed, a street show has the potential to bring hope in its ways of showing emotions and dealing with them. Thus, this occupation might be perceived as emotional labor (Hochschild, 2003), where the emotions are being managed to be sold as labor. It is a kind of work usually undertaken by women and generally belonging to the private sphere (Folbre, 2003). There are many complex problems related to this kind of work, such as issues of defining, legalizing and rewarding it. Although emotional labor is time-consuming and requires personal involvement, there is still a tendency to underrate it. That is why many jobs may seem to be related to emotional labor, and that may include street performances in the context of the experience economy concept (Pine and Gilmore, 1999).

During the show, street performers use their talents and skills to awake in people definite emotions and reactions, which let them play their episodic but meaningful roles. Performers also refer to feelings while presenting various stories, creating moods and communicating messages. Their work may consist of many stages of preparation, which mostly can be done single-handedly. However, they seldom are done this way in practice, since street performers appreciate the opportunity to build communities, share ideas and give support. These stages, such as creation of a theoretical idea, technical preparation, legal matters, procurement, logistics and promotion, require an entirely different form of communication and behavior than that of the street show itself. At that stage, buskers can show their artistic images, composed of nicknames, outfits, motions and manners, typical just of created characters. After all, the performance has to display a world different than the real one and to create situations which do not happen normally. Thanks to it, people may interact with performers in a different way than they usually do with anyone else.

Street performers have to make contact with strangers easily, engage their trust and sympathy, display understanding and develop an ability to foresee their reactions. Moreover, they have to create for their audience an atmosphere of safety and comfort, even if the show turns out to be surprising, including for themselves. When we are spectators, we may not really be sure if an accident was planned in advance by the performer or happened unintentionally. In spite of my rich experience in watching street shows, I have made such mistakes plenty of times. Once, I made the assumption that a man who proposed to his girlfriend during the show had secretly planned the moment with the performer earlier, but this assumption was wrong. Another time, I thought that people dancing in front of the guitarist were good friends, but later I realized they had met only a short while before. I often heard from the crowd the conviction that a volunteer was an associate of the artist, although this was not the case. A musician once stopped playing just to walk over to a woman he did not know to ask why she was crying while listening to his music. As performers highlight, the unforeseeable occurrences are essential elements of performances in the urban sphere. That is why performers have to accept them and to work out the best solutions, rather than working against them.

Since Hochschild (2003) diversifies emotional labor into an equal relation in the private sphere and an unequal relation in the public sphere, I believe street performances – though taking place in the public sphere – as emotional labor are much closer to private life. In the foregoing stories the hope comes from the truly engaged attitude of the performers. They are conscious of the emotive influence of their shows and naturally curious about the reception of the shows. Moreover, they leave a space for spectators to reveal their emotions, which further enriches the collective experience. While realizing the wide range of preparations for each street performance, which usually has to look as though it happens accidentally, we may feel hope for human creativity, vulnerability and good intentions for our feelings and needs.

OVERVIEW

Street shows provide many examples of hope in human life in the urban sphere, showing the positive ways local communities and societies benefit from them. First of all, street performances seen as human interaction present an activity which may teach us about human values such as support, trust, cooperation, kindness, creativity and one's own involvement. These values have an essential meaning not only in relations with other people but also generally in building the atmosphere of the public sphere, where, after all, we all spend time. Secondly, street performances perceived as artistic self-realization show traditional human activities that belong to an intangible cultural heritage. They present the right to live life independently of the economic mainstream and social life expectations.

Finally, street performances might be perceived as emotional enactment. Street shows are usually watched by people of different ages, but especially by children, for whom the performances may become important memories of their childhood. When they are adults, they can refer to these memories while thinking about the way to use and change the urban sphere. That is why, I believe, performative street art with its social, cultural and educational meaning has unrevealed potential to inspire good practices for human life.

What is worth highlighting is that there are certain aspects which might seem to be close to the issue of street performances (Połeć, 2018c) but which are nevertheless different, such as begging practices and children's work. Undeniably, they have an impact on urban life and also may lead to implementation of limitations for street performers. However, the definition of street performance should be clarified to strengthen its meaning. A street performance poses a universal, non-consumption way of spending time and plays a crucial role in the majority of urban festivals. Owing to the fact that street shows cannot compete with the commercial initiatives which overwhelm public space, they do not especially require any specific kind of support other than easier legal requirements and less strict regulations.

I am sure street performances are worth appreciating mainly because of their human facets, as they state a common, easily accessible and diversified phenomenon. Kostera believes that humanistic management has its philosophical roots in Kant (cited in Kostera, 2015, p. 9). This means that a person should never be considered the means to an end. A human being is an end in him- or herself. Street shows are created to entertain people and to interact with them. I believe that street performances bring hope for the future of the urban sphere, because the stories of the performers are inspiring and deserve respect and support. Through presentation of the wide range of this activity and its significance, it may become easier to perceive it more thoughtfully. If we could live in the same way as we behave during the street show, it would definitely be – as I profoundly hope – a more friendly, interactive, mindful and trustful life.

16. There is hope in organizing: Dialogic imagination against linearity

Michał Izak and Monika Kostera

INTRODUCTION

Subverting linearity is an activity at the heart of what organization theorist Heather Höpfl (2013) used to regard as the necessary, redeeming resistance against a morbid system, and for a desired future, beyond linearity. As such, it brings hope in a situation defined by its hopelessness. In this chapter *we propose to consider imagination to replace linear thinking as inspiration for the conceiving of new directions for organizing* in times when systems and discourses seem to run dry or come to an end. By doing so we are compelled to accept two consequences, which we feel are contingent upon this aim: that the nature of our proposal be categorical in a sense of rejecting the status quo (we do take a position); and that at times – specifically when an alternative to linearity is considered – the style of our discussion will need to render its subject, thus eschewing linearity in our writing.

To achieve our aim – conscious of the irony entailed by sequential discourse in this context – we will first state our understanding of linearity and imagination and its consequences for sociological reflection and consciousness. Then we explain what we mean by the metaphorical mode of organizing, a dialogically imaginative one. We conclude by offering some images from ethnographic research of organizations that admit imagination and bear hope for a non-linear future.

AGAINST LINEARITY

Following thinkers such as Zygmunt Bauman (2017a) and Wolfgang Streeck (2016), we see the current social world as ruled by a crumbling, morbid system. Old social institutions are failing and no new ones have yet emerged. This state in between ruling institutions has been labeled the interregnum by Zygmunt Bauman (2012), using Antonio Gramsci's metaphor. The morbidity and rigidity of the failing system are linked to framing by cleansing out of everything outside of the one dominant mode, limiting of complexity (Bøås and McNeill, 2003). The system poses as one to which, in Margaret Thatcher's famous dictum, "There is no alternative." In Heather Höpfl's (1994, 1995) terms, this is management by rhetorics: an activity that aims to order everything in a simple clearly defined thrust. Gibson Burrell (1997) speaks of linearity: a thin narrative line, devoid of depth or complexity, unambiguous, a desperate claim to understand and sort out the world. It is an optimistic and morbid activity, proposing to cleanse the world of all ambivalence and eradicate twists, hesitations and everything that is poetic and baroque. It brings objectivity and distance from the self. It promises Apollonian enlightenment, an end to depression and melancholia. But – "linearity kills," warns Burrell (1997, p. 50). Life is the enemy of linearity as linearity is the enemy of life. What lives cannot and will not be is linear. Conscious life is able to find redemption outside of the straight line. Everything that mocks it and defies it – melancholy, meandering, winding, complexity – can save our minds from dullness, and our organizations from the morbid and profitable path to death: environmental destruction, exploitation and spiritual austerity. "Flatlining" takes many shapes and forms, including termination of activity and subsequent physical decay in the case of the individual organism: the antithesis of life. Yet, in the organizational context, involving social exchange and embracing some sort of alterity enabling new understanding to emerge from meaningful social interaction, the "death by linearity" means denying both components: the newness of understanding and meaningfulness of interaction. We shall subsequently explore both and begin scoping a frame for discussion of alternatives. The existing body of work on imagination and dialogue, as well as the role of metaphor in both, will guide our inquiry.

IMAGINATION, METAPHOR AND DIALOGUE

"The *imagination* is not a state: it is the human existence itself," said visionary and poet William Blake (2008, p. 132) more than 200 years ago. Imagination makes us human and helps us to shape worlds around us which transcend the limitations of sheer biological determinism, by bringing together existing elements into something new, yet inexistent and unthought of and so always opening up spaces and possibilities to become. Imagination is an ability, as well as a process: a kind of creativity or, rather, the non-external space where creativity can take place. It involves both the mind and the feelings, body and soul, reflection and dream. With Gaston Bachelard (1969) we consider it "a major power of human nature" (p. xxx), which produces not just images, but multidirectional reverberations and very real, spatial consequences for human existence.

The use of imagination creates a radical breach from linear reality by showing its superficiality and putting it into a broader context. Charles Wright Mills ([1959] 2007) proposes imagination to be central to the human ability to transcend current limitations. His notion of sociological imagination is the ability to combine individual experiences with social structures, by making it possible to see connections between the singular and the social. Evan Willis (1993) listed four types of factors that influence sociological imagination: historical, cultural, structural and critical. They help the human being to make links between immediate personal issues and the bigger picture. Each adds another dimension to the situation, working together to reveal and support the multifariousness of social life. The derivative idea of organizational imagination (Kostera, 1996; Mir and Mir, 2002) is also a radical notion of contextualizing the individual and unique to achieving a bridge between reflection and practice and back to reflection again (Kostera, 1996); it is a state of mind enabling organizers, theorists and consultants to find ways of understanding and influencing organizational processes (Mir and Mir, 2002). Through imagination people are equipped to deal with complexity in organizational life, a way of thinking outside of the social structure while remaining conscious of its role (Morgan, [1993] 2002).

Imagination is, in itself, highly complex and ambivalent. Many organizations[1] claiming to support imagination are, in fact, only maintaining what Karl Weick (2005) calls "fancy," a superficial creative re-arranging of known objects in an often playful or decorative way. Imagination, by contrast, is unpredictable. Weick describes it as an ability based on concurrence, allowing ideas to grow exponentially, producing associations of simultaneity. In this process the profane encounters the sublime in the act of organizational carrying (of meaning) – the metaphor (Höpfl, 1994). A linear managerial approach can be subverted by what lies beyond the straightforward strategic thrust: images and sensations, metaphors that move us (Höpfl, 1995).

Such a mode of knowing marks a radical break with fragmented ordering, lying at the heart of linearity. It brings about the sense of being in relation to the Other through openness and imagination, and about the ability to embrace alterity, or "the spaces of unknowingness and betweenness where new possibilities, new questions, new ways of seeing, being and acting arise" (Cunliffe, 2018, p. 20). Getting to know oneself and at the same time letting new ideas and actions emerge result in the adoption of a dialogical attitude and strategy of engagement (Cunliffe, 2002). This has profound implications for organizing.

METAPHOR AND DIALOGIC IMAGINATION

Metaphor extends understanding, makes it richer and more profound. In the process of constructing (and selecting) a particular theoretical representation of a certain subject (Weick, 1989), where complex and often abstract phenomena are represented through "metaphorical images," metaphors in fact play a paramount role in sensemaking. The metaphorical language enables a creative and often novel correlation of two concepts (Cornelissen, 2006), forcing us to make semantic leaps to create an understanding (Coulson, 2001). In this view a metaphor becomes the vehicle through which imagination takes place, and it becomes a source for theoretical representation (Cornelissen, 2006).

This association of imagination with the (creative use of) metaphor is, we find, crucial for delving into the imagination's role in creating space for hope. Metaphors are restless creatures: they are all about movement (Höpfl, 2000). Metaphors offer the possibility of creating a new understanding, not by surpassing or obliterating the existing one but by enabling one to see an object or a phenomenon in a different "light," allowing for new connections to present themselves. Unfreezing the established semantic connections yet enrooting this process of re-imagining or re-theorizing within a certain context – tentatively stabilized by certain (e.g. aesthetic) wholes – makes metaphor a perfect vehicle for intersubjective exchange, facilitating a joint effort to communicate and thus, in some cases at least, to organize. Metaphor explodes the linear and invites communication. Crucially, the semantic ferment occasioned by such communicative organizing – at its inception at least, that is before the metaphor becomes sedimented in social imagination and thus "symbolized" – precludes *monologic violence* and enforces liberating *dialogue* (see for example Kociatkiewicz, 2000, for performative demonstration), to which we shall turn next.

In Mikhail Bakhtin's essay on *dialogic imagination*, the "preconditioned" attitude towards language in which "word" has a particular and normalized meaning, ignores its semantic and expressive layers (Bakhtin, 1981, p. 279), which "in the actual life of speech" are always active (1981, p. 282). Certainly, the distinction between monologic and dialogic discourses (Bakhtin, 1981) was never meant as purely linguistic: The process in which languages, jargons and so on are created is often intentional and always social: the exchanges ongoing between and within different social strata form "social heteroglossia" (Bakhtin, 1981, p. 285), thus becoming a precondition for the dialogue. The capacity and willingness of the speaker to slacken the web of meanings and expose him- or herself to different discourses, different languages, different meaning-making strategies – to "switch on" imagination – are what makes the communication dialogically meaningful.

A dialogic–monologic distinction is useful for distinguishing those types of communication which aim to simply relay some sort of truth deemed absolute, thus assuming an overlap between the speaker's understanding and the listener's interpretation (monologism), from those which make no such assumption: hence there is a space in the communication process for the new meaning to appear (dialogism). Consequently, those accounts are polarized in their assessment of divergence within the communication process. In monologic communication, lack of meaning overlap between the speaker and the listener is a flaw, and ensuing communication is deemed ineffective; in dialogism, on the other hand, such divergence is a basic precondition for the communication to be meaningful (Lotman, 1988). In communicational terms, therefore, immunizing the signal sent by the speaker against interference and transformation – ensuring that it is transparent and unequivocal – turns the communicational process into an "absolute harmony of similarities" (Brown, 2002, p. 6), which is inconceivable as long as communication is to be deemed meaningful (Serres, 1982).

This brings us back to non-linear modes of organizational sensemaking. If organizing can be seen as a vehicle for socially mediated understandings and as a reflection of societal processes, then questions such as how organizations intersubjectively construe their enacted realities, how those enactments circulate and thus what and how organizations – broadly speaking – "communicate" become crucial for understanding organizational processes and thus constitute valid aspects of organizational inquiry (Kuhn, 2012). These can recreate the current dominant order or break away from linearity (Burrell, 1997).

Non-linear organizing is relational and oriented towards the Other; it opens up the potential to engage with alterity, as Ann Cunliffe (2018) points out. It means that the Other becomes a compass for sensemaking and in the making of decisions. Dialogical organizations elevate intersubjectivity to strategic significance: social creation of organization is *an embodied and situated dialogue* (Cunliffe, 2002). The emerging structure is not linear but can be driven by the dialogic imagination in how it enables meaningful exchange. It holds a potential to question (and be responded to) without undermining or obliterating social construction. It is, by the same token, well suited for the management of complexity.

PICTURES FROM THE FIELD

The material we are referring to here was collected by one of us (Monika Kostera) during an ethnographic study (Van Maanen, 1988; Czarniawska, 2014) still in progress. It started in 2012 and focuses on alterative organizations (35 in all) based in Poland (16) and in the North of England (18), as well as one from Sri Lanka. The organizations provide sustenance to their employees and fulfill economic roles, but the organizers regard themselves as primarily oriented towards value-driven aims. The field includes a variety of organizational and ownership types: informal, social, cooperative and privately run. They represent a wide range of types and activities, from adult education to independent journal to restaurant.

The methods used in the study include the wide ethnographic variety, such as interviews (both formal and informal – with more formal interviews during the first five years and then more informal ones – and collective and individual), observation (participant, non-participant and direct), and shadowing, as well as text analysis (Kostera, 2007). To date, 110 formal transcribed interviews have been carried out, a large number of informal interviews, and 131 longer and 50 shorter observations. However, we present the material in a narrative form, focusing on telling an illustrative tale, rather than just quoting and ordering formal interviews or transcripts.

Imagination is valued and explicitly used in all the organizations, in some more emphatically than others. It is used to envisage and plan new activities. For example, Weronika,[2] one of the key organizers of Folk Village, an ecological tourism and crafts project, talks about the active use of imagination as the key way in which she looks for ideas about how to develop the organization. One of Folk Village's recent and most successful projects, a "living museum," where guests can take part in the (re)creation of a cultural tradition, materialized as the result of a dream that Weronika had and then continued to imagine into a plan together with her co-organizer Andrzej:

> I dreamed up the whole thing, the place, the museum building. I had wanted to [create a folk museum] for a long time. . . . [In a dream vision] I saw the cottage, beautiful and oblong, with light blue windows. In front of the cottage there was a white dog sleeping. And not even one month later, there was the dog. A friend brought me a dog from a shelter, big and white, just like in the dream. Okay, I say, the dog is here, so the museum will happen too. (Weronika, Folk Village)

Some organizers talk unabashedly about dreaming and inspiration, and others are more down to earth about how imagination is used. For example, Aurelia, one of the founders of the vegan restaurant Eat Well in central Warsaw, likes to narrate the story of how the restaurant was imagined into being by herself and her partner, both as a vision and desire and as a series of quite practical events, such as the organization of parties for friends and family:

> So we also wanted to make it a way of life. So we created a business, but this business never has been our real aim. The aim was promoting vegetarianism, and it began when we ourselves became vegetarians, started to cook vegetarian meals, to invite friends to common dinners. Feasts. (Aurelia, Eat Well)

She likes to imagine different new dishes and she particularly enjoys fantasizing about pastry and cakes. Sometimes an idea for a new cake can come to her when she is sleeping. Then she gets up and makes a note about it, which she later develops into a recipe.

This mode of interweaving more or less bold acts of imagination, experimentation and practical problem solving is typical for most if not all of the studied organizations. Whenever a challenge or a problem presents itself, the organizers turn first to imagination for ideas about how it can be dealt with or solved, sometimes individually but always eventually through discussing it collectively. For example, Ania from EduGames, an organization offering education for adults in the form of face-to-face games, explains that the organizers always look for inspiration to their inventive and imaginative minds, but as soon as something occurs to them they meet and talk about it, until it takes concrete form. It also happens sometimes that new ideas emerge directly from group conversations. The people in the team know how to inspire each other and try to be respectful and not to kill the "spirit of inventiveness." This collective active imagination within the organization is one very common way to use imagination together with others. Another one, occurring more often in some of the organizations, involves people from outside, such as clients or neighbors, in imaginative processes. For example, Marlena, founder of the Little Green Croc kindergarten, considers the children and their parents to be important partners in imaginative processes. When the adults play with the children, they use not just "real" toys but other items that the children want to use in their games, such as old kitchen utensils, stones or everyday objects.

The members of a collective of squatters, Radical House, invite neighbors and passers-by to join in their inventive activities just for the pleasure but also to develop and practice sociological imagination. For example, they organize sessions of collective sewing to which they invite neighbors, help each other to repair rather than throw things away, invent new uses for old clothes and learn from each other about different sewing techniques and methods. At the same time, they involve the others in thinking in terms of recycling, a no-waste culture and a setting where it is acceptable for men to enjoy sewing and crocheting.

There is also an everyday level of imaginative work. People refer to imagination and speak in respectful tones of something being imagined or dreamed up. "Imaginative" is almost exclusively used as a term of praise, never as a put-down. But so is "practical." In fact, these two qualities are often seen to go hand in hand. A child playing with an old spoon at Little Green Croc is seen as brilliant: both practical and imaginative. A sudden insight about how a vegan version of a traditional Polish bun can be prepared without losing any of its distinctive taste is regarded as a sound and down-to-earth revelation at Eat Well. New participants are encouraged to use their imagination not instead of procedures but in addition to them. All sincere and respectful ways of performing the role are good. A lack of ability to imagine is seen as a failure, something "brought in" from the outside corporate world. Those who seem to lack imagination are usually educated and more or less insistently supported to develop their imagination. Dave, an interviewee from a local independent magazine in the North of England, told me the story of Chris, who was a really good person but was unable to think imaginatively, expecting instead that things would somehow become organized in the way he was used to from the corporate world where he worked before. The organizers tried to educate him, but he would not – or could not – play along. Eventually, they proposed that he quit working with the organization, as his aims and ideas were not compatible with theirs. The Wave, a collective of artists and makers located in the North of England, shared with me the tale of Susan, who had been working with them for a longer time and shared their convictions and most of their ideals, but used her visions only to promote herself. She also liked to make public statements about the cooperative over which she did not consult with the others, using metaphors and images that she had invented herself and with which the others did not identify themselves. In this case it was they who did their best to play along. In the end she left to become a private entrepreneur, and the others breathed a sigh of relief.

The organizers also use their imagination to distinguish their organizations from what they view as the dominant order of the world outside, which we label the linear mode of organizing. On numerous occasions, both in interviews and in everyday conversations, they prolifically used metaphors, some well known from public discourses with organizations of the common good, and others more original and tailor made for their purposes. Many, especially the Polish ones, used the word "home" (*dom*) or "our place" (*u nas*), when referring to their organization, interchangeably with "office," "work" or "shop."

The artists from the Wave once, in a collective conversation, presented themselves as a rhizomatic organization, explaining that they, and other organizations like them, are as resilient and self-organized as weeds, often invisible on the surface of things and thus able to work in their own way outside of the (capitalist) system's control. Marianna from EduGames described it as an anarchist organization, where things happen effectively but without the need for hierarchy. Mariola from the Dragon Coop in southern Poland, selling produce from local farmers to the inhabitants of Kraków, called her organization a "cornucopia." What it does is the management of abundance.

The ethnographer also witnessed many instances when the neoliberal world outside was described in a strongly metaphorical way. In the vivid language of the artists from the Wave, "Neoliberalism is like waking in a flat full of things from Poundland" (Robert, the Wave). Daniel from a Polish organization described it as a compost heap: "Capitalism is a huge compost heap and we are sprouting on it, using whatever is healthy for us to use and recycling it" (Daniel, Good Cooperative). And, indeed, they occasionally take over actively some of the notions of the outside world and recycle them for their own purposes, somehow turning the metaphors they are based on and making them work in accordance with their own ideas. Quite boldly, Krzysiek from Arkadia used the word "profit" to mean "gain of goodness" and claimed that his organization is making profit measured in sociality and relationships. Bogna from Green Bazaar, which organizes an ecological marketplace for local farmers to sell their produce independently of corporate chains, proposed using the word "market" in its original sense – as a physical place where people meet to buy and sell (a revitalized metaphor?). An employee from the vegan restaurant used the word "marketing" in a new sense to convey what she saw as central for her organization: "Our marketing . . . is our goodness. We do good things" (Ania, Eat Well).

DISCUSSION

Rather than attempting to propose a framework, we wish to commence a discussion regarding how dialogic imagination – and the appreciation of metaphorical thinking as its much desired "by-product" – may inform emerging organizational forms, which by and large manage to eschew the most acute organizational ailments (as identified above): in a word we wish to explain why there may yet be hope in organizing.

To start with, we believe, the presented case material illustrates the spectrum of organizational dynamics unfolding when imagination is enabled to kick in: when the organizational processes unravel freely, emergent patterns are candidly scrutinized for cues and learned from. The seemingly or allegedly haphazard events and actor performances, including those – especially those – not fitting the preconceived picture, are inspected, yet not in order to sanitize and remove them but rather to take them on board and allow them to inform the never-final organizational form. Those looming shapes turn into meaningful "conclusions" regarding what an organization is or can become; likely, different conclusions can be reached in the future, as what is meaningful – or, in this case, what the organization is about – is never set in stone.

The second lesson to learn is that linear discourse does not allow for the social imagination to thrive: at best it allows for one preconceived personal pattern to exist, overshadowing and marginalizing others (the stories of Chris and Susan are cases in point). The dialogic attitude, on the other hand, understood well beyond mere verbal exchange, and including a more general proneness to remain open to being impressed, surprised, inspired and so on by the unexpected, enables organizations to develop and change despite no design being present. A series of meetings, parties, discussions and other events (as we saw in the accounts above), if approached as an opportunity for gathering new experiences and understanding other points of view, sometimes provide all the momentum needed to turn the loose set of people's egos, desires and motivations into an organization.

Another important aspect of such grass-roots emergence devoid of design or a stifling agenda is that, more often than not, a "big picture" is allowed tentatively to frame and impact an organization's existence, since the meetings between wider sets of convictions or ideologies (anti-systemic, anti-neoliberal) often drive the above-mentioned dialogical mechanism. The possibility of ideologizing such an organization following a "success-ful" takeover by one set of convictions – thus effectively turning it into a monologic organization – is real, yet mitigated by the inherently dynamic nature of such undertakings (with typically a high turnover of individuals) and by the fact that interests vested in them will not be exclusive ones for most of the actors involved (many of whom will be volunteers and/or people with a different "day job").

In this vein, yet more fundamentally perhaps, the social creation of such an organization (as we already mentioned) is an embodied and situated dialogue: a meaning of what the organization is emerges from a range of interactions and often, apparently, metaphorical negotiations as to what things mean and why. This opens up a range of possibilities to define and redefine the basic terms and notions holding the organization together, without precluding the possibility of reformulating them constantly and thus (re)finding what it is about. It is for instance allowed for the by-standing actors to be considered co-creators of the organization, for example children and their parents in the case of Little Green Croc, thus imaginatively opening the organization not only to internal but likewise to external dialogue – a dialogue made possible by enabling links to be made that are not merely non-obvious but likely not even yet existent or emergent, rather than limiting one's vision to a range of palpably "real" connections or patterns.

And therein lies our hope. It is hope not defined, as it sometimes is, as an "expectation and desire for a particular thing to happen" (*Oxford Living Dictionaries*, 2018), but, rather, as a desire motivated by the forlorn state of much of the organizational world as it is today and justified by, we find, a range of empirical examples, some of which we have discussed in this chapter, that *no particular thing needs to happen with any necessity*. We wish that no singular visions are fulfilled, that no utopian agendas devised for the benefit of some and demise of others are followed, and that no "best solutions" are ever universally applied. While such a wish is, of course, utopian in itself, it comes, we believe, a little bit closer to being partially fulfilled if a cue is taken from how the organizers in our ethnographic material enable dialogic imagination with regard to what they do and are about.

ORGANIZATIONAL IMAGINATION AS A SOURCE OF HOPE

By the rejection of linearity and obsessive ordering, dialogic imagination helps reclaim the desire for movement, transportation and hope. In terms proposed by the short review of concepts above, and in reference to the theme of this volume, such an angle warrants understanding of the "crumbling of social institutions" in terms of the "monologic mode," whereby communication becomes streamlined, with "noise" removed from it, thus rendering it a mere exchange of preconceived contents ongoing between agency-devoid social "actors." While such linearity "kills" (Burrell, 1997) organizing processes, it all too often still enables their empty shells to be confused with organizations as they were once construed. As recently proposed by Thompson, imagination has two mutually reinforcing aspects: firstly, it blends and unifies one's immediate sensory experiences with memories, thus enabling the perception of something as full of possibilities and emotional meaning; and, secondly, it extends into the conscious ability to perceive something not currently present (Thompson, 2018). On both counts it is therefore preconditioned by dialogic thinking, either because it enables us to see something in some productive way differently than presented, or because it enables us to see that which does not (as yet) present itself to us at all. If there is "hope" in this respect, then "organizing it" needs to embrace the dialogic approach: allow for diversity to flourish, for new meanings to emerge, and for the positive conceptual ferment ensured by imagination and use of metaphors in making sense of organizational realities, such as those presented in our empirical material, to be accepted.

NOTES

1. Understood here as systems, therefore equipped with agency (even if not with consciousness).
2. All names of protagonists and organizations have been changed to protect the field's identity and privacy.

17. Good labour: Affirmative work awareness and hope

Małgorzata Ćwikła

Inspiration comes of working every day. (Charles Baudelaire)

Work is a culturally rooted phenomenon, whose shape and form, which have been changing over the centuries, illustrate how humanity has evolved (Komlosy, 2018). Work can take various forms. It can be done out of necessity or genuine passion, take few or many hours of the day, and lead to loneliness or satisfy one's need to be around people. Regardless of its shape or form, work is a marriage of different characteristics: on the one hand, it is performed by almost everyone; on the other hand, a small proportion of working people are privileged at the expense of the rest.

'Work' is also a strongly symbolic keyword. People look for work, change it, pursue it. They often criticize it. When scrutinizing this issue, one can get an overwhelming impression that there are more examples of work unhappiness than work joy, and also that it is job dissatisfaction that has been documented by history and cultural texts in more detail. It is enough merely to look at the fate of various revolutions or the struggles of Dilbert. People tend to point out that their job is too laborious, poorly paid, or unpleasant, or that it robs them of their leisure time (Weeks, 2011; Frayne, 2015; Bregman, 2018). At the same time, one should not assume that work is associated only with negative factors. It often brings joy, generates social and cognitive value, and gives hope for the fulfilment of individual and shared dreams. As described in this chapter, the attempt to look at the positive side of work from a scientific perspective, without moralizing and advising, is therefore a reaction to the observed marginalization of this topic in both research and the social domain.

This chapter presents the perspective of a selected group of employees who were asked to describe only what is positive about their job. The aim of the chapter is to make researchers and practitioners interested in the affirmative approach to work that is based on a deep reflection upon what we consider good and hopeful in our professional careers. The concept of affirmation used at the stage of analysis refers to 'affirmative deconstruction', which stems from feminist reflection (Braidotti, 2005). In addition, the chapter indicates on which issues the current scientific debates on work are focused. They were used as a background to formulate the initial conclusion about how 'good work' is understood from the perspective of an individual in order to show the potential that lies in one's affirmative understanding of work. The attempt to move away from the trends fixated on the negative factors at work and on the fear of change and the unknown leads to the notion of hope, understood here as one of the tools used to design the future of work and to voice the individual needs and aspirations of employees.

CURRENT DISCUSSIONS ABOUT WORK AND ITS CONTEXT

Work appeared as a subject of reflection as early as antiquity. In the modern world, however, one can get the impression that what we have now is a complexity of issues and breakthroughs that shape the fate of individuals to a greater extent than was the case in the past. As part of modern societies, we feel lost, because we are short of reference points (Bauman, 2012), we devise fictitious social realities (Taylor, 2004), the pace of our lives has madly accelerated (Rosa, 2005), and the position of the individual in late capitalism is constantly evolving (Reckwitz, 2017). The chapter discusses some of the currently emerging topics associated with work, which are the background for the empirical analysis. As shown by the results, noticing the difference between the individual perspective and the problems affecting society in a broader sense is of great importance for the modern understanding of work. In comparison with the popular themes discussed in the literature on the subject, some research conclusions turned out to be surprising. I decided to highlight these discrepancies in order to illustrate both the ambivalent nature of the subject and the potential that lies in finding good and hope.

Inequalities, Exploitation, Blurred Boundaries, and Pointlessness

The issue of work is associated with the context of mature capitalism and the criticism thereof as a solution biased mainly in favour of the most wealthy people. The current point in history, which Bauman (2012) calls 'interregnum', is a period devoid of clear-cut indicators of the direction in which the world is going, which breeds feelings of uncertainty and readiness to accept solutions disadvantageous to employees. One of the forms of work abuse that we can observe is extended working hours, as well as making people available to employers round the clock by giving it the appearance of flexibility. In *Modern Times, Ancient Hours: Working Lives in the Twenty-First Century*, Basso (2003) claims that never before in history have we worked so hard as we work today, losing the sense of boundaries between work and private time. As noted by Frayne (2015) in the first pages of *The Refusal of Work*, 'the time has come to challenge the work-centred nature of modern society' (p. 5). Such an approach is by no means in praise of a laziness that negates the meaning of work. It derives from the desire to shed light on the paradoxes and abuses. For example, Dennis Nørmark and Anders Fogh Jensen describe in *Pseudoarbejde* (Pseudo-work) (2018) the immense number of superfluous and time-consuming activities performed at work, for example reading (and deleting) CC e-mails or attending meetings that do not lead to any conclusions. Another problematic phenomenon involves deliberate working for the sake of appearances, so as to receive a salary without performing any significant tasks. A great example is provided by Roland Paulsen (2014) in *Empty Labor*. In *Bullshit Jobs*, David Graeber (2018) took an even more literal approach to the issue of work nonsense and meaninglessness by categorically criticizing the existence of unnecessary professions and specializations. The main tendencies addressed in the literature mostly concern groups. There is often a lack of an individual perspective emphasized in the presented research. However, as was found, opinions of individuals may deviate from wide-ranging analyses.

A Good Organization

On the opposite pole from the tendencies described above, there is an emerging trend associated with a positive attitude to work and employees. The relationship between employees and their superiors should be based on mutual trust, empowerment, and respect. In recent years, the literature on management, by referring to the idea of a good organization, has stressed the narrative element and diversity. The former is associated with fantasy and relationships formed in the invisible layer of language which builds symbolic networks that bind the organization together. Attention is paid to inconspicuous discourses and narrations that shed a completely different light on the issue of the organizational good (Addleson, 2010). This approach moves away from performance orientation and striving to quickly achieve set goals. A different perspective on the matter of good is offered by Heather Höpfl (2003), who pays attention to the lack of balance in creating organizational identity. Her aspiration to embody organizational experiences as well as her referring to the (m)other figure was based on the need to embrace and understand otherness (Flory et al.,

2017). The concept of a good organization is associated with good labour, although it mainly concerns the relations shaped between working groups. Other important factors directly related to good labour as a valuable and satisfying phenomenon include motivation and meaning (Moch, 1980). As indicated by the famous MOW International Research Team studies from 1987, combining meaning with work, and thus determining the symbolic value of labour, is conditioned by a number of cultural and social factors. It is still a topical issue with a wide scope that allows for factoring in new elements, for example good and hope, as was done in the presented research.

The Future of Work

The issue of hope in the context of labour is connected with developing a vision of what is to come. Thus, the chapter refers to the recently popular subject of the future of work, and hence disappearing professions (Kaplan, 2015; Susskind and Susskind, 2015; M. Ford, 2016). It stems from the breakneck technological advancement as well as the streamlining of artificial intelligence. What is a particularly alarming vision is the possibility of full automatization (Srnicek and Williams, 2016) and programming machines in such a way that they are able to imitate emotions (Martíanez-Miranda and Aldea, 2005). However, it should be emphasized that the ongoing breakthrough as a result of which the machines are becoming more and more capable of taking over from humans resembles the once-feared Industrial Revolution (Makridakis, 2017). As we know today, even though some of the jobs disappeared as a result of the popularization of the steam engine or assembly lines, there were new professions that came on the scene, and the progress itself did not make human workers redundant. The tasks to be done are also changing now, and so is the working environment. The expansion of artificial intelligence in the context of the organizational world evokes justified uncertainty, which, however, does not necessarily have to lead to a paralysing fear but to creative adjustment and organizational flexibility. Owing to the research design and the selection of respondents, the issue of technological advancement was of secondary importance. It should be borne in mind, however, that there are sectors in which this issue plays a key role and, for example, can be combined with the issue of people's hopes of retaining their work or their ability to adapt to the new conditions co-created by machines.

RESEARCH DESIGN

In order to find an answer to the question of what employees believe is good about their work, the decision was made to conduct a qualitative study. Because the main question is very general and can lead to different associations, it was obvious that the study would only illustrate certain trends and identify issues that could be further researched in the future. At present, nearly 3.5 billion people from all over the world remain employed (World Bank, 2018). Each of them works in different conditions, being subjected to various forms of treatment in their organizations. A comprehensive analysis of what is good and brings hope at work would therefore have to take into account a myriad of factors. Since a research scope this broad was infeasible, the objective was to show the good at the micro scale, but still striving for a certain degree of diversity. The research proper was preceded by a pilot study. It lasted one month and involved short daily interviews with three employees about what good happened to them at work each day. The answers were used to formulate questions for the purpose of the study itself. The respondents were selected by means of purposive, convenience sampling based on the following criteria: university education, and age from 30 to 50. The research sample included people working: in Poland (25), Germany (3), Cambodia as part of a contract with a European organization (1), and the United States (1). One question during the interviews was of particular significance: 'When I leave home for work on Monday morning, I'm happy that . . .'. The task of the participants was to finish the sentence in any way they wanted, preferably in anecdotal form. The answers could be based on their own experiences or imagined. This resembles the method of the narrative collage (Kostera, 2006), although the perspective was complementary rather than leading in nature. Reference has been made also to the idea of 'anecdotal evidence', according to which organizations may be researched through humorous stories told by the employees (Jemielniak et al., 2018). The answers were analysed qualitatively. While compiling the material, I drew inspiration from discourse analysis and thematic analysis, which made it possible to identify certain patterns in the respondents' answers and to shed light on the elements left unsaid (Boyatzis, 1998; Rapley, 2007). The entire study focused on the positive elements perceived by the respondents in their work. Hence, this implied that such elements in fact existed. There was no one who refused to take part because they were convinced there was nothing good about their job.

WHAT IS GOOD ABOUT MY JOB?

When asked about what determines the presence of positive aspects in their jobs, the majority of respondents pointed to an interesting range of duties, which, however, does not bear any hallmarks of a common generalization. The next two most popular responses were the relations between employees and the way management treats employees. On the other hand, the significance of social responsibility and of successes was mentioned only by a few. Three people answered 'salary', and one participant stated that she was satisfied with all the categories (relations between employees, treatment of employees by management, social responsibility, an interesting range of duties, and numerous successes) except salary. At this point, it is necessary to stress the disparity between the responses given by the employees from Poland and Germany. The respondents from Germany mentioned 'salary' as one of the most vital factors much more frequently, while the Polish employees focused more on career development opportunities, which apparently compensate for lower income. Naturally, increased job satisfaction in well-educated high earners is not a rule. This also applies to the category of 'good', which the employees defined in their own individual way, for example as the possibility of eating together with their colleagues.

When considering the key study issues in more detail, the respondents were asked to provide five features of their job that they considered 'good' (see Table 17.1). The analysis of the entire material strove to spot any recurrent patterns illustrating several basic phenomena linking the five features. Once they had been identified, more general categories were developed.

From the discourse analysis perspective, it is worth paying attention to the order in which individual features are listed and to the elements left unsaid (Gee, 2004). The first associations, in most cases, concerned the possibility of pursuing one's own passions or self-development. This coincided with the previous answers regarding the actual range of work duties, changeability, and autonomy. Subsequently, the participants mentioned the relations formed within the team, appreciating the fact of synergy. The conclusions from the closed-ended part were also corroborated: few people spoke about financial satisfaction and relations with superiors. One curious and virtually unvoiced element was the relationship with the external environment. Only two answers were about the possibility of dealing with clients. In other cases, the world outside the organization was left unmentioned, and what the employees considered 'good' included mainly factors conditioning their self-development, i.e. performing interesting tasks and creative interactions with colleagues.

This observation has been confirmed by the analysis of the answers to a

Table 17.1   'Good' elements in organizations

Category	Interview samples
Interpersonal relations	'Friendly atmosphere', 'opportunity to meet interesting people', 'contact with a foreign language', 'shared Friday meals', 'professionalism of colleagues'.
Range of duties	'Changeability of tasks', 'uniqueness of projects', 'mobility', 'possibility of abandoning certain tasks for other (more interesting) tasks', 'continuous inspiration'.
Factors designed by the organization	'Flexible working hours', 'security', 'comfort', 'workplace equipment', 'frequent training'.
Personal attitude	'Purposefulness of what I do', 'personal development', 'social approval of being a nerd', 'possibility of helping others'.
Other	'Discipline', 'respect for others', 'no corporate dependencies', 'freedom of choosing the right tools for a task', 'daily meetings with the best students in the Galaxy'.

different question about the sense of 'a job well done'. Most participants focused their responses on their own satisfaction with having completed a project or met expectations. Therefore, the emphasis was on individual achievements. Furthermore, in the case of creative jobs, the respondents were satisfied with the positive feedback on for example a theatre play or a scientific paper. One person mentioned the fact of having their own work appreciated by subordinate employees, and the other one talked about the success of their subordinates. Most of them, however, focused on grand accomplishments. Interestingly, young employees had a sense of 'a job well done' much more frequently than their senior colleagues.

Taking into account the topicality of the question about the future of work, an attempt was made to establish which aspects of their job the research participants would never change. It was based on the assumption that these factors might show what gives employees hope in an uncertain future, at the same time making it possible to design their own visions of the world of tomorrow. Several trends can be identified based on the answers provided by the study participants. In their opinion, the most crucial factors include (from the most to the least important): flexibility in choosing tasks and defining the time and place of work; independence; scope of duties; and possibility of continuous development. One person gave the following answer: 'I would never choose anyone else to be my boss over my current one.' Someone else replied jokingly: 'I would never want to sit with my back to the door.' Once again, what can be readily noticed is the respondents' concentration on themselves and their own development, while aspects associated with team-playing or interaction with the environment are disregarded. Another deduction made from the analysis of this aspect of the study is connected with the glorification of flexibility and the opportunity to make independent decisions about when and where the work is done. The fact that these ambivalent privileges of late capitalism are the things the respondents found so hard to give up is indeed fascinating. As mentioned in the theoretical part of the chapter, flexible working hours have led many people to work 'round the clock' and blurred the line between work and private life (Crary, 2014). It is also worth emphasizing that in the opinion of Cooper (2014) the responsibility for shaping flexible working time rests equally on employees and employers.

'WHEN I LEAVE HOME FOR WORK ON MONDAY MORNING, I'M HAPPY THAT . . .'

The statement was deliberately formulated in such a way as to depart from the typical pattern of associating this day of the week with pessimism. The Monday blues is perpetuated by pop culture: since the late 1970s, the melancholy song 'I Don't Like Mondays' by the Boomtown Rats has enjoyed great popularity. The comic character Garfield also became known for his hostility towards Mondays. Hence, looking at Monday as the first day of interesting work was supposed to be something other than simply counting down time until Friday. The answers focused on the following phenomena:

- *Time*: Monday is considered the starting point of a new stage of work; it refers to planning, treating time as a resource, and taking an orderly approach to the time allocated for work and rest (e.g. 'It gives you at least five days (sometimes seven) to start or finish something important. Fridays are worse, because then the time is up' – Project Manager).
- *Interactions*: There were frequent answers saying that on Monday a given person would meet with co-workers, and that it would be possible to have dinner together or talk over coffee; such social aspects were emphasized much more often here than in the replies to the previous questions (e.g. 'I'm about to sip some good coffee and chat with the girls about the weekend and the upcoming business trip to Ireland. It's going to be a good week' – Academic Teacher).
- *Tasks*: A few people mentioned that they were happy about the challenges to come, that Monday is like the promise of change and new tasks; one person also said that they were going to learn something new again; and one person noted that they were excited about the

awaiting tasks, because they could 'get away from the hullabaloo' they had at home (Diversity Manager).

● *Freedom*: To a few respondents, it did not matter which day of the week it was, because their job allowed them to plan their own activities individually; similarly, certain organizations had a different work schedule, for instance a theatre employee answered that they would not ask themselves this question until Tuesday; once again, the flexibility factor was rated as positive.

In general, one can get the impression that the study participants were very happy about the fact that virtually each new week brought them the opportunity to do something interesting and was not merely an upsetting necessity to halt the weekend rest (provided the profession allowed it). The issue of hope has been reduced to the perspective of micro-development, which turned out to be the dominant element in this research.

SUMMARY

The analysis of the research gives answers to the question of what employees perceive as positive and where hope is placed in the context of labour. As shown, employees are willing to talk about the good aspects of their work, pointing to various factors, which can be considered as indicating key issues that should not be missing in the future dimension of work. At the same time, it should be noted that the research results mainly reveal self-development, which might mean that people's hope for job satisfaction is conditioned by their personal attitude and achieving their own goals. This particular outlook on work is, to a large extent, a continuation of the education process, during which people acquire new knowledge and skills. It guarantees the mobility of imagination and freedom, which was greatly valued by the respondents. Hope means the opportunity to fulfil one's plans.

When seeking an answer to the question of what good aspects the respondents see in their work, a division was made into several phenomena that grouped the majority of answers: interpersonal relations, the range of duties, factors designed by the organization, and personal attitude. As mentioned earlier, the 'good' was predominantly associated with the personal situation at work, particularly related to the substantive scope of the duties performed. Social factors, including interactions with colleagues, were recognized as 'good' less often. Finally, there was no mention of the external context of the organization, such as the issue of social responsibility. Most of the research participants did their job willingly, recognized its meaning, and were far from treating it as an unpleasant duty. On Monday morning, they enjoyed the opportunity to complete the tasks they had started, to pursue new challenges, or to meet colleagues. To them, their work had many good elements encoded in it, because it remained in alignment with their needs. The most salient conclusions can be summarized as follows:

1. Employees feel a great need to talk about the good factors at their work; even if their daily small talk focuses on the negative phenomena such as exploitation (as demonstrated by the pilot study), a more in-depth reflection helps shift the perspective and allow them to see the true purpose of their own work.
2. There is a noticeable gradual disappearance of orientation towards cooperation, and more emphasis is put on self-development.
3. The social, economic, and cultural contexts of the organization are less important than a specific task being performed at a given moment.
4. Employees appreciate the flexibility and the possibility of tailoring their work schedule to their individual needs; nevertheless, none of the research participants mentioned the associated trap of finding it difficult to separate work time from leisure time.

It is also worth emphasizing that the participants approached the interviews with tremendous openness and enthusiasm. This conclusion shows that this type of research is practical and can change employees' attitudes, thus positively influencing organizations by shedding light on the needs to be addressed. As for the question of whether there is hope for work, it seems justified to conclude that learning the opinions of employees might contribute to the creation of optimal work conditions, where nobody is just counting down until the weekend when they can finally get out of the office. This process, conditioned by the involvement of a management team interested in the well-being of employees, could be interpreted as an ongoing event, during which there is a shift in the way employees think about their work. As a result, it allows people not to lose hope in the meaning of work. It is facilitated, on the one hand, by employees' awareness of organizational phenomena that are oriented to change and subject to being shaped and, on the other hand, by the ability to pause in one's thoughts and critically reflect upon both the inconspicuous and the noticeable factors that make our work good. Such orientation resembles the postulate of 'affirmative deconstruction' (Braidotti, 2005, p. 173). Its premise is to move away from the standard way of thinking and from adopting certain patterns as a dogma, for example claiming that Monday is the worst day of the week. It seems that what is much more valuable to individual employees as well as to organizations is a different attitude that embraces new possibilities and gives hope for doing something meaningful. It is recognizing the meaning of their own work that motivates employees to perform tasks and combine work with hope, which deviates significantly from Graeber's (2018) conclusions. The affirmative awareness of one's actions is particularly important in the context of discussions about the future of work. However, the focus on the fates of individuals is surprising, as it is in opposition to the ongoing debates about the meaning of the collective dimension of work and the need to separate work from private life. Perhaps the 'good' of work lies in strong, self-confident employees who truly understand professional flexibility by being ready to perform tasks at different times of the day. This 'good' gives employees hope for self-development, humanity hope to remain superior to the ever-evolving technology, and managers hope to have all the tasks completed. Thus the question that arises from the research presented here is how to capitalize on the potential lying in the will to self-develop in order to solve the more general problems signalled in the theoretical part of the chapter, including fear, poverty, exploitation of labour, the blurred boundary between work and 'non-work', and automatization. In conclusion, hope in the context of labour lies in individual human needs determined by people's dreams. They can be the foundation for building a better tomorrow. Hope is a projection of the world in which we want to live. The affirmative view promoted in the chapter does not have to refer only to the world of labour, but it can shape a general attitude towards social phenomena. This stems from the tradition of critical thinking, which stipulates that big changes can begin on a micro scale. All one needs to do is answer a simple question: 'What good has happened to me today and what good might happen to me tomorrow?'

18. Actors of goodness and hope in action
Aneta Milczarczyk

INTRODUCTION

Hope is a drive that lies behind almost all actions that people perform. People need to have at least a slight amount of faith in the successful accomplishment of their efforts; otherwise no rational explanation can be offered for their acting. When they relate the results of their undertakings, they usually include something positive, believing that the achievement of what they have planned brings something good to them or others. It gives them fulfilment. Therefore hope for them, after Nuland (1995, p. 9), is 'the anticipation of a good that is yet to come'. People define the good that they want to create, establish tangible measures, plan the way to achieve it, and carry out the required action. They are led by hope throughout the whole process, because they have, as translated from Old English *hopa*, 'confidence in the future' (*Online Etymology Dictionary*, 2018).

There are people who do not agree with what they see and experience and who have enough strength and courage to do something about it. Such individuals are able to spot problems others may encounter and to come up with ideas of how to solve them. They are good people, as they want to make the world a better place and they actually do something about it. With hope that they are able to bring about positive social change, they try to respond to social and environmental needs and problems. Their beliefs are similar to those of the famous Polish singer Czesław Niemen, who sang: 'Strange is this world, where there is still so much evil. . . . But there are more people of goodwill and I strongly believe that this world will never die thanks to them.' Many want to be those people of goodwill who save the world. Therefore they surrender to the constant inward urge they feel and allow it to lead them toward the path of social action.

In this chapter I tell stories presenting such people, the actors of a social enterprise – the Southend Credit Union (SCU)[1] – who are idealists full of compassion for others and driven by hope that they might bring about positive change and encourage others to follow them.

UNIQUE INDIVIDUALS – THOSE WITH THE URGE TO ACT FOR OTHERS BECAUSE THEY CARE

There are a lot of social and environmental issues in the world that always need to be tackled. Governments are expected to respond to these needs and problems, but they often fail to do so for various reasons. Such incapacity makes people feel marginalized and powerless, and it kills their trust and hope that their governments can effectively handle matters that are important to them and others, if they can handle them at all (Courville and Piper, 2004). But this incapacity of governments also gives impetus to particular groups of people who both notice the problems and have enough motivation and strength to respond to them. People realize at some point of their lives that it is up to them to do something about things that concern them (Bornstein, 2004). Such people are often linked to the social economy sector,[2] as this sector principally aims to tackle social and environmental issues that have not been satisfactorily addressed or have been neglected.

A social entrepreneur is recognized as a leader in the social economy who uses entrepreneurial tools and approaches to run social projects (Defourny and Develtere, 1999). Social entrepreneurs and their followers act through social enterprises, using social entrepreneurship, which is a method of action for pursuing their social goals (Milczarczyk, 2017). They are able to spot and use opportunities unnoticed by others and pioneer new solutions to create a better society; thus they are change agents for society (Dees, 2001; Ashoka, 2008). Bornstein (2004, p. 3) clearly states that important social change usually begins with an individual with entrepreneurial skills and determination, an 'obsessive individual who sees a problem and envisions a new solution, who takes the initiative to act on that vision, who gathers resources and builds organizations to protect and market that vision'. Changing systems is extremely difficult, since social entrepreneurs must change attitudes, expectations and behaviours and overcome disbelief, prejudice and fear; therefore they have to be able to 'persuade, inspire, seduce, cajole, enlighten, touch hearts, alleviate fears, shift perceptions, articulate meanings' and cleverly manoeuvre their ideas through systems (Bornstein, 2004, p. 92). Only people with great motivation who believe in the rightness of what they are doing, who are obsessed with their goals and who are ready to put their ideas into action can bring about essential change (Bornstein, 2004, p. 92). It means that social entrepreneurs need to be highly motivated by altruism, social responsibility and their values and beliefs (Prabhu, 1999). This is the explanation of why they are not satisfied with the existing state of affairs and therefore act accordingly and as a result change society (Prabhu, 1999; Bornstein, 2004).

Actors of the social economy are certainly able to develop vision and introduce it to others, and to develop confidence in other people (Swamy, cited in Prabhu, 1999) that a desired outcome can be achieved. Not only do they have a vision of a better world but, most importantly, they have hope that this vision can be realized. Hope is behind every performed activity, because hope 'based on a positive imagination of the future' (Bar-Tal, 2001, p. 605) is 'the energizer of our actions' (Braithwaite, 2004, p. 129) and 'a powerful resource for social change', as it activates motivation to pursue positive change and 'an alternative future' (Courville and Piper, 2004, p. 42). Cartwright (2004, p. 167) claims that 'hope is essentially future oriented, focused toward some desired goal'. Nevertheless hope does not build on an unreal future ideal but confronts reality (Lashaw, cited in K. Rogers, 2013). Hence hope does not guarantee that all goals can be attained; it just suggests that change is possible (Lueck, 2007) when hope entails setting real goals, choosing pathways to attain those goals, and following those pathways (McGeer, 2004).

People of the social economy are able to convey their hopes to others, initiate relevant actions to achieve the goals behind these hopes and pursue them. According to Bar-Tal (2001) and Braithwaite (2004), combined hope that consists of the hopes of individuals who share a vision of social change and who see the possibility for its realization is the motivating power towards attaining a set goal. Thus cooperation is a result of collective hope (Lueck, 2007), because, when individuals pursue an outcome as a group, hope is certainly involved (Braithwaite, 2004). Courville and Piper (2004) argue that shared feelings of injustice, ideas for change, empowerment through organizing, and collective action are the essential elements that allow the hope present in social movements to achieve its objectives. The example of social activity discussed below presents social entrepreneurs with ideas that are further conveyed between local people in order to trigger shared hope, which next activates collective actions resulting in social change (Courville and Piper, 2004).

PEOPLE OF THE SOUTHEND CREDIT UNION – ACTORS OF NEW HOPE

This section presents a study of hope shared by a group of people that came out of ideas of how to change reality in Southend-on-Sea so that people who lived on the margin of society could get back on track with their lives.

The Southend Credit Union (SCU) was set up by people who noticed injustice in their local community. They observed people who struggled in their lives, had financial problems and even if they tried to escape difficult situations could not overcome the obstacles. These people were marginalized, and the system did not want them. The banks and building societies they turned to for help rejected them. Therefore they often got engaged with and trapped by people and organizations called doorstep lenders or loan sharks. This often led to more problems. SCU actors could not accept the existing situation and decided to give such people a chance so that they could straighten out their finances and consequently their lives. Although determined to fight injustice, the people of the SCU did not have a concrete plan how to do it. A plan slowly crystallized as they visited various institutions and organizations, talked to a number of people and finally realized that they needed to unite themselves into an organized structure in order to gain empowerment to be more effective and get legitimacy for their actions. A credit union seemed like a natural choice, since through this type of organization they could reach people they wanted to support and provide the help the local community required. Moreover, the SCU actors knew that these less privileged people, after years of negligence by society, needed to feel valued and respected again. They had a chance to gain that by joining the credit union, since apart from receiving needed support they would have the right to decide about the operation and future of the organization as its co-owners. Thus a credit union structure was chosen by the SCU actors as their solution to local problems and their idea for change.

Setting up a credit union in Southend-on-Sea was a complicated and long process, but its actors decided to get the project up and running, as they did not want to disappoint those many people in need of the services of this particular type of organization. It was not an easy task in a situation where credit unions did not have recognition in the area and where their cognitive and socio-political legitimacy was not clear. The steering group formed voluntarily to work on the project had to work hard, think entrepreneurially and use entrepreneurial abilities to set up the SCU. They contacted many local institutions, organizations and people who might help them with the task. They attended various meetings and conferences to learn more about credit unions and related topics. They did everything to collect enough money to set the organization up, including working on obtaining financial support from the European Social Fund and other sources. They also had to convince local people about their idea, so they promoted the credit union in various local places. They organized different events such as 'Strictly Come Dancing' evenings, chocolate testing and tea parties in order to inform people about the new credit union. Although they did not get much response to their promotional activities, which led to some members of the steering group feeling disappointed and leaving, those who stayed continued the project and managed to get new people on board.

All the efforts undertaken to offer a long-run solution for the particular needs and problems of the local community finally paid off. The credit union was introduced to the Southend community after five years of collective and devoted work. During this period, people who dedicated themselves to the project sacrificed their time, energy, knowledge, expertise, ideas, skills and experience, not expecting anything in return. The group struggled with the many tasks they had to perform, encountered many problems and together experienced sad moments and a big loss when three people who were very much engaged in the project died in one year. But, despite all of that, they did not even think about giving up, because they believed that what they were doing was right and justified, and because they had hope in a positive outcome. They knew there was a need for a credit union in the Southend community, since there were a lot of people who were desperate for the help that could be offered by the organization. Hence the SCU was created thanks to a group of individuals who noticed the difficult life situations of other people and who were not indifferent to others' problems and misfortune. They empathized with those who were struggling in their lives and because of that they could not accept the status quo and had to act accordingly. The SCU is the result of their collective hope and work.

The actors' collective action resulted in creating the organization through which they are able to support members of the local community by offering them fair financial services. The credit union proposes the terms and conditions under which money is provided to optimize the benefits to the recipients of such funding and to enable them to better integrate in society. The SCU actors teach local people money management through saving schemes that come automatically from the credit union's rules. Moreover, they run such schemes for children in schools and, although the credit union does not earn much from that, they are determined to continue this activity. They claim it is very important to show people from childhood how to handle their money properly so that they can avoid getting into debt. SCU actors are also able to help its volunteers gain experience and start to believe in themselves. Volunteers obtain new knowledge and skills that may make it easier to return to the labour market. The SCU actors have created an encouraging, supportive and friendly environment to make work more congenial and to help volunteers (re)gain confidence. The case of a boy – who was introverted, very timid and quiet – sent by the Young Men's Christian Association (YMCA) to the SCU on work placement demonstrates that. Initially he felt most comfortable staying in the back office and scanning documents, but with the support of other people at the SCU he gradually became more open to others and clearly started to gain confidence.

SCU actors try to accommodate everyone wanting to volunteer at the credit union in terms of office organization and conditions. There was not a problem finding a place for a volunteer who had problems with carrying out a job in the office or at the reception desk because of her deafness. They managed to organize her work in the office in such a way that she did not need to take phone calls but mainly dealt with documents on the computer. This definitely raised her self-esteem and confidence. Volunteers at the SCU admit that they started volunteering at the credit union mainly because they wanted to contribute actively to a project that helps other people and supports the local community. This contribution to something good that is serving the local community brings them satisfaction and self-fulfilment. Quite a lot of them have a charity background and have previously worked and/or volunteered in non-profit organizations. Some of the SCU volunteers have even started their own social projects, such as a justice and peace group to help third world countries. They are undoubtedly distinguished by their sensitivity to others' misery and by a willingness to help those in need.

The fact that a number of SCU actors have experienced various problems or have known somebody who has struggled in life makes them additionally motivated to help other people. They feel that they need to give something back to the community. The hope and motivation of the SCU actors are also strengthened when they manage to solve people's problems and help them straighten their lives out. They always perceive it not only as a success of the organization but also as their personal success. Such outcomes give them satisfaction and pride in what they do as well as prove that their work is meaningful, has a deeper sense and is worth pursuing. The SCU people feel that they are taking part in something important, as they touch other people's lives. The story of a woman in her 70s who was with Provident for years and could not get out of a circle of rising debts is only one of many examples. The woman first used Provident's services when her children were small and she had to buy uniforms and other school necessities for them. Since then she had given Provident a significant proportion of her income, and yet she was struggling to pay off her continuously growing debts. When her income barely covered a loan instalment, her social worker took her to the Citizens Advice Bureau for advice, and its solicitor brought her to the SCU. The woman became a member of the credit union and got a special emergency loan (although the organization does not usually grant such loans, especially to people who have not yet fulfilled membership conditions). The SCU bought her debts and paid off all she owed Provident, and she started paying the credit union an amount she could afford. The woman also started saving a few pounds a week, which she had not previously been able to do. Most importantly, after so many years she regained peace of mind and a sense of freedom.

SCU actors also had no doubts about helping another person who did not fulfil the conditions to obtain a loan from the credit union. The woman had moved to the Southend area after her divorce and let her house in Yorkshire, but, when she learnt that tenants had ruined the house, she decided to put it up for sale. Unfortunately, just before she signed the contract with a buyer, she was informed that she needed to pay a £12 000 penalty for selling the house earlier than the mortgage conditions allowed. All the banks she visited to try to get a loan in order to pay the penalty rejected her request, since she already had a mortgage. The only financial organization that agreed to help her was the SCU.

The stories above show that the SCU actors treat each person individually, and therefore they are able to effectively help people to get out of poverty and difficult life situations. But most of all the stories confirm that the credit union values people much more than rules, because its actors are prepared to make exceptions to set criteria when it is required and right. This is because every person matters to them, and they see in every person a human being and not simply an account number. They recognize that every person is different, with different life situations and different problems, and, because the SCU actors feel for others, they try to be as flexible as they can in order to support all the people who come to them. The SCU is open even to such vulnerable groups as the homeless, which is the exception in the banking system, as banking institutions operate to get as much as they can out of business while perfectly protecting themselves. Therefore they do not even consider the homeless or people without enough income as potential clients. This results in these people finding themselves beyond the system and thus becoming alienated from society. The SCU actors do not reject anybody, but welcome everybody who is willing to join the credit union. These are the premises the people who created the SCU established and always respect. Both employees and volunteers of the credit union empathize with people who struggle in their lives, and they never judge anybody. They see in every person a human being with potential that needs to be revealed, freed and directed in the right way. They are ready to listen patiently to the problems of every person who looks for help, and support them to overcome their difficulties.

The SCU actors do not only concentrate on achieving the credit union's social goals but also support other social initiatives if possible. For example, the organization collects stamps for charities or serves as a work placement for people sent by the YMCA, to whom its actors give their time and with whom they share knowledge. Another feature characterizing the social enterprise, and thus its actors, is that it is ethical in everything it does. It has an account in a cooperative bank, because the SCU actors believe this bank has more principles than mainstream banks. It is important for them that the bank does not invest in questionable and unethical enterprises such as armaments but behaves ethically, sympathizes with people and supports social initiatives. They do not want to be involved even indirectly in something that is not good by definition.

As the stories above demonstrate, the SCU actors, with goodness and continuous hope reflected in their actions and approaches, certainly change others' lives. Moreover, they have brought new hope into the local community. Through their activity they have participated in constructing a strong, stable and confident community with people feeling safe, happy and in control of their own lives. The ultimate goal of the steering group members was to make unprivileged people feel that they were fully fledged members of society again and people who deserved to be respected. The SCU actors have undoubtedly achieved what they planned to achieve through a long-term solution to local problems – the Southend Credit Union.

DISCUSSION – PEOPLE AWED BY GOODNESS, LED BY HOPE

The case of the SCU described above depicts that the organization was created on the foundation of a trust deficit as to public institutions being able to efficiently address particular problems, if they can address them at all. In today's world, economic factors prevail over social ones as multinational corporations that are set up to gain as much as they can increase in power, whereas the state's capability to safeguard the values of a caring society deteriorates (Courville and Piper, 2004). Because of that, people have lost hope in the state's ability and/or willingness to effectively tackle social and environmental issues and thus to bring about positive social change. But they still have hope deriving from a force they notice in the world that they want to exploit because they do not accept the existing situation and want to build another, better world (Holloway, 2014). For this reason they organize themselves and act through social initiatives, whether non-governmental organizations (NGOs) or social movements, to work towards solving problems they have noticed (Courville and Piper, 2004).

The SCU is an organization of the social economy, the sector that by nature challenges the current order and follows the path of introducing change, a sector full of people with hope of creating a better world (Courville and Piper, 2004). Local social entrepreneurs who saw social problems in Southend-on-Sea decided to help those who struggled in life by offering fair banking services. They managed to convey their vision and hope to other local people, and through collective action they created the credit union. They worked hard to bring the organization into being, encountering many barriers they had to overcome, but they were very determined to continue their activity. People of the SCU knew where they wanted to get to, and even if they were struggling to achieve their objective they did not give up but stuck to their chosen path. They had hope that they could achieve what they intended, and therefore they methodically planned their next steps to move the project forward and overcome the obstacles. According to Drahos (cited in Lueck, 2007), hope entails planning to achieve the desired outcome and combat the problems encountered on the way. The steering group members constantly had to analyse the situation and use their creativity to adjust to changing conditions to be able to gain their goal. Bar-Tal (2001) claims that hope requites both thinking, from which ideas are derived, and skills such as creativity and flexibility. 'In hoping, we create a kind of imaginative scaffolding that calls for the creative exercise of our capacities and so, often, for their development' (McGeer, 2004, p. 105). Hence hope is essential to bringing about social change, but it needs to be projected in actions channelled towards obtaining social justice objectives (Courville and Piper, 2004).

The SCU actors also needed to convince local people, organizations and institutions about the idea of a credit union in Southend-on-Sea. This was not an easy task, since a credit union was a new concept for the local community, who did not know much about this type of organization or misunderstood it. The steering group members, who knew that 'hope requires conceiving of new behaviours to achieve the desired, positively valued goal' (Bar-Tal, 2001, p. 605), proposed new approaches to win local people's support for their actions and to enkindle hope for a better future for the local community. They managed to convince the local people that the credit union would help people get back on track with their lives. The case shows that social organizations can 'play a critical role as bridges between people, translating individual hopes into combined efforts of action through organising' (Courville and Piper, 2004, p. 57).

Setting up the credit union was a long process full of hope and good times as well as disappointment and sad moments. Sometimes all the efforts seemed to be useless, as nothing came of them for a long time. But, although 'these actions can be regarded as hopeless, the fact that they happen can inspire hope even in the direst of contexts' (Courville and Piper, 2004, p. 44). The SCU actors never lost hope that they might create a better world through positively changing the lives of other people. They sometimes felt disheartened for a short period, after which they resumed action, because it was hope that brought them together and helped them persevere in difficult moments (Lee, cited in Rogers, 2013).

The social enterprise puts people above rules. It makes every effort to work for people in every possible way. The SCU people try to get to know the organization's members and their life situations, so that they can offer them the help and support relevant to their situations. People are more motivated to be engaged in and carry out social actions when they are directly linked to those whose lives they manage to positively affect by their work (Blau and Scott, cited in Michaelson et al., 2014; Katz and Kahn, cited in Michaelson et al., 2014). The SCU actors admit that such close interaction with people they help is important to them. It allows them to better understand people's needs, but most of all it keeps their collective hope strong and motivates them to further actions.

The organization attempts to create meaningful work for its employees and volunteers, which is seen as 'a fundamental human need' through which people can experience such values as freedom, dignity and autonomy (Yeoman, 2014, p. 235). It is crucial for the SCU actors to know that through their work at the credit union they participate in something significant – changing others' lives. This make them feel needed, important and fulfilled. People can also find their work meaningful if they have an opportunity to develop appropriate abilities (Yeoman, 2014), and the SCU offers such a chance to its volunteers. Meaningful work grounded in the logic of deontology represents the approach that 'one should always treat persons as an end and not merely as a means' (Michaelson et al., 2014). This is an attitude social movements and organizations reflect, and the SCU as an example practises it in every aspect of its operation. Thus hope for realizing something good is more vivid in NGOs and their actors, since they are purely directed toward the generation of good and tend to make the world better through their social actions. Social movements and groups that possess collective hope create opportunities for change as a result of their pursuit of given social goals (Lueck, 2007). This is possible because organized groups give their members a sense of empowerment and a confidence that together they can succeed. As Moyer (cited in Rogers, 2013) argues, hope that is grounded in reality is a vital component of empowerment for people working on attaining social goals and for preserving social movements leading to social change.

The whole history of the SCU illustrates that its actors' ideas triggered hope, which activated appropriate action, since the SCU was created and is run thanks to collective action stimulated by the collective hope that is crucial for effectively building a better world (Courville and Piper, 2004).

The case of the SCU proves that collective hope 'is a stimulus for social change' (Lueck, 2007, p. 253). This collective hope shared by the SCU actors is reflected in 'a shared desire for a better society, articulated through a broad set of agreed-upon goals and principles, developed and elaborated though socially inclusive dialogue' (Braithwaite, 2004, p. 146). All the actions of the social enterprise prove that its people, led by goodness and hope, have worked towards generation of social change. Their attitude and activity made it possible for the SCU to achieve its ultimate goal, which is to allow people of the Southend community rejected by society to return to society as full members who deserve respect. The credit union is a pathway that the SCU actors chose in order to implement desired goals and is one of the 'social institutions that are available for groups wishing to pursue collective action' (Braithwaite, 2004, p. 134). In the form of a credit union, a new solution to tackle local problems in Southend-on-Sea, its actors have been able to introduce positive changes as a consequence of their collective actions hinged on shared hope, because it is hope that is the essence of social change (McGeer, 2004).

NOTES

1. A social enterprise in England involved in the author's ethnographic study on the identity of the social enterprise conducted from May 2008 to October 2008.
2. The social economy sector is often referred to as the third sector, the non-profit sector, the charitable sector, the voluntary sector or the independent sector (Borzaga and Defourny, 2001).

Postscript: Avalanche

Karolina Matyjaszkowicz

Hope helps us to survive. It evokes an avalanche of feelings, emotions and sometimes also experiences which can be very real. It makes creativity more profound, it invokes images and invites imagination, and they help to create something new that can be real, good and invigorating.

Imagination brings immediate relief here and now, whereas hope seems to be inextricably linked to the future.

What my imagination gives birth to, I transfer to the canvas.

People often tell me that my paintings bring out something good and powerful in them. This gives me strength and hope for the future . . .

And so a "magic circle" perpetuates itself which, I hope, will never be broken. I don't want anything to break this circle.

Hope gives birth to imagination and leads directly into art.

Nothing can possibly give as much hope as art can do.

*Photo 19.1   Karolina Matyjaszkowicz, "There Is Probably Another World
. . .," 2018 (mixed media/computer graphics, 90 × 63/64 cm).*

References

Adamiak, P., Charycka, B., and Gumkowska, M. (2016). *Kondycja sektora organizacji pozarządowych w Polsce 2015. Raport z badań.* Warszawa: Stowarzyszenie Klon/Jawor.

Addleson, M. (2010). What is good organization? Learning organizations, community and the rhetoric of the "bottom line." *European Journal of Work and Organizational Psychology*, 9(2), 233–252.

Adler, P., Forbes, L., and Willmott, H. (2007). Critical management studies. *Academy of Management Annals*, 1(1), 119–179.

Adorno, T.W. ([1936] 1989). On jazz. *Discourse*, 12(1), 44–69.

Adorno, T.W., and Horkheimer, M. ([1944] 1997). *Dialectic of enlightenment.* London: Verso.

Alderman, J. (2001). *Sonic boom: Napster, MP3 and the new pioneers of music.* London: Fourth Estate.

Allen, J. (2013). *14 street art terms – illustrated!* Retrieved September 10, 2018 from http://mentalfloss.com/article/51583/14-street-art-terms%E2%80%94illustrated

Altheide, D. (1996). *Qualitative media analysis.* Thousand Oaks, CA: Sage.

Alvesson, M. (2014). *The triumph of emptiness: Consumption, higher education, and work organization.* Oxford: Oxford University Press.

Amabile, T.M. (1988). A model of creativity and innovation in organizations. In B.M. Staw and L.L. Cummings (Eds.), *Research in organizational behavior*, Vol. 10, (pp. 123–167). Greenwich, CT: JAI Press.

Amabile, T.M. (1996). *Creativity in context.* Boulder, CO: Westview Press.

Anderson, P. (1974). *Passages from antiquity to feudalism.* London: New Left Review Books.

Anderson, R., Baxter, L.A., and Cissna, K.N. (2004). Texts and contexts of dialogue. In R. Anderson, L.A. Baxter, and K.N. Cissna (Eds.), *Dialogue: Theorizing difference in communication studies* (pp. 1–17). Thousand Oaks, CA: Sage.

Angrosino, M. (2015). *Badania etnograficzne i obserwacyjne.* Warszawa: PWN.

Apple, M.W., and Beane, J.A. (Eds.). (1999). *Democratic schools: Lessons from the chalk face.* Buckingham: Open University Press.

Arias-Maldonado, M. (2016). The Anthropocenic turn: Theorizing sustainability in a postnatural age. *Sustainability*, 8(10), 1–17.

Aristotle. (2013). *Aristotle's Politics*. Chicago, IL: University of Chicago Press.

Ashoka. (2008). *What is the social entrepreneur?* Retrieved November 16, 2018 from https://www.ashoka.org/social_entrepreneur

Attali, J. ([1977] 1985). *Noise: The political economy of music*. Manchester: Manchester University Press.

Bachelard, G. (1969). *The poetics of space*. Boston, MA: Beacon Press.

Bakhtin, M.M. (1981). *The dialogic imagination: Four essays*. Austin: University of Texas Press.

Balfour, C. (2018). Workers' participation in Western Europe. In C. Balfour (Ed.), *Participation in industry* (pp. 181–212). London: Routledge.

Balu, R. (2001). How to bounce back from setbacks. *Fast Company*, 45, 148–156.

Banerjee, S.B. (2008). Necrocapitalism. *Organization Studies*, 29(12), 1541–1563.

Banks, J.A. (2004). Teaching for social justice, diversity, and citizenship in a global world. *Educational Forum*, 68(4), 296–305.

Barclay-Goddard, R., King, J., Dubouloz, C.J., and Schwartz, C.E. (2012). Building on transformative learning and response shift theory to investigate health-related quality of life changes over time in individuals with chronic health conditions and disability. *Archives of Physical Medicine and Rehabilitation*, 93(2), 214–220.

Barker, W. (2001). *The adages of Erasmus*. Toronto: University of Toronto Press.

Barkham, P. (2018). We're doomed: Mayer Hillman on the climate reality no one else will dare mention. *The Guardian*, April 26. Retrieved April 30, 2018 from https://www.theguardian.com/environment/2018/apr/26/were-doomed-mayer-hillman-on-the-climate-reality-no-one-else-will-dare-mention?utm_source=dlvr.it&utm_medium=facebook

Barone, T., and Eisner, E.T. (2012). *Arts based research*. Thousand Oaks, CA: Sage.

Barro, R. (1997). *Macroeconomics*. Cambridge, MA: MIT Press.

Bar-Tal, D. (2001). Why does fear override hope in societies engulfed by intractable conflict, as it does in the Israeli society? *Political Psychology*, 22(3), 601–627.

Bartlett, C., and Ghoshal, S. (1994). Changing the role of top management: Beyond strategy to purpose. *Harvard Business Review*, 72(6), 79–88.

Baskin, J. (2015). Paradigm dressed as epoch: The ideology of the Anthropocene. *Environmental Values*, 24, 9–29.

Basso, P. (2003). *Modern times, ancient hours: Working lives in the twenty-first century.* London: Verso.

Basu, S. (2017). *Corporate purpose: Why it matters more than strategy.* London: Routledge.

Bateson, G. (1972). *Steps to an ecology of mind.* Chicago, IL: University of Chicago Press.

Battilana, J., Fuerstein, M., and Lee, M. (2017). New prospects for organizational democracy? How the joint pursuit of social and financial goals challenges traditional organizational designs. In S. Rangan (Ed.), *Capitalism beyond mutuality* (pp. 256–288). Oxford: Oxford University Press.

Bauman, Z. (1989). *Modernity and the Holocaust.* Cambridge: Polity.

Bauman, Z. (1998). *Work, consumerism and the new poor.* Buckingham: Open University Press.

Bauman, Z. (2007). *Liquid times.* Cambridge: Polity.

Bauman, Z. (2011). *Collateral damage.* Cambridge: Polity.

Bauman, Z. (2012). Times of interregnum. *Ethics and Global Politics*, 5(1), 49–56.

Bauman, Z. (2016). Private communication with Monika Kostera, Leeds.

Bauman, Z. (2017a). *Retrotopia.* Cambridge: Polity.

Bauman, Z. (2017b). O wszystkim, co najważniejsze. *Gazeta Wyborcza*, January 10. Retrieved July 12, 2018 from http://wyborcza.pl/51,75398, 21222206.html?i=0

Baunsgaard, V., and Clegg, S. (2012). Dominant ideological modes of rationality: Organizations as arenas of struggle over members' categorization devices. In D. Courpasson, D. Golsorkhi, and J. Sallaz (Eds.), *Rethinking power in organizations, institutions, and markets* (pp. 199–232). Bingley: Emerald.

BBC. (2018). Macron to US Congress: "There is no Planet B." *BBC News*, April 25. Retrieved April 30, 2018 from http://www.bbc.com/news/av/world-us-canada-43900009/macron-to-us-congress-there-is-no-planet-bbed.

Belbin, M. (1993). *Team roles at work.* Oxford: Butterworth-Heinemann.

Belfrage, C., and Kallifatides, M. (2018a). Financialisation and the new Swedish model. *Cambridge Journal of Economics*, 42(4), 875–900.

Belfrage, C.A., and Kallifatides, M. (2018b). The politicisation of macroprudential regulation: The critical Swedish case. *Environment and Planning A: Economy and Space*, 50(3), 709–729.

Benhabib, S. (1986). *Critique, norm and utopia: A study of the foundations of critical theory.* New York: Columbia University Press.

Bible. Authorized King James version. (1997). (R. Carroll and S. Prickett, Eds.). Oxford: Oxford University Press.

Björkegren, D. (1996). *The culture business: Management strategies for the arts-related business.* London: Routledge.

Blake, W. (2008). Milton. In *The complete poetry and prose of William Blake*, ed. D.V. Erdman and H. Bloom. Berkeley: University of California Press.

Bloch, E. ([1959] 1986). *The principle of hope* (Vol. 1). Cambridge, MA: MIT Press.

Bøås, M., and McNeill, D. (2003). *Global institutions and development: Framing the world?* London: Routledge.

Bogacz-Wojtanowska, E. (2013). *Zdolności organizacyjne a współdziałanie organizacji pozarządowych.* Kraków: Wydawnictwo ISP UJ.

Bogacz-Wojtanowska, E. (2016). Istota i podstawowe zasady funkcjonowania organizacji pozarządowych. In E. Bogacz-Wojtanowska and S. Wrona (Eds.), *Zarządzanie organizacjami pozarządowymi* (pp. 11–27). Kraków: Wydawnictwo ISP UJ.

Bornstein, D. (2004). *How to change the world: Social entrepreneurs and the power of new ideas.* Oxford: Oxford University Press.

Borzaga, C., and Defourny, J. (Eds.). (2001). *The emergence of social enterprise.* London: Routledge.

Boyatzis, R.B. (1998). *Transforming qualitative information thematic analysis and code development.* Thousand Oaks, CA: Sage.

Boyle, D. (1996). *Trainspotting.* PolyGram.

Braidotti, R. (2005). A critical cartography of feminist post-postmodernism. *Australian Feminist Studies*, 20(47), 169–180.

Braithwaite, V. (2004). The hope process and social inclusion. *Annals of the American Academy of Political and Social Science*, 592(1), 128–151.

Bregman, P. (2018). The next time you want to complain at work, do this instead. *Harvard Business Review*, May 17. Retrieved May 17, 2018 from https://hbr.org/2018/05/the-next-time-you-want-to-complain-at-work-do-this-instead

Brown, S.D. (2002). Michel Serres: Science, translation and the logic of the parasite. *Theory, Culture and Society*, 19(3), 1–27.

Burchell, B.J. (2003). *Identifying, describing and understanding financial aversion: Financial phobes.* Report for EGG. Retrieved April 24, 2019 from http://people.ds.cam.ac.uk/bb101/FinancialAversionReportBurc hell.pdf

Burrell, G. (1997). *Pandemonium: Towards a retro-organization theory.* London: Sage.

Burrell, G., and Morgan, G. (1979). *Sociological paradigms and organisational analysis.* London: Heinemann.

Busby, J.S. (2006). Failure to mobilize in reliability-seeking organizations:

Two cases from the UK railway. *Journal of Management Studies*, 43(6), 1375–1393.

Butler, M. (2001). Transformative hope: A pedagogical vision. *Counterpoints*, 94, 265–285.

Caldwell, I., and Thomason, D. (2004). *The rule of four*. New York: Dial Press.

Carlsen, A., and Pitsis, T. (2009). Experiencing hope in organizational lives. In L.M. Roberts and J. Dutton (Eds.), *Exploring positive identities and organizations: Building a theoretical and research foundation* (pp. 77–98). New York: Psychology Press.

Carlsen, A., Hagen, A.L., and Mortensen, T.F. (2012). Imagining hope in organizations. In K.S. Cameron and G.M. Spreitzer (Eds.), *The Oxford handbook of positive organizational scholarship* (pp. 288–303). New York: Oxford University Press.

Cartwright, J. (2004). Aquinas to Zwelethemba: A brief history of hope. *Annals of the American Academy of Political and Social Science*, 592 (1), 166–184.

Cassel, D. (2012). *The pavement stage: Perspectives on street theatre*. Berlin: Pace Station Press.

Cataluna, L. (2016). Re: The purpose of life is not happiness: It's usefulness. [Reader comment]. Retrieved October 15, 2019 from https://medium.com/p/65064d0cdd59/responses/show

Cederström, C., and Fleming, P. (2012). *Dead man working*. Winchester: Zero Books.

Cera, A. (2017). The Technocene or technology as (neo)environment. *Techné: Research in Philosophy and Technology*, 21(2–3), 243–281.

Chandler, D. (2018). *Ontopolitics in the Anthropocene*. London: Routledge.

Chaney, D. (2012). The music industry in the digital age: Consumer participation in value creation. *International Journal of Arts Management*, 15(1), 42–52.

Choi, H., and Burnes, B. (2013). The internet and value co-creation: The case of the popular music industry. *Prometheus*, 31(1), 35–53.

Christianson, M.K., Farkas, M.T., Sutcliffe, K.M., and Weick, K.E. (2009). Learning through rare events: Significant interruptions at the Baltimore and Ohio Railroad Museum. *Organization Science*, 20(5), 846–860.

Christophers, B. (2013). A monstrous hybrid: The political economy of housing in early twenty-first century Sweden. *New Political Economy*, 18(6), 885–911.

Clegg, S. (2016). The East India Company: The first modern multinational. In C. Dörrenbächer and M. Geppert (Eds.), *Multinational corpora-*

tions and organization theory: Post millennium perspectives (pp. 43–67). Bingley: Emerald.

Cohen, S., and Taylor, L. ([1976] 1992). *Escape attempts.* London: Routledge.

Comor, E. (2010). Contextualizing and critiquing the fantastic prosumer: Power, alienation and hegemony. *Critical Sociology*, 37(3), 309–327.

Connolly, K. (2012). Ikea says sorry to East German political prisoners forced to make its furniture. *The Guardian*, November 16. Retrieved from 15 October, 2019 http://www.theguardian.com/business/2012/nov/16/ikea-regrets-forced-labour-germany

Cooper, C. (2014). There are two sides to flexibility. *HR Magazine*, October 29. Retrieved August 7, 2018 from http://www.hrmagazine.co.uk/article-details/cary-cooper-there-are-two-sides-to-flexibility

Cornelissen, J.P. (2006). Making sense of theory construction: Metaphor and disciplined imagination. *Organization Studies*, 27(11), 1579–1597.

Costas, J., and Fleming P. (2009). Beyond dis-identification: A discursive approach to self-alienation in contemporary organizations. *Human Relations*, 62, 353–378.

Coulson, S. (2001). *Semantic leaps: Frame-shifting and conceptual blending in meaning construction.* Cambridge: Cambridge University Press.

Council of Europe. (1998). Education for citizenship, the basic concepts and core competences. DECS/CIT (98) 7 def. Council for Cultural Co-operation, Council of Europe.

Courpasson, D. (2017). The politics of everyday. *Organization Studies*, 17, 843–859.

Courville, S., and Piper, N. (2004). Harnessing hope through NGO activism. *Annals of the American Academy of Political and Social Science*, 592(1), 39–61.

Coutu, D.L. (2002). How resilience works. *Harvard Business Review*, 80(5), 46–55.

Craig, R.T., and Muller, H.L. (2007). *Theorizing communication: Readings across traditions.* Thousand Oaks, CA: Sage.

Crary, J. (2014). *24/7: Late capitalism and the ends of sleep.* London: Verso.

Crick, B. (Chair). (1998). *Education for citizenship and the teaching of democracy in schools: Final report of the Advisory Group on Citizenship and the Teaching of Democracy in Schools.* London: QCA.

Crick, B. (2000). *Essays on citizenship.* London: Continuum.

Cronon, W. (1992). A place for stories: Nature, history and narrative. *Journal of American History*, 78(4), 1347–1376.

cummings, e.e. (2019). Voices to voices, lip to lip. In *e.e. cummings: Three poems.* Retrieved July 19, 2019 from https://www.sccs.swarthmore.edu/users/03/cdisalvo/cummings2/voices2.html

Cunha, M.P., Rego, A., Simpson, A.V., and Clegg, S. (2019). *Positive organizational behavior*. London: Routledge.

Cunliffe, A.L. (2002). Social poetics: A dialogical approach to management inquiry. *Journal of Management Inquiry*, 11(2), 128–146.

Cunliffe, A.L. (2018). Alterity: The passion, politics and ethics of self and scholarship. *Management Learning*, 49(1), 8–22.

Czarniawska, B. (2014). *Social science research: From field to desk*. Los Angeles, CA: Sage.

Dany, C. (2013). *Global governance and NGO participation*. New York: Routledge.

Davies, I., and Issitt, J. (2005). Reflections on citizenship education in Australia, Canada and England. *Comparative Education*, 41(4), 389–410.

Davis, D., Kaplinsky, R., and Morris, M. (2018). Rents, power and governance in global value chains. *Journal of World-Systems Research*, 24(1), 43–71.

De Angelis, D. (2017). *Omnia sunt communia*. London: Zed Books.

Dees, G.J. (2001). *The meaning of social entrepreneurship*. Retrieved November 7, 2005 from http://community-wealth.org/content/meaning-social-entrepreneurship

Deetz, S. (1992). *Democracy in an age of corporate colonization: Developments in communication and the politics of everyday life*. Albany: State University of New York Press.

Deetz, S. (1998). Discursive formations, strategized subordination and self-surveillance. In A. McKinley and K. Starkey (Eds.), *Foucault, management and organizational theory* (pp. 151–172). London: Sage.

Deetz, S., and McClellan, J.G. (2009). Critical studies. In F. Bargiela-Chiappini (Ed.), *The handbook of business discourse* (pp. 119–131). Edinburgh: University of Edinburgh Press.

Deetz, S., and Simpson, J. (2004). Critical organizational dialogue: Open formation and the demand of "otherness." In R. Anderson, L.A. Baxter, and K.N. Cissna (Eds.), *Dialogue: Theorizing difference in communication studies* (pp. 141–158). Thousand Oaks, CA: Sage.

Defourny, J., and Develtere, P. (1999). Social economy: The worldwide making of a third sector. In J. Defourny, P. Develtere, and B. Fonteneau (Eds.), *Social economy: North and South* (pp. 25–56). Brussels: De Boeck University.

Dewey, J. ([1916] 1980). *The middle works: 1899–1924* (Vol. 9: *1916: Democracy and education*), ed. J.A. Boydston. Carbondale: Southern Illinois University Press.

Dewey, J. (1989). *The later works: 1925–1953* (Vol 16: *1949–1952*), ed. J.A. Boydston. Carbondale: Southern Illinois University Press.

Dewey, J. (1997). *How we think*. Boston, MA: Houghton Mifflin.

Dewey, J. ([1922] 2008). *The middle works: 1899–1924* (Vol. 14), ed. J.A. Boydston. Carbondale: Southern Illinois University Press.

Diamond, J. (1999). *Guns, germs and steel*. New York. Norton.

Dickinson, E. (1999). *"Hope" is the thing with feathers*. Retrieved April 24, 2019 from https://www.poetryfoundation.org/poems/42889/hope-is-the-thing-with-feathers-314

Doumpa, V., and Broad, N. (2014). Buskers as an ingredient of successful urban places. Future of Places Conference, Buenos Aires.

Duchêne, A., and Waelbroeck, P. (2006). The legal and techno-logical battle in the music industry: Information-push versus information-pull technologies. *International Review of Law and Economics*, 26, 565–580.

Dunn, E. ([2004] 2017). *Prywatyzując Polskę. O bobofrutach, wielkim biznesie i restrukturyzacji pracy* [Privatizing Poland: Baby food, big business and the remaking of labor]. Warszawa: Wydawnictwo Krytyki Politycznej.

Easterlin, R.A., and Angelescu, L. (2012). Modern economic growth and quality of life: Cross-sectional and time series evidence. In K.C. Land, A.C. Michalos, and M.J. Sirgy (Eds.), *Handbook of social indicators and quality of life research* (pp. 113–136). London: Springer.

Edley, P., Hylmo, A., and Newsom, V. (2004). Alternative organizing communities: Collectivist organizing, telework, home-based inter-net businesses, and online communities. *Annals of the International Communication Association*, 28(1), 87–125.

Einarsson, S., and Kallifatides, M. (2017). *Parternas bolag – ett diskus-sionsunderlag*. Stockholm: Stockholm School of Economics Institute for Research.

Ellmeier, A. (2003). Cultural entrepreneurialism: On the changing relation-ship between the arts, culture and employment. *International Journal of Cultural Policy*, 9(1), 3–16.

Ericsson, D. (2007). *Musikmysteriet. Organiserade stämningar och mot-stämningar* [The music mystery: Organized moods and countermoods]. Stockholm: Economic Research Institute at the Stockholm School of Economics.

Ericsson, D. (2010a). *Scripting creativity*. Stockholm: Economic Research Institute at the Stockholm School of Economics.

Ericsson, D. (2010b). Constellations of another other: The case of Aquarian Nation. In F. Bill, B. Bjerke, and A.W. Johansson (Eds.), *(De)Mobilizing the entrepreneurship discourse: Exploring entrepreneurial thinking and action* (pp. 179–200). Cheltenham, UK and Northampton, MA, USA: Edward Elgar Publishing.

Erixon, L. (2015). Can fiscal austerity be expansionary in present-day Europe? The lessons from Sweden. *Review of Keynesian Economics*, 3(4), 567–601.

European Commission. (1998). *Education and active citizenship in the European Union*. Luxembourg: Office for Official Publications of the European Communities.

Fairhurst, G.T., and Putnam, L. (2004). Organizations as discursive constructions. *Communication Theory*, 14, 5–26.

Feyerabend, P. (1987). *Farewell to reason*. London: Verso.

Feyerabend, P. ([1975] 1993). *Against method*. London: Verso.

Fiala, A. (2010). Nero's fiddle: On hope, despair, and the ecological crisis. *Ethics and the Environment*, 15(1), 51–68.

Figueroa, P. (2000). Citizenship education for a plural society. In A. Osler (Ed.), *Citizenship and democracy in schools: Diversity, identity, equality* (pp. 47–62). Stoke-on-Trent: Trentham Books.

Fleming, P. (2017). *The death of homo economicus: Work, debt and the myth of endless accumulation*. London: Pluto Press.

Fleming, P. (2019). *The worst is yet to come: A post-capitalist survival guide*. London: Repeater.

Fletcher, B.J. (2016). "Stars and Bars": Understanding right-wing populism in the USA. *Socialist Register*, 2016, 296–311.

Flint, D. (2009). It's a crime? A novel attack on copyright. *Business Law Review*, 30(1), 5–6.

Florida, R. (2002). *The rise of the creative class and how it's transforming work, leisure, community and everyday life*. New York: Perseus.

Florida, R. (2003). Cities and the creative class. *City and Community*, 2(1), 3–19.

Florida, R. (2017). *The new urban crisis: How our cities are increasing inequality, deepening segregation, and failing the middle class – and what we can do about it*. New York: Basic Books.

Flory, M., Durant, R., Magala, S., Boje, D., and Downs, A. (2017). Heather Höpfl's storytelling. *Culture and Organization*, 23, 110–117.

Folbre, N. (2003). *Praca opiekuńcza*. Retrieved January 1, 2018 from www.transversal.at/transversal/0805/folbre/po/folbre-po.pdf

Ford, C.M. (1996). A theory of individual creative action in multiple social domains. *Academy of Management Review*, 21, 1112–1142.

Ford, M. (2016). *Rise of the robots: Technology and the threat of a jobless future*. New York: Basic Books.

Foroux, D. (2016). The purpose of life is not happiness: It's usefulness. *Medium*, October 3. Retrieved April 24, 2019 from https://medium.com/darius-foroux/the-purpose-of-life-is-not-happiness-its-usefulness-65064d0cdd59

Forslund, D. (2008). *Hit med pengarna! Sparandets genealogi och den finansiella övertalningens vetandekonst.* Stockholm: Carlsson.

Foucault, M. (1972). *The archaeology of knowledge.* New York: Pantheon.

Foucault, M. (1980). *Power/knowledge.* New York: Pantheon.

Foucault, M. (1988). Technologies of the self. In L.H. Martin, H. Gutman, and P.H. Hutton (Eds.), *Technologies of the self: A seminar with Michel Foucault* (pp. 16–49). Amherst: University of Massachusetts Press.

Frayne, D. (2015). *The refusal of work: Rethinking post-work theory and practice.* London: Zed Books.

Freeman, R.E. (1984). *Strategic management: A stakeholder approach.* London: Pitman.

Freeman, S.F., Hirschhorn, L., and Maltz, M. (2004). The power of moral purpose: Sandler O'Neill & Partners in the aftermath of September 11th, 2001. *Organization Development Journal,* 22, 69–81.

Freire, P. (1970). *The pedagogy of the oppressed.* Harmondsworth: Penguin.

Friedman, M. (1970). The social responsibility of business is to increase its profits. *New York Times,* September 13, 17–21.

Fukuyama, F. (1992). *The end of history and the last man.* New York: Free Press.

Gabriel, Y. (2005). Glass cages and glass palaces: Images of organization in image-conscious times. *Organization,* 12, 9–27.

Gabriel, Y., and Lang, T. (1995). *The unmanageable consumer: Contemporary consumption and its fragmentations.* London: Sage.

Gadamer, H.G. (2004). *Truth and method.* London: Continuum.

Gee, J.P. (2004). *An introduction to discourse analysis: Theory and method.* London: Routledge.

Gehmann, U. (2004). Prometheus unleashed. In Y. Gabriel (Ed.), *Myths, stories, and organizations* (pp. 165–175). Oxford: Oxford University Press.

Geoghegan, V. (1996). *Ernst Bloch.* London: Routledge.

Ghoshal, S. (2005). Bad management theories are destroying good management practices. *Academy of Management Learning and Education,* 4(1), 75–91.

Gibson-Graham, J.K. (1996). *The end of capitalism (as we knew it): A feminist critique of political economy.* Oxford: Blackwell.

Gibson-Graham, J.K. (2006). *A postcapitalist politics.* Minneapolis: University of Minnesota Press.

Gill, J., and Johnson, P. (1997). *Research methods for managers.* London: Sage.

Gittell, J.H., Cameron, K., Lim, S., and Rivas, V. (2006). Relationships, layoffs, and organizational resilience: Airline industry responses to September 11. *Journal of Applied Behavioral Science,* 42(3), 300–329.

Glaeser, E. (2004). Book review of Richard Florida's "The Rise of the Creative Class." Retrieved July 19, 2018 from https://scholar.harvard.edu/glaeser/publications/book-review-richard-floridas-rise-creative-class

Global Journal. (2018). Retrieved April 24, 2019 from http://www.theglobaljournal.net

Goffman, E. (2000). *Człowiek w teatrze życia codziennego.* Warszawa: Wydawnictwo KR.

Gorz, A. (1969). *Réforme et révolution.* Paris: Editions du Seuil.

Graeber, D. (2015). *The utopia of rules: On technology, stupidity, and the secret joys of bureaucracy.* New York: Melville House.

Graeber, D. (2018). *Bullshit jobs: A theory.* New York: Simon & Schuster.

Gramsci, A. (1971). *Selections from the prison notebooks.* London: Lawrence & Wishart.

Gray, J. (2002). *Straw dogs: Thoughts on humans and other animals.* London: Granta.

Grygier, E. (2012). Muzyk(a) ulicy. *Pomiędzy sztuką, a żebractwem.* Retrieved March 12, 2018 from www.cyfrowaetnografia.pl/dlibra/doccontent?id=4744&dirids=1

Guillet de Monthoux, P. (1983). *Action and existence: Anarchism for business administration.* New York: Wiley.

Guillet de Monthoux, P. (1991). *Action and existence: Art and anarchism for business administration.* Munich: ACCEDO.

Guillet de Monthoux, P. (2014). Terrorist/anarchist/artist: Why bother? *Ephemera,* 14(4), 973–979.

Hahn, C. (2005). Diversity and human rights learning in England and the United States. In A. Osler (Ed.), *Teachers, human rights and diversity: Educating citizens in multicultural societies* (pp. 23–40). Stoke-on-Trent: Trentham Books.

Hällgren, M., Rouleau, L., and de Rond, M. (2018). A matter of life or death: How extreme context research matters for management and organization studies. *Academy of Management Annals,* 12(1), 111–153.

Hamilton, C. (2013). *Earthmasters: Playing God with the climate.* Crows Nest, NSW: Allen & Unwin.

Hamilton, C. (2017). *Defiant Earth: The fate of humans in the Anthropocene.* Cambridge: Polity.

Hanlon, G., and Fleming, P.P. (2009). Updating the critical perspective on corporate social responsibility. *Sociology Compass,* 3(6), 937–948.

Hardin, G. (1968). The tragedy of the commons. *Science,* 13(162), 1243–1248.

Harmes, A. (1998). Institutional investors and the reproduction of neoliberalism. *Review of International Political Economy,* 5(1), 92–121.

Havel, V. (1990). *Disturbing the peace: A conversation with Karel Hvízdala.* New York: Vintage Books.

Head, L. (2016). *Hope and grief in the Anthropocene: Re-conceptualising human–nature relations.* London: Routledge.

Heikkurinen, P., Rinkinen, J., Jarvensivu, T., Wile, K., and Ruuska, T. (2016). Organising in the Anthropocene. *Journal of Cleaner Production,* 113, 705–714.

Henderson, D. (2001). *Misguided virtue: False notions of corporate social responsibility.* Wellington: New Zealand Business Roundtable.

Hochschild, A.R. (2003). *The managed heart: Commercialization of human feeling.* Berkeley: University of California Press.

Hoggett, P. (2006). Conflict, ambivalence, and the contested purpose of public organizations. *Human Relations,* 59(2), 175–194.

Holgersson, M. (2018). *Finans och existens.* Växjö: Linnaeus University Press.

Holloway, J. (2014). A note on hope and crisis. *Sociology,* 48(5), 1070–1072.

Höpfl, H. (1994). Learning by heart: The rules of rhetoric and the poetics of experience. *Management Learning,* 25(3), 463–474.

Höpfl, H. (1995). Organisational rhetoric and the threat of ambivalence. *Studies in Cultures, Organizations and Societies,* 1(2), 175–187.

Höpfl, H. (2000). On being moved. *Studies in Cultures, Organizations and Societies,* 6(1), 15–34.

Höpfl, H. (2003). Good order: On the administration of goodness. *Tamara,* 2(3), 28–35.

Höpfl, H. (2013). Private communication with Monika Kostera, Sheffield.

Hornborg, A. (2017). Alf Hornborg om klimatkrisen: En global minoritet förstör planeten. *Dagens Nyheter,* August 28.

Hornborg, A., McNeill, J.R., and Martinez-Alier, J. (Eds.). (2007). *Rethinking environmental history: World-system history and global environmental change.* Lanham, MD: Altamira.

Houston, D., Findlay, A., Harrison, R., and Mason, C. (2008). Will attracting the "creative class" boost economic growth in old industrial regions? A case study of Scotland. *Geografiska Annaler: Series B, Human Geography,* 90(2), 133–149.

Howe, C. (2013). Anthropocenic ecoauthority: The winds of Oaxaca. *Anthropological Quarterly,* 87(2), 381–404.

Illich, I. (1970). *Deschooling society.* London: Marion Boyars.

Ingold, T. (2013). Prospect. In T. Ingold and G. Palsson (Eds.), *Biosocial becomings: Integrating social and biological anthropology* (pp. 1–21). Cambridge: Cambridge University Press.

Jameson, F. (1994). *The seeds of time*. New York: Columbia University Press.

Jameson, F. (2016). *An American utopia: Dual power and the universal army*. London: Verso.

Jamrog, J.J., McCann, J.E.I., Lee, J.M., Morrison, C.L., Selsky, J.W., and Vickers, M. (2006). *Agility and resilience in the face of continuous change*. Atlanta, GA: American Management Association.

JD. (2018). *Ostateczna decyzja co do przyszłości kopalni Sośnica po pierwszym półroczu 2018 roku*. Retrieved August 10, 2018 from https://gornictwo.wnp.pl/ostateczna-decyzja-co-do-przyszlosci-kopalni-sosnica-po-pierwszym-polroczu-2018-roku,320704_1_0_0.html

Jemielniak, D., Przegalińska, A., and Stasik, A. (2018). Anecdotal evidence: Understanding organizational reality through organizational humorous tales. *Humor*, 31(3), 539–561.

John, G. (2014). Bullying in higher education: It's time to hold the sector to account. *The Guardian*, December 16. Retrieved December 1, 2018 from https://www.theguardian.com/higher-education-network/2014/dec/16/bullying-higher-education-university-managers

Kallifatides, M., and Larsson, A. (2017). Neoliberal "sustainability" in the UK: The case of regulating domestic pension funds. In M. Kallifatides and L. Lerpold (Eds.), *Sustainable development and business* (pp. 129–153). Stockholm: Stockholm School of Economics Institute for Research.

Kanter, R.M. (2011). How great companies think differently. *Harvard Business Review*, 89(11), 66–78.

Kaplan, J. (2015). *Humans need not apply: A guide to wealth and work in the age of artificial intelligence*. New Haven, CT: Yale University Press.

Kemmis, S., and Smith, T. (2008). Praxis and praxis development. In S. Kemmis and T. Smith (Eds.), *Enabling praxis: Challenges for education* (pp. 3–13). Rotterdam: Sense.

Klein, N. (2004). *No space, no choice, no jobs, no logo*. Izabelin: Świat Literacki.

Klein, N. (2014). *This changes everything: Capitalism vs the climate*. New York: Simon & Schuster.

Klemsdal, L., Ravn, J.E., Amble, N., and Finne, H. (2017). The organization theories of the industrial democracy experiments meet contemporary organizational realities. *Nordic Journal of Working Life Studies*, 7(S2), 1–15.

Kociatkiewicz, J. (2000). Dreams of time, times of dreams. *Studies in Cultures, Organizations, and Societies*, 6(1), 71–86.

Kolb, D. (1984). *Experiential learning: Experience as the source of learning and development*. Englewood Cliffs, NJ: Prentice Hall.

Komlosy, A. (2018). *Work: The last 1,000 years*. London: Verso.

Korten, D.C. (1987). Third generation NGO strategies: A key to people-centered development. *World Development*, 15, 145–159.

Korten, D.C. (1995). *When corporations rule the world*. London: Earthscan.

Korten, D.C. (2015). *Change the story, change the future: A living economy for a living Earth*. Oakland, CA: Berrett-Koehler.

Kostera, M. (1996). *Postmodernizm w zarządzaniu*. Warszawa: PWE.

Kostera, M. (2006). The narrative collage as research method. *Storytelling, Self, Society*, 2(2), 5–27.

Kostera, M. (2007). *Organisational ethnography: Methods and inspirations*. Lund: Studentlitteratur.

Kostera, M. (2014). *Occupy management! Inspirations for self-management and self-organization*. London: Routledge.

Kostera, M. (2015). Wstęp. In M. Kostera (Ed.), *Metody badawcze w zarządzaniu humanistycznym* (pp. 9–24). Warszawa: Wydawnictwo Akademickie SEDNO.

Kostera, M. (2018). Organizacje jak stada ptaków. *Magazyn Kontakt*, 218. Retrieved April 24, 2019 from http://magazynkontakt.pl/organizacje-jak-stada-ptakow.html

Kotler, P. (1986). The prosumer movement: A new challenge for marketers. *Advances in Consumer Research*, 13, 510–513.

Krzyworzeka, P. (2015). Etnografia. In M. Kostera (Ed.), *Metody badawcze w zarządzaniu humanistycznym* (pp. 27–36). Warszawa: Wydawnictwo Akademickie SEDNO.

Kuhn, T. (2009). *The structure of scientific revolutions*. Chicago, IL: University of Chicago Press.

Kuhn, T. (2012). Negotiating the micro–macro divide: Thought leadership from organizational communication for theorizing organization. *Management Communication Quarterly*, 26(4), 543–584.

Kuisma, M., and Ryner, M. (2012). Third Way decomposition and the rightward shift in Finnish and Swedish politics. *Contemporary Politics*, 18(3), 325–342.

Küpers, W. (2012a). Embodied transformative metaphors and narratives in organisational life-worlds of change. *Journal of Organizational Change Management*, 26(3), 494–528.

Küpers, W. (2012b). Inter-communicating – Phenomenological perspectives on embodied communication and contextuality in organization. *Journal for Communication and Culture*, 2(2), 114–138.

Küpers, W. (2013). The art of practical wisdom – Phenomenology of an embodied, wise inter-practice in organisation and leadership. In Küpers, W., and D. Pauleen (Eds.), *A handbook of practical wisdom: Leadership, organization and integral business practice* (pp. 19–45). London: Ashgate Gower.

Küpers, W. (2014). Embodied inter-affection in and beyond organisational life-worlds. *Cultural Horizons: A Journal of Philosophy and Social Theory*, 15(2), 150–178.

Küpers, W., and Gunnlaugson, O. (2017). Introduction: Contexts and complexities of wisdom learning in management and business education. In W. Küpers and O. Gunnlaugson (Eds.), *Wisdom learning: Perspectives on wising-up management and business education* (pp. 1–38). London: Routledge.

Latour, B. (1999). *Pandora's hope*. Cambridge, MA: Harvard University Press.

Laughey, D. (2010). User authority through mediated interaction: A case of eBay-in-use. *Journal of Consumer Culture*, 10(1), 105–128.

Law, A., and Mooney, G. (2009). Thinking beyond the hybrid: "Actually-existing" cities "after neoliberalism" in Boyle et al. *Geografiska Annaler: Series B, Human Geography*, 91(3), 289–294.

Le Guin, U.K. (1974). *The dispossessed*. New York: Harper & Row.

Lecher, W., Platzer, H.W., and Weiner, K.P. (2018). *European Works Councils: Development, types and networking*. London: Routledge.

Lee, J.Y., and Gallagher, M.W. (2017). Hope and well-being. In M.W. Gallagher and S.J. Lopez (Eds.), *The Oxford handbook of hope* (pp. 287–298). Oxford: Oxford University Press.

Lee, M.Y., and Edmondson, A.C. (2017). Self-managing organizations: Exploring the limits of less-hierarchical organizing. *Research in Organizational Behavior*, 37, 35–58.

Lemmens, P., Blok, V., and Zwier, J. (2017). Toward a terrestrial turn in philosophy of technology. *Techné: Research in Philosophy and Technology*, 21(2–3), 114–126.

Lengnick-Hall, C., and Beck, T. (2003). Beyond bouncing back: The concept of organizational resilience. Paper presented at the National Academy of Management meetings, Seattle, WA.

Lengnick-Hall, C., and Beck, T. (2005). Adaptive fit versus robust transformation: How organizations respond to environmental change. *Journal of Management*, 31(5), 738–757.

Lengnick-Hall, C., Beck, T., and Lengnick-Hall, M. (2011). Developing a capacity for organizational resilience through strategic human resource management. *Human Resource Management Review*, 21(3), 243–255.

Lenin, V.I. ([1902] 1975). *What is to be done? Burning questions of our movement*. Peking: Foreign Languages Press.

Lessig, L. (2004). *Free culture: How big media uses technology and the law to lock down culture and control creativity*. New York: Penguin.

Levitas, R. (2010). *The concept of utopia*. Oxford: Peter Lang.

Levitas, R. (2013). *Utopia as method: The imaginary reconstitution of society*. Basingstoke: Palgrave Macmillan.

Libudzka, A. (2014). Dr Tupieka: muzycy uliczni zasługują na uwagę i szacunek. *wyborcza.pl*, April 20. Retrieved May 12, 2019 from www.wyborcza.pl/1,91446,15830738,Dr_Tupieka__muzycy_uliczni_zaslu guja_na_uwage_i_szacunek.html

Lindqvist, M. (2001). *Is i magen. Om ekonomins kolonisering av vardagen*. Stockholm: Natur och Kultur.

Linebaugh, P. (2008). *The Magna Carta manifesto*. Oakland: University of California Press.

Łobodziński, F. (2011). Giganci piosenki chodnikowej. *Newsweek.pl*, August 24. Retrieved June 2, 2019 from www.muzyka.newsweek.pl/ giganci-piosenki-chodnikowej,81068,1,1.html

Lockhart, K. (2016). Don't create a sense of urgency, foster a sense of purpose. *Medium*, February 10. Retrieved April 24, 2019 from https:// medium.com/@kimber_lockhart/don-t-create-a-sense-of-urgency-foster-a-sense-of-purpose-724e309ecdb0

Lorenz, E. (1963). Deterministic nonperiodic flow. *Journal of the Atmospheric Sciences*, 20(2), 130–141.

Lotman, Y.M. (1988). Text within a text. *Soviet Psychology*, 26(3), 32–51.

Ludema, J., Wilmot, T., and Srivastava, S. (1997). Organizational hope: Reaffirming the constructive task of social and organizational inquiry. *Human Relations*, 50(8), 1015–1052.

Lueck, M.A. (2007). Hope for a cause as cause for hope: The need for hope in environmental sociology. *American Sociologist*, 38(3), 250–261.

Lyotard, J.-F. ([1979] 1986). *The postmodern condition: A report on knowledge*. Manchester: Manchester University Press.

Mackey, J., and Sisodia, R.S. (2013). *Conscious capitalism: Liberating the heroic spirit of business*. Boston, MA: Harvard Business Press.

Makridakis, S. (2017). The forthcoming artificial intelligence (AI) revolution: Its impact on society and firms. *Futures*, 90, 46–60.

Malm, A., and Hornborg, A. (2014). The geology of mankind? A critique of the Anthropocene narrative. *Anthropocene Review*, 1(1), 62–69.

Mandeville, B. (1714). *The fable of the bees: Or, private vices, publick benefits*. Retrieved July 20, 2019 from https://web.archive.org/ web/20060510150308/http://pedagogie.ac-toulouse.fr/philosophie/text es/mandevillethefableofthebees.htm

Marcuse, H. (1964). *One-dimensional man*. London: Routledge & Kegan Paul.

Markusen, A. (2006). Urban development and the politics of a creative class: Evidence from a study of artists. *Environment and Planning A*, 38(10), 1921–1940.

Marshall, L. (2013). The 360 deal and the "new" music industry. *European Journal of Cultural Studies*, 16(1), 77–99.

Marshall, P. (1993). *Demanding the impossible: A history of anarchism.* London: HarperCollins.

Martínez-Miranda, J., and Aldea, A. (2005). Emotions in human and artificial intelligence. *Computers in Human Behavior*, 21(2), 323–341.

Marx, K. (2015). *Das Kapital.* Sydney: Media Galaxy.

Mattox, R. (2012). *Dealers in hope: How to lead change and shape culture.* Lulu.com.

Matyja, R. (2018). *Wyjście awaryjne: O zmianie wyobraźni politycznej.* Warszawa: Karakter.

Mbembe, A. (2008). Necropolitics. In S. Morton and S. Bygrave (Eds.), *Foucault in an age of terror* (pp. 152–182). London: Palgrave Macmillan.

McCann, J. (2004). Organizational effectiveness: Changing concepts for changing environments. *Human Resource Planning*, 27(1), 42–50.

McClellan, J.G. (2011). Reconsidering communication and the discursive politics of organizational change. *Journal of Change Management*, 11, 465–480.

McClellan, J.G., and Deetz, S. (2012). A politically attentive discursive analysis of collaborative talk. In J. Aritz and R. Walker (Eds.), *Discourse perspectives on organizational communication* (pp. 33–58). Madison, NJ: Fairleigh Dickinson University Press.

McGeer, V. (2004). The art of good hope. *Annals of the American Academy of Political and Social Science*, 592(1), 100–127.

McGurl, M. (2012). The posthuman comedy. *Critical Inquiry*, 38(3), 533–553.

McLaughlin, T.H. (2000). Citizenship education in England: The Crick Report and beyond. *Journal of Philosophy of Education*, 34(4), 541–570.

McLuhan, M., and Nevitt, B. (1972). *Take today: The executive as dropout.* San Diego, CA: Harcourt Brace Jovanovich.

Meiksins Wood, E. (2002). *The origin of capitalism: A longer view.* London: Verso.

Meiksins Wood, E. (2005). *Empire of capital.* London: Verso.

Meirav, A. (2009). The nature of hope. *Ratio* (new series), XXII, 216–233.

Merleau-Ponty, M. (2003). *Nature.* Evanston, IL: Northwestern University Press.

Mezirow, J. (1975). *Education for perspective transformation: Women's reentry programs in community colleges.* New York: Center for Adult Education, Teachers College, Columbia University.

Mezirow, J. (1991). *Transformative dimensions of adult learning*. San Francisco, CA: Jossey-Bass.

Mezirow, J. (1997). Transformative learning: Theory to practice. *New Directions for Adult and Continuing Education*, 1997(74), 5–12.

Mezirow, J. (2003). Transformative learning as discourse. *Journal of Transformative Education*, 1(1), 58–63.

Mezirow, J. (2009). Transformative learning theory. In J. Mezirow, E. Taylor, and Associates (Eds.), *Transformative learning in practice: Insights from community, workplace and higher education* (pp. 18–31). San Francisco, CA: Jossey-Bass.

Michaelson, C., Pratt, M.G., Grant, A.M., and Dunn, C.P. (2014). Meaningful work: Connecting business ethics and organization studies. *Journal of Business Ethics*, 121(1), 77–90.

Milberg, W. (2008). Shifting sources and uses of profits: Sustaining US financialization with global value chains. *Economy and Society*, 37(3), 420–451.

Milczarczyk, A. (2017). Dignity restoration: The indirect goal of social enterprises' activity. In M. Kostera and M. Pirson (Eds.), *Dignity and the organization* (pp. 125–148). London: Palgrave Macmillan.

Mill, J.S. (1978). *On liberty*. London: Penguin.

Millett, P. (2002). *Lending and borrowing in ancient Athens*. Cambridge: Cambridge University Press.

Mills, C. Wright ([1959] 2007). *Wyobraźnia socjologiczna* [Sociological imagination]. Warszawa: PWN.

Mintzberg, H. (2004). *Managers not MBAs*. Harlow: FT Prentice Hall.

Mir, R., and Mir, A. (2002). The organizational imagination: From paradigm wars to praxis. *Organizational Research Methods*, 5(1), 105–125.

MIW. (2015). *Rząd o górnictwie: cztery kopalnie do likwidacji, 5 tysięcy pracowników kopalń do zwolnienia*. Retrieved September 10, 2018 from https://dziennikzachodni.pl/rzad-o-gornictwie-cztery-kopalnie-do-likwi dacji-5-tysiecy-pracownikow-kopaln-do-zwolnienia/ar/3706820

Moberg, V. (2013). *Utvandrarna* [The emigrants]. Stockholm: Bonnier Pocket.

Moch, M. (1980). Job involvement, internal motivation, and employees' integration into networks of work relationships. *Organizational Behavior and Human Performance*, 25(1), 15–31.

Montgomery, C. (2015). *Miasto szczęśliwe: Jak zmienić nasze życie, zmieniając nasze miasta*. Kraków: Wysoki Zamek.

Moore, G. (2012). Virtue in business: Alliance Boots and an empirical exploration of MacIntyre's conceptual framework. *Organization Studies*, 33(3), 363–387.

Moore, J.W. (2016). *Anthropocene or Capitalocene? Nature, history, and the crisis of capitalism*. Oakland, CA: PM Press.

Morgan, G. ([1993] 2002). *Imaginization: New mindsets for seeing, organizing and managing*. Thousand Oaks, CA: Sage.

Morsing, M., Schultz, M., and Nielsen, K.U. (2008). The "Catch 22" of communicating CSR: Findings from a Danish study. *Journal of Marketing Communications*, 14(2), 97–111.

Morton, T. (2013). *Hyperobjects: Philosophy and ecology after the end of the world*. Minneapolis: University of Minnesota Press.

Morton, T. (2016). *Dark ecology: For a logic of future coexistence*. New York: Columbia University Press.

Mouton, A., and Montijo, M.N. (2017). Hope and work. In M.W. Gallagher and S.J. Lopez (Eds.), *The Oxford handbook of hope* (pp. 327–340). Oxford: Oxford University Press.

MOW International Research Team. (1987). *The meaning of work*. London: Academic Press.

Muller, J.Z. (2003). *The mind and the market: Capitalism in Western thought*. New York: Anchor.

Naval, C., Print, M., and Ruud, V. (2002). Education for democratic citizenship in the New Europe: Context and reform. *European Journal of Education*, 37(2), 107–128.

Neyrat, F. (2018). *The unconstructable Earth: An ecology of separation*. New York: Fordham.

Nietzsche, F. (2006). *Thus spoke Zarathustra*. Cambridge: Cambridge University Press.

Nixon, T. (2015). Resolving the awkward paradox in Frederic Laloux's Reinventing Organisations. *Medium*, April 14. Retrieved October 14, 2019 from https://medium.com/maptio/resolving-the-awkward-parad ox-in-frederic-laloux-s-reinventing-organisations-f2031080ea02

Niżyńska, A. (2011). *Street art jako alternatywna forma debaty publicznej w przestrzeni miejskiej*. Warszawa: Trio.

Noddings, N. (2010). Moral education and caring. *Theory and Research in Education*, 8(2), 145–151.

Normann, R. (2001). *Reframing business: When the map changes the landscape*. London: Wiley.

Nørmark, D., and Jensen, A.F. (2018). *Pseudoarbejde. Hvordan vi fik travlt med at lave ingenting* [Pseudo-work: How we became busy doing nothing]. Copenhagen: Gyldendal.

Nuland, S.B. (1995). *How we die: Reflections on life's final chapter*. Toronto: Vintage Books.

Nyqvist, A. (2015). *Ombudskapitalisterna: institutionella ägares röst och roll*. Stockholm: Liber.

OECD. (2018). *Trust in government.* Retrieved April 24, 2019 from http://www.oecd.org/gov/trust-in-government.html

Ollman, B. (2005). The utopian vision of the future (then and now): A Marxist critique. *Monthly Review,* 57(3), 78–102.

Ong, A.D., Standiford, T., and Deshpande, S.R. (2017). Hope and stress resilience. In M.W. Gallagher and S.J. Lopez (Eds.), *The Oxford handbook of hope* (pp. 255–286). Oxford: Oxford University Press.

Online Etymology Dictionary. (2018). Hope. Retrieved August 20, 2018 from https://www.etymonline.com/word/hope

Osler, A., and Starkey, H. (2006). Education for democratic citizenship: A review of research, policy and practice 1995–2005. *Research Papers in Education,* 21(4), 433–466.

Ostrom, E. (1990). *Governing the commons.* Cambridge: Cambridge University Press.

Oxford Living Dictionaries. (2018). Hope. Retrieved September 7, 2018 from https://en.oxforddictionaries.com/definition/hope

Packard, M. (2018). Why I am not a performativist (yet). *Journal of Business Venturing Insights,* 9, 39–44.

Parker, M. (Ed.). (2002a). *Utopianism and organization.* Oxford: Blackwell.

Parker, M. (2002b). Utopia and the organizational imagination: Outopia. In M. Parker (Ed.), *Utopia and organization* (pp. 1–8). Oxford: Blackwell.

Parker, M. (2011). *Alternative business: Outlaws, crime and culture.* Oxford: Routledge.

Parker, M. (2016). Organization and philosophy: Vision and division. In R. Mir, H. Willmott, and M. Greenwood (Eds.), *Companion to philosophy in organization studies* (pp. 491–498). London: Routledge.

Parker, M. (2018). *Shut down the business school: What's wrong with management education.* London: Pluto Press.

Parker, M., Fournier, V., and Reedy, P. (2007). *The dictionary of alternatives: Utopianism and organization.* London: Zed Books.

Parker, S., and Parker, M. (2017). Antagonism, accommodation and agonism in critical management studies: Alternative organizations as allies. *Human Relations,* 70(11), 1366–1387.

Paulsen, R. (2014). *Empty labor: Idleness and workplace resistance.* Cambridge: Cambridge University Press.

Pearce, J. (2012). Building research equipment with free, open-source hardware. *Science,* 337(6100), 1303–1304.

Pearl, A., and Knight, T. (1999). *The democratic classroom: Theory to inform practice.* Cresskill, NJ: Hampton Press.

Peck, J. (2005). Struggling with the creative class. *International Journal of Urban and Regional Research,* 29(4), 740–770.

Petriglieri, G. (2012). Are business schools clueless or evil? *Harvard*

Business Review Blog. Retrieved October 19, 2018 from https://hbr.org/2012/11/are-business-schools-clueless

Pine, J., and Gilmore, J. (1999). *The experience economy: Work is theatre and every business a stage.* Boston, MA: Harvard Business School Press.

P.M. (2014). *"The power of the neighbourhood" and the commons.* New York: Autonomedia.

Podolny, J.M., Kester, W.C., Kerr, S., Sutton, R.I., Kaplan, S., and Martin, R. (2009). Are business schools to blame? *Harvard Business Review,* 87(6), 106–108.

Połeć, M. (2016). Festiwale sztuki ulicznej: Przedmiot instytucjonalizacji i forma uspołeczniania miasta. *Zarządzanie Mediami,* 4(1), 23–38.

Połeć, M. (2017). *Kontrolowana (?) kultura: Etnografia krakowskich występów ulicznych.* Kraków: Wydawnictwo Uniwersytetu Jagiellońskiego.

Połeć, M. (2018a). *Artyści uliczni polskich miast.* Kraków: Wydawnictwo Uniwersytetu Jagiellońskiego.

Połeć, M. (2018b). Kto dba o występy uliczne? Niematerialne dziedzictwo w zinstytucjonalizowanej aktywności artystów ulicznych. In Ł. Gaweł and M. Kostera (Eds.), *Etnografie instytucji dziedzictwa kulturowego* (pp. 149–164). Kraków: Wydawnictwo Uniwersytetu Jagiellońskiego.

Połeć, M. (2018c). Ethnographic approach for street performers as cultural entrepreneurs. *International Journal of Humanities and Social Sciences,* 12(8), 2107–2110.

Ponting, C. (2007). *A new green history of the world: The environment and the collapse of great civilizations.* New York: Penguin.

Porter, M.E., and Kramer, M.R. (2006). Strategy and society: The link between competitive advantage and corporate social responsibility. *Harvard Business Review,* 84(12), 78–92.

Prabhu, G.N. (1999). Social entrepreneurial leadership. *Career Development International,* 4(3), 140–145.

Prahalad, C.K., and Ramaswamy, V. (2004). The co-creation connection. *Strategy and Business,* 28(2), 51–60.

Prus, B. (1953). *Placówka* [The outpost]. Warszawa: PIW.

QCA. (1998). *Education for citizenship and the teaching of democracy in schools: Final report of the Advisory Group on Citizenship* (the Crick Report). London: QCA.

Ramanujam, R. and Roberts, K.H. (Eds.). (2018). *Organizing for reliability.* Stanford, CA: Stanford University Press.

Rapley, T. (2007). *Doing conversation, discourse and document analysis.* London: Sage.

Ratajczakowa, D. (2015). *Galeria gatunków widowiskowych, teatralnych i dramatycznych.* Poznań: Uniwersytet im. Adama Mickiewicza w Poznaniu.

Reckwitz, A. (2017). *Die Gesellschaft der Singularitäten: Zum Strukturwandel der Moderne.* Frankfurt: Suhrkamp.

Reddick, R., Bukoski, B., Smith, S., Valdez, P., and Wasielewski, M. (2014). A hole in the soul of Austin: Black faculty community engagement experiences in a creative class city. *Journal of Negro Education,* 83(1), 61–76.

Reedy, P., King, D., and Coupland, C. (2016). Organizing for individuation: Alternative organizing, politics and new identities. *Organization Studies,* 37, 1553–1573.

Rego, M. (2016). 7 movements that will help you understand the future of work. *LeadWise,* December 14. Retrieved April 24, 2019 from https://journal.leadwise.co/7-movements-that-will-help-you-understand-the-future-of-work-a65624c4afd1

Reinecke, J., and Donaghey, J. (2015). After Rana Plaza: Building coalitional power for labour rights between unions and (consumption-based) social movement organisations. *Organization,* 22(5), 720–740.

Riemer, N., Simon, D.W., and Romance, J. (2013). *The challenge of politics.* Washington, DC: Sage.

Ritzer, G. (1999). *Enchanting a disenchanted world: Revolutionizing the means of consumption.* Thousand Oaks, CA: Pine Forge Press.

Ritzer, G., and Jurgenson, N. (2010). Production, consumption, prosumption: The nature of capitalism in the age of the digital "prosumer." *Journal of Consumer Culture,* 10(1), 13–36.

Ritzer, G., Dean, P., and Jurgenson, N. (2012). The coming of age of the prosumer. *American Behavioral Scientist,* 56(4), 379–398.

Robins, N. (2007). This imperious company. *Journal of Corporate Citizenship,* 27, 31–42.

Rogers, H. (2013). *Green gone wrong: Dispatches from the front lines of eco-capitalism.* London: Verso.

Rogers, K. (2013). Hope springs fraternal: Engendering hope in anti-poverty activism. *Canadian Social Work Review,* 30(2), 217–234.

Rosa, H. (2005). *Beschleunigung. Die Veränderung der Zeitstrukturen in der Moderne.* Frankfurt: Suhrkamp.

Ryner, J.M. (2007). The Nordic model: Does it exist? Can it survive? *New Political Economy,* 12(1), 61–70.

Salomon, L., and Anheier, H. (1992). *In search of the nonprofit sector II: The problem of classification.* Working Papers of the Johns Hopkins Comparative Nonprofit Sector Project. Retrieved April 24, 2019 from http://ccss.jhu.edu/wp-content/uploads/downloads/2011/09/CNP_WP3_1993.pdf

Sandel, M. (2004). The case against perfection: What's wrong with designer children, bionic athletes, and genetic engineering. *Atlantic Monthly*, 293(3), 50–54.

Sands, D., and Tennant, M. (2010). Transformative learning in the context of suicide bereavement. *Adult Education Quarterly*, 60(2), 99–121.

Sardo, M. (2019). *Remain faithful to the earth: Resentment, responsibility and political theory in the Anthropocene*. Unpublished PhD. Evanston, IL: Northwestern University.

Schumacher, E. (1973). *Small is beautiful*. London: Blond & Briggs.

Scott, J. (1998). *Seeing like a state*. New Haven, CT: Yale University Press.

Scranton, R. (2015). *Learning to die in the Anthropocene*. San Francisco, CA: City Light Books.

Selznick, P. (1949). *TVA and the grass roots: A study in the sociology of formal organization*. Berkeley: University of California Press.

Sennett, R. (2006). *The culture of the new capitalism*. New Haven, CT: Yale University Press.

Serres, M. (1982). *The parasite*. Baltimore, MD: Johns Hopkins University Press.

Shackle, G.L.S. (1974). *Keynesian kaleidics*. Edinburgh: Edinburgh University Press.

Shantz, J. (2013). *Commonist tendencies: Mutual aid beyond communism*. New York: Punctum Books.

Sigrún, D. (2003). Kärleken i det flytande samhället. *Dagens Nyheter*, August 15.

Skinner, Q. (1996). *Reason and rhetoric in the philosophy of Hobbes*. Cambridge: Cambridge University Press.

Skoglund, A. (2015). Climate social science: Any future for "blue sky research" in management studies? *Scandinavian Journal of Management*, 31(1), 151–167.

Slaughter, R.A. (2004). *Futures beyond dystopia: Creating social foresight*. London: Routledge.

Smith, A. (1776). *An inquiry into the nature and causes of the wealth of nations*. London: Cass.

Smith, A. (2010). *The theory of moral sentiments*. New York: Penguin.

Smith, P. (2017). *Devotion*. New Haven, CT: Yale University Press.

Snyder, C.R. (Ed.). (2000). *Handbook of hope*. Cambridge, MA: Academic Press.

Snyder, C.R. (2002). Hope theory: Rainbows in the mind. *Psychological Inquiry*, 13(4), 249–275.

Snyder, C.R., Irving, L., and Anderson, J.R. (1991). Hope and health: Measuring the will and the ways. In C.R. Snyder and D.R. Forsyth

(Eds.), *Handbook of social and clinical psychology: The health perspective* (pp. 285–305). Elmsford, NY: Pergamon.

Sobczyk, I. (2015). *Mural z górnikami robi furorę, a autorka komentuje: "Tata się uśmiecha, bo mi się pomyliło."* Retrieved July 19, 2018 from http://katowice.wyborcza.pl/katowice/1,35063,18180057,Mural_z_gornikami_robi_furore__a_autorka_komentuje_.html

Solnit, R. (2016). *Hope in the dark.* New York: Nation.

Sorge, A. (2018). Management in Germany, the dynamo of Europe. In R.A. Crane (Ed.), *The influence of business cultures in Europe* (pp. 69–113). London: Palgrave Macmillan.

Spicer, A., Alvesson, M., and Kärreman, D. (2009). Critical performativity: The unfinished business of critical management studies. *Human Relations*, 62(4), 537–560.

Spicer, A., Alvesson, M., and Kärreman, D. (2016). Extending critical performativity. *Human Relations*, 69(2), 225–249.

Spreitzer, G. (2007). Giving peace a chance: Organizational leadership, empowerment, and peace. *Journal of Organizational Behavior*, 28(8), 1077–1095.

Srnicek, N., and Williams, A. (2016). *Inventing the future: Postcapitalism and a world without work.* London: Verso.

Steffen, W., Grinevald, J., Crutzen, P., and McNeill, J. (2011a). The Anthropocene: Conceptual and historical perspectives. *Philosophical Transactions of the Royal Society A*, 369, 842–867.

Steffen, W., Persson, Å., Deutsch, L., Zalasiewicz, J., Williams, M., Richardson, K., Crumley, C., Crutzen, P., Folke, C., Gordon, L., Molina, M., Ramanathan, V., Rockström, J., Scheffer, M., Schellnhuber, H.J., and Svedin, U. (2011b). The Anthropocene: From global change to planetary stewardship. *Ambio*, 40(7), 739–761.

Stewart, J., Zediker, K.E., and Black, L. (2004). Relationships among philosophies of dialogue. In R. Anderson, L.A. Baxter, and K.N. Cissna (Eds.), *Dialogue: Theorizing difference in communication studies* (pp. 21–38). Thousand Oaks, CA: Sage.

Streeck, W. (2016). *How will capitalism end? Essays on a failing system.* London: Verso.

Surowiec, Ł. (2016). *Od dziecka chciałem robić rzeczy ważne. Rozmowa z Łukaszem Surowcem, rozmawiała Magda Grabowska.* Retrieved July 19, 2018 from https://sztukapubliczna.pl/pl/od-dziecka-chcialem-robic-rzeczy-wazne-lukasz-surowiec/czytaj/6

Surowiec, Ł. (2018). Interview with Łukasz Surowiec, August 3, Kraków.

Susskind, R., and Susskind, D. (2015). *The future of professions.* Oxford: Oxford University Press.

Sussman, E. (2014). *The new rules of social journalism.* Retrieved April

24, 2019 from https://pando.com/2014/03/29/the-new-rules-of-social-journalism-a-proposal/

Sutcliffe, K.M. (2018). Mindful organizing. In R. Ramanujam and K.H. Roberts (Eds.), *Organizing for reliability* (pp. 61–89). Stanford, CA: Stanford University Press.

Swyngedouw, E. (2013). Apocalypse now! Fear and doomsday pleasures. *Capitalism Nature Socialism*, 24(1), 9–18.

Swyngedouw, E. (2014). Anthropocenic politicization: From the politics of the environment to politicizing environments. In K. Bradley and J. Hedrén (Eds.), *Green utopianism, perspectives, politics and micropractices* (pp. 24–37). London: Routledge.

Swyngedouw, E., and Ernstson, H. (2018). Interrupting the Anthropo-obScene: Immuno-biopolitics and depoliticising ontologies in the Anthropocene. *Theory, Culture and Society*, 35(6), 3–30.

Talani, L.S. (2011). The impact of the global financial crisis on the City of London: Towards the end of hegemony? *Competition and Change*, 15(1), 11–30.

Tapscott, D., and Williams, A.D. (2006). *Wikinomics: How mass collaboration changes everything*. New York: Portfolio.

Tawney, R.H. (1926). *Religion and the rise of capitalism*. New Brunswick, NJ: Transaction.

Taylor, C. (2004). *Modern social imaginaries*. Durham, NC: Duke University Press.

Teanor, B. (2018). Hope in the age of the Anthropocene. *Analecta Hermeneutica*, 10, 43–65.

Thedvall, R. (2017). Affective atmospheres of hope: Management model training in public reforms. *Journal of Organizational Ethnography*, 6(2), 87–99.

Thomas, A. (1996). *Rhodes: The race for Africa*. New York: St. Martin's Press.

Thompson, N.A. (2018). Imagination and creativity in organizations. *Organization Studies*, 39(2–3), 229–250.

Toffler, A. (1980). *The third wave*. New York: William Morrow.

Tolsma, R. J. v Inspecteur der Omzetbelasting Leeuwarden, March 3, 1994. Judgment of the Court (Sixth Chamber). Reference for a preliminary ruling. Case C-16/93 (1994), EUR-Lex. Retrieved April 3, 2018 from www.eur-lex.europa.eu/legal-content/EN/TXT/?uri=CELEX:61993CJ0016

Tonkinwise, C. (2018). *This time, it is really happening: Democracy must be defended, by undemocratic design specifications*. Retrieved April 24, 2019 from www.academia.edu/download/55656731/De-Democracy_II.pdf

TVN24. (2015). *"Tato nie płacz."* *Jak rysunek 5-latki stał się muralem.* Retrieved July 19, 2018 from https://www.tvn24.pl/katowice,51/tato-nie-placz-rysunek-5-latki-na-scianie-familoka,553394

Twomey, S. (2012). *Street performance as a rhetorical art form.* Retrieved November 10, 2018 from www.academia.edu/1651134/Street_Perform ance_as_a_Rhetorical_Art_Form

Tyszka, J. (1998). *Obywatelski protest i karnawał uliczny: Serbia, 17 listopada 1996 – 20 marca 1997.* Poznań: Wydawnictwo Fundacji Humaniora.

Unknown, (2015). "Tato, nie płacz." Poruszający mural powstał w Załężu. Retrieved July 19, 2018 from http://wyborcza.pl/1,75248,18141781,_ Tato__nie_placz___Poruszajacy_mural_powstal_w_Zalezu.html

van der Pijl, K. (2005). *Transnational classes and international relations.* London: Routledge.

Van Maanen, J. (1988). *Tales of the field: On writing ethnography.* Chicago, IL: University of Chicago Press.

Vattimo, G., and Rovatti, P.A. (Eds.). ([1983] 2012). *Weak thought.* New York: SUNY Press.

Vaughan, J. (2015a). A pluralist paradigm for business schools: The multicultural learning group. British Academy of Management Conference, Portsmouth.

Vaughan, J. (2015b). Developing an entrepreneurial imagination. Conference on Enterprise Marketing and Globalization, Singapore.

Veldhuis, R. (1997). *Education for democratic citizenship: Dimensions of citizenship, core competencies, variables and international activities.* Strasbourg: Council of Europe.

Verdenius, W. (1985). *A commentary on Hesiod.* Leiden: Brill.

Veugelers, W. (2007). Creating critical-democratic citizenship education: Empowering humanity and democracy in Dutch education. *Compare,* 37(1), 105–119.

Veugelers, W., and Zijlstra, H. (2004). Networks of schools and constructing citizenship in secondary education. In F. Hernandez and I.F. Goodson (Eds.), *Social geographies of educational change* (pp. 65–77). Dordrecht: Kluwer.

Warriner, C. (1965). The problem of organizational purpose. *Sociological Quarterly,* 6(2), 139–146.

Weber, A. (2013). *Enlivenment: Towards a fundamental shift in the concepts of nature, culture and politics.* Berlin: Heinrich-Böll-Stiftung.

Weber, M. (1930). *The Protestant ethic and the spirit of capitalism and other writings.* London: Routledge.

Weedon, C. (1997). *Feminist practice and poststructuralist theory.* Oxford: Blackwell.

Weeks, K. (2011). *The problem with work: Feminism, Marxism, antiwork politics, and postwork imaginaries.* Durham, NC: Duke University Press.
Weick, K.E. (1979). *The social psychology of organizing.* Topics in Social Psychology. Columbus, OH: McGraw-Hill Humanities.
Weick, K.E. (1988). Enacted sensemaking in crisis situations. *Journal of Management Studies*, 25, 305–317.
Weick, K.E. (1989). Theory construction as disciplined imagination. *Academy of Management Review*, 14, 516–531.
Weick, K.E. (1990). The vulnerable system: Analysis of the Tenerife air disaster. *Journal of Management*, 16, 571–593.
Weick, K.E. (1993). The collapse of sensemaking in organizations: The Mann Gulch disaster. *Administrative Science Quarterly*, 38, 628–652.
Weick, K.E. ([1995]2016). *Tworzenie sensu w organizacjach* [Sensemaking in organizations]. Kraków: Wydawnictwo Uniwersytetu Jagiellońskiego.
Weick, K.E. (2005). Organizing and failures of imagination. *International Public Management Journal*, 8(3), 425–438.
Weick, K.E., and Sutcliffe, K.M. (2003). Hospitals as cultures of entrapment: A re-analysis of the Bristol Royal Infirmary. *California Management Review*, 45(2), 73–84.
Weick, K.E., and Sutcliffe, K.M. (2015). *Managing the unexpected: Sustained performance in a complex world.* Hoboken, NJ: Wiley.
Weick, K.E., Sutcliffe, K.M., and Obstfeld, D. (1999). Organizing for high reliability: Processes of collective mindfulness. In B. Staw and R. Sutton (Eds.), *Research in organizational behavior*, Vol. 21, (pp. 81–123). Greenwich, CT: JAI.
Weick, K.E., Sutcliffe, K.M., and Obstfeld, D. (2005). Organizing and the process of sensemaking. *Organization Science*, 16, 409–421.
Wheeler, D., Fabig, H., and Boele, R. (2002). Paradoxes and dilemmas for stakeholder responsive firms in the extractive sector: Lessons from the case of Shell and the Ogoni. *Journal of Business Ethics*, 39(3), 297–318.
Whiteley, P. (2005). *Citizenship education: The political science perspective.* Research Report RR631. London: Department for Education and Skills.
Whyte, W.H. (1961). *The organization man.* Harmondsworth: Penguin.
Wilkins, C. (2003). Teachers and young citizens: Teachers talk about their role as social educators. *Westminster Studies in Education*, 26(1), 63–75.
Willis, E. (1993). *The sociological quest: An introduction to the study of social life.* Sydney: Allen & Unwin.
Williston, B. (2015). *The Anthropocene project.* Oxford: Oxford University Press.

Wilson, S. (1993). Historicism. *The year's work in critical and cultural theory*, 3(1), 164–189.

Wolf, M. (2004). *Why globalization works*. New Haven, CT: Yale University Press.

Wolff-Jontofsohn, U. (2002). *Learning the language of democracy with Betzavta*. Retrieved November 12, 2018 from http://www.academia. edu/4006075/Learning_the_Language_of_Democracy_with_Betzavta

Wood, J. (1997). Deep roots and far from a soft option. In T. Dickson and G. Bickerstaffe (Eds.), *Mastering Management* (pp. 217–224). London: FT/Pitman.

Woodman, R.W., Sawyer, J.E., and Griffin, R.W. (1993). Toward a theory of organizational creativity. *Academy of Management Review*, 18, 293–321.

World Bank. (2018). Employers, total (% of total employment) (modeled ILO estimate). Retrieved September 10, 2018 from https://data.world bank.org/indicator/SL.EMP.MPYR.ZS

Wright, E.O. (1997). *Class counts: Comparative studies in class analysis*. Cambridge: Cambridge University Press.

Wright, E.O. (2010). *Envisioning real utopias*. London: Verso.

Yeoman, R. (2014). Conceptualising meaningful work as a fundamental human need. *Journal of Business Ethics*, 125(2), 235–251.

Žižek, S. (2002). *Welcome to the desert of the Real! Five essays on September 11 and related dates*. London: Verso.

Zuidervaart, L. (2011). *Art in public: Politics, economics, and a democratic culture*. Cambridge: Cambridge University Press.

Zylinska, J. (2014). *Minimal ethics for the Anthropocene*. Ann Arbor, MI: Open Humanities Press.

Index

244 *Organizing hope*

self-subordination
  Christian 152
  practices of 7, 49, 53, 59
  and self-alienation 52–4
Shackle, G.L.S. 17–18
Smith, Adam 64
  commercial society 64
  *Inquiry into the Nature and Causes
    of the Wealth of Nations, An*
    (1776) 62, 64
  on need for a moral order 64
  on process of primitive
    accumulation 63
social economy 28, 200, 201, 206
social entrepreneur 6, 200–201, 207
social inclusion, problem of 6, 9, 153,
  165
socialism 30–31, 33, 103, 127, 129
social relations 28, 87, 89, 95
social responsibility, significance of
  193, 200
social stratification 108, 118
Socrates (Greek philosopher) 62
standard of living 35, 64, 66
Streeck, Wolfgang 1, 6, 109, 176
Surowiec, Łukasz 11, 157–64

Tabiś-Hubka, Zosia 158
Thatcher, Margaret 2, 31, 35, 98, 177

There is no alternative! (TINA) 2, 7,
  31, 35, 88, 177
Toffler, Alvin 10, 19, 143
transformative learning 10
  Betzavta 134–41
  process of 133
  theory of 134–6

urban economy 63, 155
urban sphere 11, 166–72, 174–5
utopia 30–36

van der Pijl, Kees 127
Voltaire 64–5, 67

Wigforss, Ernst 128, 130
Willis, Evan 178
wisdom 8, 41, 75–6, 82, 142
  collective 44
  conventional 90
  hope and 80–81
  practical 73–4
Wood, Ellen Meiksins 120
  definition of organisational
    behaviour 44
  on levels of analytic abstraction 44
Wright, Erik Olin 7, 34, 127

Zawisza, Marcelina 158